AF777717

Whillans's Tax Tables

Budget 2010 Edition

Edited by

Mary Hyland
CA CTA (Fellow)

Kevin Walton
MA

LexisNexis®

Members of the LexisNexis Group worldwide

United Kingdom	LexisNexis, a Division of Reed Elsevier (UK) Ltd, Halsbury House, 35 Chancery Lane, London, WC2A 1EL, and London House, 20-22 East London Street, Edinburgh EH7 4BQ
Australia	LexisNexis Butterworths, Chatswood, New South Wales
Austria	LexisNexis Verlag ARD Orac GmbH & Co KG, Vienna
Benelux	LexisNexis Benelux, Amsterdam
Canada	LexisNexis Canada, Markham, Ontario
China	LexisNexis China, Beijing and Shanghai
France	LexisNexis SA, Paris
Germany	LexisNexis Deutschland GmbH, Munster
Hong Kong	LexisNexis Hong Kong, Hong Kong
India	LexisNexis India, New Delhi
Italy	Giuffrè Editore, Milan
Japan	LexisNexis Japan, Tokyo
Malaysia	Malayan Law Journal Sdn Bhd, Kuala Lumpur
New Zealand	LexisNexis NZ Ltd, Wellington
Poland	Wydawnictwo Prawnicze LexisNexis Sp, Warsaw
Singapore	LexisNexis Singapore, Singapore
South Africa	LexisNexis Butterworths, Durban
USA	LexisNexis, Dayton, Ohio

First published in 1948

© Reed Elsevier (UK) Ltd 2010

Published by LexisNexis
This is a Tolley title

All rights reserved. No part of this publication may be reproduced in any material form (including photocopying or storing it in any medium by electronic means and whether or not transiently or incidentally to some other use of this publication) without the written permission of the copyright owner except in accordance with the provisions of the Copyright, Designs and Patents Act 1988 or under the terms of a licence issued by the Copyright Licensing Agency Ltd, Saffron House, 6–10 Kirby Street, London EC1N 8TS. Applications for the copyright owner's written permission to reproduce any part of this publication should be addressed to the publisher.
Warning: The doing of an unauthorised act in relation to a copyright work may result in both a civil claim for damages and criminal prosecution.

Crown copyright material is reproduced with the permission of the Controller of HMSO and the Queen's Printer for Scotland. Parliamentary copyright material is reproduced with the permission of the Controller of Her Majesty's Stationery Office on behalf of Parliament. Any European material in this work which has been reproduced from EUR-lex, the official European Communities legislation website, is European Communities copyright.
A CIP Catalogue record for this book is available from the British Library.

[Seventy-ninth edition] ISBN for this volume 9781405748940

Printed in the UK by CPI William Clowes Ltd, Beccles, NR34 7TL

Visit LexisNexis at www.lexisnexis.co.uk

Administration

Bank base rates

Period	*Rate*
from 5 March 2009	**0.50%**
5 February 2009–4 March 2009	1.00%
8 January 2009–4 February 2009	1.50%
4 December 2008–7 January 2009	2.00%
6 November 2008–3 December 2008	3.00%
8 October 2008–5 November 2008	4.50%
10 April 2008–7 October 2008	5.00%
7 February 2008–9 April 2008	5.25%
6 December 2007–6 February 2008	5.50%
5 July 2007–5 December 2007	5.75%
10 May 2007–4 July 2007	5.50%
11 January 2007–9 May 2007	5.25%
9 November 2006–10 January 2007	5.00%
3 August 2006–8 November 2006	4.75%
4 August 2005–2 August 2006	4.50%
5 August 2004–3 August 2005	4.75%
10 June 2004–4 August 2004	4.50%
6 May 2004–9 June 2004	4.25%
5 February 2004–5 May 2004	4.00%
6 November 2003–4 February 2004	3.75%
10 July 2003–5 November 2003	3.50%
6 February 2003–9 July 2003	3.75%
8 November 2001–5 February 2003	4.00%
4 October 2001–7 November 2001	4.50%
18 September 2001–3 October 2001	4.75%
2 August 2001–17 September 2001	5.00%
10 May 2001–1 August 2001	5.25%
5 April 2001–9 May 2001	5.50%
8 February 2001–4 April 2001	5.75%
10 February 2000–7 February 2001	6.00%
13 January 2000–9 February 2000	5.75%
4 November 1999–12 January 2000	5.50%
8 September 1999–3 November 1999	5.25%
10 June 1999–7 September 1999	5.00%
8 April 1999–9 June 1999	5.25%
4 February 1999–7 April 1999	5.50%
7 January 1999–3 February 1999	6.00%
10 December 1998–6 January 1999	6.25%
5 November 1998–9 December 1998	6.75%
8 October 1998–4 November 1998	7.25%
4 June 1998–7 October 1998	7.50%
6 November 1997–3 June 1998	7.25%
7 August 1997–5 November 1997	7.00%
10 July 1997–6 August 1997	6.75%

Due dates of tax

Capital gains tax

Normally 31 January following end of year of assessment. (TMA 1970 s 59B)

(See also *Extended due dates* under **Income tax**, below.)

Corporation tax

Generally

9 months and 1 day after end of accounting period. (FA 1998 Sch 19 para 29)

Instalments for larger companies (TMA 1970 s 59E, SI 1998/3175)

(A 'large company' is one whose taxable profits exceed £1.5m a year, divided by 1 plus the number of any active associated companies.) For most large companies (those with no ring fence profits) the amount of each instalment for a 12 month accounting period will be one quarter of its total liability. The amount of each instalment for any accounting period longer than 3 months but shorter than 12 months is calculated using the formula 3 x CTI/n where CTI is the amount of a company's total liability for that accounting period n is the number of months in the accounting period. The due dates of instalments are as follows:

1st instalment: 6 months and 13 days from start of accounting period (or date of final instalment if earlier);
2nd instalment: 3 months after 1st instalment, if length of accounting period allows;
3rd instalment: 3 months after 2nd instalment, if length of accounting period allows;
Final instalment: 3 months and 14 days from end of accounting period.

Close companies: tax on loans to participators

9 months and 1 day after the end of the accounting period. To be included in instalment payments for large companies (TMA 1970 s 59E(11), see above).

Income tax

Payments on account (TMA 1970 s 59A)

A payment on account is required where a taxpayer was assessed to income tax in the immediately preceding year to an amount exceeding the amount of tax deducted at source in respect of that year (subject to a de minimis limit, see below).

The payment on account is made in 2 equal instalments due on:

(a) 31 January during the year of assessment, and
(b) 31 July in the following year of assessment.

No payments on account are required where either:

(a) the aggregate of the liability (including Class 4 NIC) for the preceding year (net of tax deducted at source) is less than £1,000 (£500 for 2008/09 and previous years (SI 2008/838)); or
(b) more than 80% of the taxpayer's income tax and Class 4 NIC liability for the preceding year was met by tax deducted at source (including PAYE).

Final payment (TMA 1970 s 59B, Sch 3ZA)

Balance of income tax due for a year of assessment (after deducting payments on account, tax deducted at source and credits in respect of dividends, etc) is due on:

31 January following end of year of assessment (TMA 1970 s 59B(4)).

Extended due dates:

(a) If a taxpayer has given notice of liability within 6 months of the end of the year of assessment , but a notice to make a return is not given until after 31 October following the end of the year of assessment, the due date is 3 months after the notice is given (TMA 1970 s 59B(3)).
(b) If tax is payable as a result of a taxpayer's notice of amendment, an HMRC notice of correction or an HMRC notice of closure following enquiry, in each case given less than 30 days before the due date (or the extended due date at (a) above), the due date is on or before the day following the end of a 30-day period beginning on the day on which the notice is given (TMA 1970 s 59B(5), Sch 3ZA).
(c) If an assessment other than a self-assessment is made, tax payable under the assessment is due on the day following the end of a 30-day period beginning on the day on which notice of the assessment is given (TMA 1970 s 59B(6)).

The extensions under (b) and (c) do *not* alter the due date for *interest purposes* (see p 5).

Interest on overdue tax see p 5.
Remission of tax see p 7.
Repayment supplement see p 8.

Inheritance tax

Chargeable transfers other than on death, made between:

6 April and 30 September	–	30 April in next year.
1 October and 5 April	–	6 months after end of month in which chargeable transfer is made.

Chargeable events following conditional exemption for heritage etc property and charge on disposal of trees or underwood before the second death

– 6 months after end of month in which chargeable event occurs.

Transfers on death

Earlier of (*a*) 6 months after end of month in which death occurs, and
(*b*) delivery of account by personal representatives.

Tax or extra tax becoming payable on death:

Chargeable transfers and potentially exempt transfers within 7 years of death.

PAYE and national insurance

Employer's tax and Class 1 national insurance payable under PAYE.	19 April following deduction year (extended to 22 April where payments after 5 April 2004 are made by electronic means).
Class 1A national insurance.	19 July following year in which contributions due.
PAYE settlement agreement and Class 1B national insurance.	19 October following year to which agreement relates.
Class 4 national insurance.	See under income tax on p 4.

Interest on overdue tax

Interest runs from the due date (see p 4) to the date of payment, on the amount outstanding. For tax resulting from amendments/corrections to returns and from discovery assessments (under TMA 1970 s 29), interest normally runs from the annual filing date for the relevant tax year.

Interest is payable gross and is not tax deductible.

Income tax, capital gains tax, NICs Class 1, 1A, 4 and (from 6.4.99) 1B, and (from 1.10.99) stamp duty, SDRT and (from 26.9.05) stamp duty land tax

Period	*Rate*
from 29 September 2009	**3.0%**
24 March 2009–28 September 2009	2.5%
27 January 2009–23 March 2009	3.5%
6 January 2009–26 January 2009	4.5%
6 December 2009–5 January 2009	5.5%
6 November 2008–5 December 2008	6.5%
6 January 2008–5 November 2008	7.5%
6 August 2007–5 January 2008	8.5%
6 September 2006–5 August 2007	7.5%
6 September 2005–5 September 2006	6.5%
6 September 2004–5 September 2005	7.5%
6 December 2003–5 September 2004	6.5%
6 August 2003–5 December 2003	5.5%

Surcharge on unpaid income tax and capital gains tax (TMA 1970 s 59C)

Where income tax or capital gains tax becomes payable and all or part of it remains unpaid the day following 28 days after the due date, the taxpayer is liable to a surcharge of 5% of the unpaid tax. A further surcharge of 5% is levied on any of the tax remaining unpaid six months and one day from the due date. Interest is payable on surcharge from the expiry of 30 days beginning on the day on which the surcharge is imposed until the date of payment chargeable at the above rate. Penalties for late filing of returns and late payment of tax are to be reformed. A new system, starting on 6 April 2010 for PAYE (see p 14), is to be introduced and the existing rules will be abolished. The new rules are to be phased in over several years.

Corporation tax

Interest runs from the due date (see p 4) to the date of payment. For instalment payments by large companies for accounting periods ending after 30 June 1999, a special rate of interest runs from the due date to the earlier of the date of payment and nine months after the end of the accounting period (after which the normal rate applies).

Corporation tax self-assessment (accounting periods ending after 30 June 1999)

Period	*Normal rate*
from 29 September 2009	**3.0%**
24 March 2009 to 28 September 2009	2.5%
27 January 2009–23 March 2009	3.5%
6 January 2009–26 January 2009	4.5%
6 December 2008–5 January 2009	5.5%
6 November 2008–5 December 2008	6.5%
6 January 2008–5 November 2008	7.5%
6 August 2007–5 January 2008	8.5%
6 September 2006–5 August 2007	7.5%
6 September 2005–5 September 2006	6.5%
6 September 2004–5 September 2005	7.5%
6 December 2003–5 September 2004	6.5%
6 August 2003–5 December 2003	5.5%
6 November 2001–5 August 2003	6.5%

Period	*Special rate for instalment payments (except where still unpaid nine months after end of accounting period)*
from 16 March 2009	**1.50%**
16 February 2009–15 March 2009	2.00%
19 January 2009–15 February 2009	2.50%
15 December 2008–18 January 2009	3.00%
17 November 2008–14 December 2008	4.00%
20 October 2008–16 November 2008	5.50%
21 April 2008–19 October 2008	6.00%
18 February 2008–20 April 2008	6.25%
17 December 2007–17 February 2008	6.50%
16 July 2007–16 December 2007	6.75%
21 May 2007–15 July 2007	6.50%
22 January 2007–20 May 2007	6.25%
20 November 2006–21 January 2007	6.00%
14 August 2006–19 November 2006	5.75%
15 August 2005–13 August 2006	5.50%
16 August 2004–14 August 2005	5.75%
21 June 2004–15 August 2004	5.50%
17 May 2004–20 June 2004	5.25%
16 February 2004–16 May 2004	5.00%
17 November 2003–15 February 2004	4.75%
21 July 2003–16 November 2003	4.50%
17 February 2003–20 July 2003	4.75%
19 November 2001–16 February 2003	5.00%

Corporation tax pay and file (accounting periods ending after 30 September 1993)

Period	*Rate*
from 29 September 2009	**3.0%**
24 March 2009– 28 September 2009	**1.75%**
27 January 2009–23 March 2009	2.75%
6 January 2009–26 January 2009	3.50%
6 December 2008–5 January 2009	4.25%

Period	*Rate*
6 November 2008–5 December 2008	5.00%
6 January 2008–5 November 2008	6.00%
6 August 2007–5 January 2008	6.75%
6 September 2006–5 August 2007	6.00%
6 September 2005–5 September 2006	5.25%
6 September 2004–5 September 2005	6.00%
6 December 2003–5 September 2004	5.25%*
6 August 2003–5 December 2003	4.25%
6 November 2001–5 August 2003	5.00%

* This rate was corrected by HMRC (see news release HMRC 27/05 of 6 September 2005) and is higher than that previously used (5%). No attempt will be made to recover any further interest which may be due unless, exceptionally, a liability is reviewed.

Income tax on company payments (due on or after 14 October 1999)

Period	*Rate*
from 29 September 2009	**3.0%**
24 March 2009– 28 September 2009	2.5%
27 January 2009–23 March 2009	3.5%
6 January 2009–26 January 2009	4.5%
6 December 2008–5 January 2009	5.5%
6 November 2008–5 December 2008	6.5%
6 January 2008–5 November 2008	7.5%
6 August 2007–5 January 2008	8.5%
6 September 2006–5 August 2007	7.5%
6 September 2005–5 September 2006	6.5%
6 September 2004–5 September 2005	7.5%
6 December 2003–5 September 2004	6.5%
6 August 2003–5 December 2003	5.5%
6 November 2001–5 August 2003	6.5%

Inheritance tax

Interest runs from the due date (see p 5) to the date of payment.

Period	*Rate*
from 29 September 2009	**3%**
24 March 2009–28 September 2009	0%
27 January 2009–23 March 2009	1%
6 January 2009 to 26 January 2009	2%
6 November 2008–5 January 2009	3%
6 January 2008–5 November 2008	4%
6 August 2007–5 January 2008	5%
6 September 2006 to 5 August 2007	4%
6 September 2005–5 September 2006	3%
6 September 2004–5 September 2005	4%
6 December 2003–5 September 2004	3%
6 August 2003–5 December 2003	2%
6 November 2001–5 August 2003	3%

Remission of tax

By concession, arrears of tax may be waived if they result from HMRC's failure to make proper and timely use of information supplied by the taxpayer or, where it affects the taxpayer's coding, by his or her employer. The concession also applies to information supplied by the Department for Work and Pensions affecting the taxpayer's entitlement to a retirement or widow's pension (see Concession A19). The concession only applies where the taxpayer could reasonably have believed that his or her affairs were in order and (unless the circumstances are exceptional) where the taxpayer is notified of the arrears more than 12 months after the end of the tax year in which HMRC received the information indicating that more tax was due.

Interest on overpaid tax

Income tax, capital gains tax, Class 1, 1A, 4 and (from 6.4.99) 1B national insurance contributions and (from 1.10.99) stamp duty and stamp duty reserve tax and (from 26.9.05) stamp duty land tax

Calculated as simple interest on the amount of tax repaid. The supplement is tax free.

Period	*Rate*
from 29 September 2009	**0.50%**
27 January 2009–28 September 2009	0.00%
6 January 2009–26 January 2009	0.75%
6 December 2008–5 January 2009	1.50%
6 November 2008–5 December 2008	2.25%
6 January 2008–5 November 2008	3.00%
6 August 2007–5 January 2008	4.00%
6 September 2006–5 August 2007	3.00%
6 September 2005–5 September 2006	2.25%
6 September 2004–5 September 2005	3.00%*
6 December 2003–5 September 2004	2.25%*
6 August 2003–5 December 2003	1.50%*
6 November 2001–5 August 2003	2.25%*

* These rates were corrected by HMRC (see HMRC 27/05, 6 September 2005) and are lower than those previously used. No attempt will be made to recover amounts overpaid by HMRC unless, exceptionally, a repayment is reviewed.

Income tax

(TA 1988 s 824; FA 1997 s 92; ITTOIA 2005 s 749)

From 1996–97 (1997–98 for partnerships whose trade, profession or business commenced before 6 April 1994) repayment supplement applies to:

(a) amounts paid on account of income tax
(b) income tax paid by or on behalf of an individual
(c) surcharges on late payments of tax
(d) penalties incurred by an individual under any provision of TMA 1970

but excluding amounts paid in excess of the maximum the taxpayer is required to pay.

Except for tax deducted at source, the repayment supplement runs *from* the date on which the tax, penalty or surcharge was paid *to* the date on which the order for repayment is issued. For tax deducted at source, repayment supplement runs from 31 January after the end of the tax year for which the tax was deducted.

Capital gains tax

(TCGA 1992 s 283)

From 1996–97 repayment supplement runs *from* the date on which the tax was paid *to* the date on which the order for repayment is issued.

Inheritance tax

(IHTA 1984 s 235)

Repayments of inheritance tax or interest paid carries interest *from* the date of payment *to* the date on which the order for repayment is issued. Before 29 September 2009 the prescribed rates for unpaid tax apply equally to repayment supplements – see p 7. From 29 September 2009, the rate is 0.5%.

Companies

Corporation tax self-assessment (accounting periods ending after 30 June 1999)

Normal rates

Rates on overpaid corporation tax in respect of periods after normal due date (SI 1989/1297 reg 3BB).

Period	*Rate*
from 29 September 2009	**0.5%**
27 January 2009– 28 September 2009	0%
6 January 2009–26 January 2009	1%
6 December 2008–5 January 2009	2%
6 November 2008–5 December 2008	3%

Period	Rate
6 January 2008–5 November 2008	4%
6 August 2007–5 January 2008	5%
6 September 2006–5 August 2007	4%
6 September 2005–5 September 2006	3%
6 September 2004–5 September 2005	4%
6 December 2003–5 September 2004	3%
6 August 2003–5 December 2003	2%
6 November 2001–5 August 2003	3%

Special rates

For instalment payments by large companies and early payments by other companies, a special rate of interest runs from the date the excess arises (but not earlier than the due date of the first instalment) to the earlier of the date the repayment order is issued and nine months after the end of the accounting period after which the normal rate of interest (as above) applies.

Rates on overpaid instalment payments and on corporation tax paid early (but not due by instalments).

Period	Rate
from 21 September 2009	**0.5%**
16 March 2009 to 20 September 2009	0.25%
16 February 2009–15 March 2009	0.75%
19 January 2009–15 February 2009	1.25%
15 December 2008–18 January 2009	1.75%
17 November 2008–14 December 2008	2.75%
20 October 2008–16 November 2008	4.25%
21 April 2008–19 October 2008	4.75%
18 February 2008–20 April 2008	5.00%
17 December 2007–17 February 2008	5.25%
16 July 2006-16 December 2007	5.50%
21 May 2007–15 July 2007	5.25%
22 January 2007–20 May 2007	5.00%
20 November 2006–21 January 2007	4.75%
14 August 2006–19 November 2006	4.50%
15 August 2005–13 August 2006	4.25%
16 August 2004–14 August 2005	4.50%
21 June 2004–15 August 2004	4.25%
17 May 2004–20 June 2004	4.00%
16 February 2004–16 May 2004	3.75%
17 November 2003–15 February 2004	3.50%
21 July 2003–16 November 2003	3.25%
17 February 2003–20 July 2003	3.50%
19 November 2001–16 February 2003	3.75%
15 October 2001–18 November 2001	4.25%
1 October 2001–14 October 2001	4.50%
13 August 2001–30 September 2001	4.75%
21 May 2001–12 August 2001	5.00%
16 April 2001–20 May 2001	5.25%
19 February 2001–15 April 2001	5.50%
21 February 2000–18 February 2001	5.75%
24 January 2000–20 February 2000	5.50%

Corporation tax pay and file (accounting periods ending before 1 July 1999)

Repayments of corporation tax, repayments of income tax in respect of payments received, payments of tax credits in respect of franked investment income received, and (before its abolition from 6 April 1999) repayments of ACT in respect of foreign income dividends made after the material date. (FA 1998 ss 31, 32, SI 1999/358.)

Calculated *from* the material date *to* the date the repayment order is issued.

For corporation tax, the material date is the later of:

(a) the date on which the tax was paid; and

(b) the date on which the tax became, or would have become, due and payable – generally, nine months and one day after the end of the accounting period.

(For ACT, the material date was the date on which corporation tax for the accounting period in which the distribution was made became, or would have become, due and payable – generally, nine months and one day after the end of the accounting period.)

For repayments of income tax in respect of payments received and payments of tax credits in respect of franked investment income received, the material date is the date on which corporation tax for the accounting period in which the payments or the franked investment income were received became, or would have become, due and payable. Again, this is generally nine months and one day after the end of the accounting period.

Where there is in any accounting period ('the later period') a non-trading deficit on a company's loan relationships and a claim is made to carry this deficit back to an earlier accounting period ('the earlier period'), then interest on any repayment of corporation tax for the earlier period (or of income tax on a payment received in the earlier period) resulting from the claim begins to run only after the date on which the corporation tax for the *later* period (the period in which the non-trading deficit arose) became due and payable. (TA 1988 s 826(7C).)

A similar rule (s 826(7) repealed for accounting periods beginning on or after 6 April 1999) applied to the carry-back of surplus ACT as applies to the carry-back of a non-trading deficit.

Trading losses carried back for more than 12 months (s 826(7A), (7B))

Where a claim is made under TA 1988 s 393A(1) to set off a loss incurred in a later period against the profits of an earlier period not falling within the 12 months immediately preceding the later period, and

(a) a repayment of corporation tax in respect of that earlier period or a repayment of income tax in respect of a payment received in the earlier period; or

(b) following a claim under TA 1988 s 242 to include surplus franked investment income in profits available for set-off, a payment of the whole or part of the tax credit comprised in franked investment income of the earlier period,

is made, interest in respect of that part of the repayment due to the claim under TA 1988 s 393A(1) or TA 1988 s 242 (so far as it relates to the claim under s 393A(1)) begins to run only after the date on which the corporation tax in respect of the later period (the lossmaking period) became, or would have become, due and payable.

Period	*Rate*
from 29 September 2009	**0.50%**
27 January 2009–28 September 2009	0.00%
6 January 2009–26 January 2009	0.50%
6 December 2008–5 January 2009	1.25%
6 November 2008–5 December 2008	2.00%
6 January 2008–5 November 2008	2.75%
6 August 2007–5 January 2008	3.50%
6 September 2006–5 August 2007	2.75%
6 September 2005–5 September 2006	2.00%
6 September 2004–5 September 2005	2.75%
6 December 2003–5 September 2004	2.00%
6 August 2003–5 December 2003	1.25%
6 November 2001–5 August 2003	2.00%

Certificates of tax deposit

Certificates are not available for purchase for use against corporation tax liabilities. Certificates are available to individuals, trustees, companies or other persons or bodies for the payment of income tax, Class 4 national insurance contributions, capital gains tax, inheritance tax, petroleum revenue tax or petroleum royalty. Minimum first deposit £500; subsequent deposits not less than £250 or amount required to bring total deposits up to £500 (ie where total deposits have fallen below that amount). Interest is paid gross and is chargeable to tax. It will only be paid for the first six years of a deposit. A deposit bears interest for the first year at the rate in force at the time of the deposit and for each subsequent year at the rate in force on the anniversary of the deposit.

Date	*Amount*	*Held for (mths in yr)*	*Pay't of tax %*	*Cashed %*
11.6.04–5.8.04	Under £100,000	no limit	1.00	0.50
	£100,000 or over	under 1	1.00	0.50
		1–under 3	3.75	1.75
		3–under 6	3.50	1.75
		6–12	3.75	1.75
6.8.04–4.8.05	Under £100,000	no limit	1.25	0.50
	£100,000 or over	under 1	1.25	0.50
		1–12	3.75	1.75
5.8.05–3.8.06	Under £100,000	no limit	1.00	0.50

Date	Amount	Held for (mths in yr)	Pay't of tax %	Cashed %
	£100,000 or over	under 1	1.00	0.50
		1–under 3	3.50	1.75
		3–under 6	3.25	1.50
		6–12	3.00	1.50
4.8.06–9.11.06	Under £100,000	no limit	1.75	0.75
	£100,000 or over	under 1	1.75	0.75
		1–under 3	4.25	2.00
		3–under 6	4.25	2.00
		6–12	4.00	2.00
10.11.06–11.1.07	Under £100,000	no limit	1.50	0.75
	£100,000 or over	under 1	1.50	0.75
		1–under 3	4.00	2.00
		3–under 6	4.00	2.00
		6–12	3.75	1.75
12.1.07–10.5.07	Under £100,000	no limit	1.50	0.75
	£100,000 or over	under 1	1.50	0.75
		1–under 3	4.25	2.00
		3–under 6	4.00	2.00
		6–12	4.00	2.00
11.5.07–5.7.07	Under £100,000	no limit	2.00	1.00
	£100,000 or over	under 1	2.00	1.00
		1–under 3	4.75	2.25
		3–under 6	4.50	2.25
		6–12	4.50	2.25
6.7.07–6.12.07	Under £100,000	no limit	2.25	1.10
	£100,000 or over	under 1	2.25	1.10
		1–under 3	5.00	2.50
		3–under 6	4.75	2.25
		6–12	4.75	2.25
7.12.07–7.02.08	Under £100,000	no limit	3.00	1.50
	£100,000 or over	under 1	3.00	1.50
		1–under 3	5.50	2.75
		3–under 6	5.00	2.50
		6–under 9	4.75	2.25
		9–12	4.50	2.25
8.02.08–10.04.08	Under £100,000	no limit	2.00	1.00
	£100,000 or over	*under 1*	2.00	1.00
		1–under 3	4.50	2.25
		3–under 6	4.25	2.00
		6–under 9	4.00	2.00
		9–12	3.75	1.50
11.04.08–8.10.08	Under £100,000	no limit	2.00	1.00
	£100,000 or over	Under 1	2.00	1.00
		1–under 3	4.75	2.25
		3–under 6	4.50	2.25
		6–under 9	4.25	2.00
		9–12	4.25	2.00
9.10.08–6.11.08	Under £100,000	No limit	2.50	1.25
	£100,000 or over	under 1	2.50	1.25
		1–under 3	5.25	2.50
		3–under 6	5.00	2.50
		6–under 9	5.00	2.50
		9–12	4.75	2.25
7.11.08–4.12.08	Under £100,000	No limit	1.75	0.75
	£100,000 or over	under 1	1.75	0.75
		1–under 3	4.50	2.25
		3–under 6	4.25	2.00
		6–under 9	4.25	2.00
		9–12	4.00	2.00
5.12.08–8.1.09	Under £100,000	No limit	0.00	0.00
	£100,000 or over	under 1	0.00	0.00

Date	Amount	Held for (mths in yr)	Pay't of tax %	Cashed %
		1–under 3	2.50	1.25
		3–under 6	2.50	1.25
		6–under 9	2.50	1.25
		9–12	2.25	1.00
9.1.09–5.2.09	Under £100,000	No limit	0.00	0.00
	£100,000 or over	under 1	0.00	0.00
		1–under 3	1.50	0.75
		3–under 6	1.25	0.50
		6–under 9	1.25	0.50
		9–12	1.25	0.50
6.2.09–5.3.09	Under £100,000	No limit	0.00	0.00
	£100,000 or over	under 1	0.00	0.00
		1–under 3	1.00	0.50
		3–under 6	1.00	0.50
		6–under 9	1.00	0.50
		9–12	0.75	0.25
6.3.09–	Under £100,000	No limit	0.00	0.00
	£100,000 or over	under 1	0.00	0.00
		1–under 3	0.75	0.25
		3–under 6	0.75	0.25
		6–under 9	0.75	0.25
		9–12	0.75	0.25

Penalties

General

Offence	*Penalty*
Careless or deliberate error in taxpayer's document Delivery of return containing a careless or deliberate error. Applies to IT, CT, CGT, CT and VAT where the return period starts on or after 1 April 2008 and the return is due to be filed on or after 1 April 2009. Applies to inheritance tax for deaths on or after 1 April 2009 or where the liability arises on or after 1 April 2010, and to stamp duty land tax where the liability arises on or after 1 April 2010 (FA 2007 s 97, Sch 24).	An amount arrived at by applying a percentage to the potential lost revenue — 30% for a careless error, 70% for a deliberate but unconcealed error and 100% for a deliberate and concealed error. Reductions may be made for unprompted disclosure, down to nil, 20% and 30% respectively and for prompted disclosure down to 15%, 35% and 50%.
Third party careless or deliberate error in taxpayer's document Careless or deliberate error in a document supplied by a taxpayer to HMRC on or after 1 April 2009 as a result of incorrect information provided by a third party (FA 2008 s 122, Sch 40).	An amount arrived at by applying a percentage to the potential lost revenue — 30% for a careless error, 70% for a deliberate but unconcealed error and 100% for a deliberate and concealed error. Reductions may be made for unprompted disclosure, down to nil, 20% and 30% respectively and down to 15%, 35% and 50% for a prompted disclosure.
Failure to notify chargeablility on or after 1 April 2010 (FA 2008 Sch 41).	An amount arrived at by applying a percentage to the potential lost revenue — 30% for a careless error, 70% for a deliberate but unconcealed error and 100% for a deliberate and concealed error. Reductions may be made for unprompted disclosure, down to nil, 20% and 30% respectively and down to 15%, 35% and 50% for a prompted disclosure.
Failure to inform HMRC of an error in an assessment to IT, CGT, CT or VAT on or after 1 April 2008 within 30 days beginning with the date of assessment. Extended to inheritance tax and stamp duty land tax, among other taxes, for tax periods beginning on or after 1 April 2009 when the filing date is on or after 1 April 2010 (FA 2007, Sch 24).	An amount arrived at by applying a percentage to the potential lost revenue — 30% for a careless error, 70% for a deliberate but unconcealed error and 100% for a deliberate and concealed error. Reductions may be made for unprompted disclosure, down to nil, 20% and 30% respectively and down to 15%, 35% and 50% for a prompted disclosure.

Personal tax and corporation tax

Offence	*Penalty*
Failure to notify chargeability to income or capital gains tax within six months of tax year or to corporation tax within one year of accounting period (TMA 1970 s 7; FA 1998 Sch 18).	Up to tax liability still unpaid after 31 January following tax year (IT or CGT) or one year after end of accounting period (CT). Repealed for failures on or after 1 April 2010.
Failure to render return for income tax or capital gains tax (TMA 1970 ss 93, 93A).	(*a*) Initial penalty of £100 (or tax due if less); (*b*) upon direction by Commissioners, further penalty up to £60 for each day failure continues; (*c*) if failure continues after six months from filing date, and no penalty imposed under (*b*), a further penalty of £100 (or tax due if less); (*d*) if failure continues after one year from filing date, a further penalty up to amount of tax due.
Failure to render return for corporation tax (FA 1998 Sch 18 paras 17, 18).	(*a*) £100 if up to three months late (£500 if previous two returns also late); (*b*) £200 if over three months late (£1,000 if previous two returns also late); (*c*) if failure continues, on final day for delivery of return or, if later, 18 months after return period, 10% of tax unpaid 18 months after return period (20% of tax unpaid at that date if return not made within two years of return period).
Failure to maintain records supporting personal and trustees' returns of partnership returns (TMA 1970 s 12B).	Up to £3,000.
Fraudulently or negligently making an incorrect statement in connection with a claim to reduce payments on account (TMA 1970 s 59A).	Up to the amount (or additional amount) payable on account if a correct statement had been made.
Fraudulently or negligently delivering incorrect return or accounts or making an incorrect claim for an allowance, deduction or relief (TMA 1970 ss 95, 95A; FA 1998 Sch 18 para 89).	Up to amount of tax underpaid by reason of incorrectness for (IT and CGT) the tax year (or following tax year and any preceding tax year) in which the return or claim is delivered, (CT) the accounting period(s) to which the return or claim relates. Repealed for returns or claims for periods to which penalty under FA 2007 Sch 24 applies (see p 12).
Failure to notify within charge to corporation tax within three months after the beginning of the first accounting period and any subsequent accounting period not following on immediately from the end of a previous accounting period. With effect for accounting periods beginning on or after 22 July 2004 (FA 2004 s 55).	(*a*) Initial penalty up to £300; and (*b*) a continuing penalty up to £60 for each day on which the failure continues. Repealed for accounting periods ending after 31 March 2010.
Failure to register as self-employed (and liable to Class 2 NIC) within three months after month in which self-employment begins (SI 2001/1004 reg 87).	Up to £100. Repealed for obligations arising after 31 March 2010.

PAYE

Offence	*Penalty*
Careless or deliberate error Delivery of return containing a careless or deliberate error where the return period starts on or after 1 April 2008 and is due to be filed on or after 1 April 2009. (FA 2007 s 97, Sch 24)	An amount arrived at by applying a percentage to the potential lost revenue — up to 30% for a careless error, up to 70% for a deliberate but unconcealed error and up to 100% for a deliberate and concealed error.
Third party error Delivery by a third party of a document containing a relevant inaccuracy on or after 1 April 2009. (FA 2007 s 97, Sch 24)	An amount arrived at by applying a percentage to the potential lost revenue — up to 30% for a careless error, up to 70% for a deliberate but unconcealed error and up to 100% for a deliberate and concealed error.
Failure to notify chargeablility on or after 1 April 2010. (FA 2008 s 123, Sch 41)	An amount arrived at by applying a percentage to the potential lost revenue — up to 30% for a careless error, up to 70% for a deliberate but unconcealed error and up to 100% for a deliberate and concealed error.
Failure to submit return P9D or P11D (benefits in kind) by due date (6 July following subsequent tax years) (TMA 1970 s 98(1)).	(*a*) Initial penalty up to £300; and (*b*) continuing penalty up to £60 for each day on which the failure continues.
Fraudulently or negligently submitting incorrect return P9D or P11D (TMA 1970 s 98(2)).	Penalty up to £3,000.

Offence	Penalty
Failure to submit returns P14 (individual end of year summary), P35 (annual return), P38 or P38A (supplementary returns for employees not on P35) by due date (19 May following tax year) (TMA 1970 s 98A).	(*a*) First 12 months: penalty of £100 for each 50 employees (or part thereof) for each month the failure continues; (*b*) failures exceeding 12 months: penalty up to amount of PAYE or NIC due and unpaid after 19 April following tax year.
Fraudulently or negligently submitting incorrect forms P14, P35, P38 or P38A (TMA 1970 s 98A).	Penalty up to the amount of tax due.
Failure to submit returns P11D(b) (Class 1A NIC returns) by due date (19 July following tax year, extended for 2000/01 only to 19 September 2001) (SI 2001/1004 reg 81).	(*a*) First 12 months: penalty of £100 for each 50 employees (or part thereof) for each month the failure continues (but total penalty not to exceed total Class 1A NIC due); (*b*) failures exceeding 12 months: a penalty not exceeding the amount of Class 1A NIC due and unpaid after 19 July following tax year.
Failure to submit information in connection with mandatory e-filing from 2004/05 onwards (SI 1993/744 as amended).	Penalty based on number of employees not exceeding £3,000 for 1,000 or more employees.
Failure to make payments on time. Applies for 2010/11 onwards to income tax and Class 1 NICs collected through in-year PAYE and to Class 1A and Class 1B NICs and student loan deductions. (FA 2009 Sch 56)	*In-year payments.* The first failure in a tax year does not count as a default. If there are one, two or three defaults during a tax year, penalty of 1% of total amount of defaults. If four, five or six defaults during a tax year, penalty of 2%; if seven, eight or nine defaults, penalty of 3%; if ten or more defaults in one tax year penalty 4%. If tax remains unpaid six months after penalty date a penalty of 5% of the unpaid amount applies; a further 5% penalty applies if tax is still unpaid after a further six months. *Class 1A, 1B NICs.* A 5% penalty applies if full amount not paid within 30 days of due date. If amount remains unpaid six months after due date a penalty of 5% applies; a further 5% penalty applies if amount is still unpaid after a further six months.

Inheritance tax returns and information

Offence	Penalty
Failure to deliver an account within 12 months of death (unless tax is less than £100 or there is a reasonable excuse) (IHTA 1984 s 245). 1 The fixed penalty in (*a*) and (*c*) relates to failures where the account is due by 22 January 2005 (FA 2004 s 295(5)). 2 Where the account is due on or before 22 July 2004, the penalty in (*d*) relates to failures continuing after 21 July 2005 (FA 2004 s 295(6)).	(*a*) Initial penalty of (up to) £100 (or the amount of tax payable if less); (*b*) further penalty up to £60 (where penalty determined by court or Special Commissioners) for each day on which the failure continues; (*c*) if failure continues after six months after the date on which account is due, and proceedings not commenced, a further penalty of (up to) £100 (or amount of tax payable if less); and (*d*) if failure continues one year after end of the period in which account is due (where the account is due after 22 July 2004), and IHT is payable, a penalty not exceeding £3,000.
Failure to submit account or notify HMRC under IHTA 1984 s 218A if a disposition on a death is varied within six months of the variation and additional tax is payable (IHTA 1984 s 245A(1A), (1B)).	(*a*) Initial penalty up to £100; (*b*) further penalty up to £60 (if determined by court or Special Commissioners) for each day on which the failure continues; (*c*) up to £3,000 if failure continues after 12 months from date notification is due (where account due after 22 July 2004).
Failure to provide documents etc under IHTA 1984 s 219A(1) or (4) (IHTA 1984 s 245A(3)).	(*a*) Initial penalty up to £50; and (*b*) further penalty up to £30 (where penalty determined by court or Special Commissioners) for each day on which the failure continues.
Taxpayer fraudulently or negligently delivering, furnishing or producing incorrect accounts, information or documents (IHTA 1984 s 247; FA 2004 s 295(4), (9)).	(Accounts etc delivered after 22 July 2004) penalty up to the amount of tax payable. Repealed for accounts etc to which penalty under FA 2007 Sch 24 applies (see p 12). (Accounts etc delivered on or before 22 July 2004) (*a*) in the case of fraud, penalty up to aggregate of £3,000 and the amount payable; and (*b*) in the case of negligence, penalty up to the aggregate of £1,500 and the amount of tax payable.

Offence	*Penalty*
Person other than the taxpayer fraudulently or negligently delivering, furnishing or producing incorrect accounts, information or documents (IHTA 1984 s 247(3); FA 2004 s 295(4), (9)).	(Accounts etc delivered after 22 July 2004) penalty up to £3,000. (*a*) in the case of fraud, penalty up to £3,000; and (*b*) in the case of negligence, penalty up to £1,500.
Incorrect return etc: Assisting in or inducing the delivery, furnishing or production of any account, information or document knowing it to be incorrect (IHTA 1984 s 247(4)).	Up to £3,000.

Special returns of information

Offence	*Penalty*
Failure to comply with a notice to deliver a return or other document, furnish particulars or make anything available for inspection under any of the provisions listed in column 1 of the table in TMA 1970 s 98.	(*a*) Initial penalty up to £300 (£3,000 in relation to TA 1988 s 765A (movements of capital between residents of EU Member States); (*b*) further penalty up to £60 (£600) for each day on which the failure continues.
Failure to furnish information, give certificates or produce documents or records under any of the provisions listed in column 2 of the table in TMA 1970 s 98.	(*a*) Initial penalty up to £300; and (*b*) further penalty up to £60 for each day on which the failure continues.
Fraudulently or negligently delivering any incorrect document, information etc required under the above provisions.	Penalty up to £3,000.
Failure to deduct income tax at source from payments of interest or royalties under TA 1988 ss 349(1), 350(1) where the exemption does not apply and the company did not believe or could not reasonably have believed that it would apply (TMA 1970 s 98(4A)–(4D)).	(*a*) Initial penalty up to £3,000; and (*b*) further penalty up to £600 for each day on which the failure continues.
Advance pricing agreements: Fraudulently or negligently making a false or misleading statement in the preparation of, or application to enter into, any advance pricing agreement (FA 1999 s 86).	Penalty up to £10,000.
Declaration of non-UK residence: Fraudulently or negligently making a false or misleading declaration of non-UK residence to a deposit-taker or building society under ITA 2007 ss 858-861 (TMA 1970 s 99B).	Penalty up to £3,000.

Other offences by taxpayers, agents etc

Offence	*Penalty*
Falsification of documents. Intentionally falsifying, concealing or destroying documents required under TMA 1970 ss 20, 20A or 20BA (TMA 1970 s 20BB).	On summary conviction, a fine up to the statutory maximum (£5,000); on conviction on indictment, imprisonment for a term not exceeding two years or a fine or both.
Failure to produce documents etc for the purposes of an enquiry under TMA 1970 s 19A or under FA 1998 Sch 18 para 27 (TMA 1970 s 97AA; FA 1998 Sch 18 para 29).	(*a*) Initial penalty of £50; and (*b*) further penalty up to £30 (if determined by HMRC) or £150 (if determined by Commissioners) for each day on which failure continues. Repealed on or after 1 April 2009.
European Economic Interest Groupings– Offences in connection with the supply of information:	
(i) failure to supply information	Initial penalty up to £300 per member of the Grouping at the time of failure and after direction by the Commissioners: continuing penalty up to £60 per member of the Grouping at the end of the day for each day on which the failure continues.
(ii) fraudulent or negligent delivery of an incorrect return, accounts or statement (TMA 1970 s 98B).	Up to £3,000 for each member of the Grouping at the time of delivery.
Assisting in the delivery of incorrect returns, accounts or information (TMA 1970 s 99).	Penalty up to £3,000.
Certificates of non-liability to income tax: Fraudulently or negligently giving such a certificate for the purposes of receiving interest gross on a bank or building society account, or failing to comply with an undertaking given in such a certificate (TMA 1970 s 99A).	Penalty up to £3,000.
Refusal to allow a deduction of income tax at source (TMA 1970 s 106).	£50.

Offence	*Penalty*
Obstruction of officer in inspection of property to ascertain its market value (TMA 1970 s 111).	Up to £50.
Construction Industry Scheme: (pre 1 April 2007 scheme) Failure by contractor to check validity of registration card (TA 1988 s 566(2B)–(2E)).	Up to £3,000.
(pre 1 April 2007 scheme) Fraudulent attempt by sub-contractor to obtain or misuse a sub-contractor's certificate (TA 1988 s 561(10), (11)).	Up to £3,000.
Construction Industry Scheme: (post 31 March 2007 scheme) Making false statements etc for the purpose of obtaining a gross payment certificate (FA 2004 s 72).	Up to £3,000.
Fraudulent evasion of income tax (FA 2000 s 144).	On summary conviction, imprisonment for up to six months or a fine up to the statutory maximum (£5,000); on conviction on indictment, imprisonment for up to seven years or a fine or both.
Enterprise investment scheme relief: Issue by a company of a certificate of approval for such relief fraudulently or negligently or without the authority of HMRC (TA 1988 s 306(6)).	Not exceeding £3,000.
Treasury consent: Creation or transfer of shares or debentures in a non-resident subsidiary company without the consent of HM Treasury (TA 1988 s 766).	On conviction on indictment— (*a*) imprisonment for not more than two years or a fine, or both; or (*b*) in the case of a UK company, a fine not exceeding the greater of £10,000, or three times the tax payable by the company attributable to income and gains arising in the previous 36 months.
Deliberately or recklessly failing to pay corporation tax due in respect of total liability of company for accounting period, or fraudulently or negligently making claim for repayment (TMA 1970 s 59E(4); SI 1998/3175 reg 13).	Penalty not exceeding twice amount of interest charged under SI 1998/3175 reg 7.
Failure of a company to maintain records (other than those only required for claims, etc, or dividend vouchers and certificates of income tax deducted where other evidence is available) (FA 1998 Sch 18 para 23).	Penalty not exceeding £3,000.
Failure to notify notifiable proposals or notifiable arrangements, or failure to notify the client of the relevant scheme reference number under the provisions of FA 2004 ss 308(1), (3), 309(1), 310 or s 312(1).	(*a*) An initial penalty not exceeding £5,000; (*b*) a continuing penalty not exceeding £600 for each day on which the failure continues after imposition of initial penalty.
Failure to notify scheme reference number etc under FA 2004 s 313(1);	Penalty of £100 in respect of each scheme to which the failure relates;
for second failure, occurring within three years from the date on which the first failure began;	penalty of £500 in respect of each scheme to which the failure relates;
for subsequent failures, occurring within three years from the date on which the previous failure began.	penalty of £1,000 in respect of each scheme to which the failure relates.
[TMA 1970 s 98C; FA 2004 s 315(1)].	

Mitigation of penalties

HMRC have discretion to mitigate or entirely remit any penalty or to stay or compound any penalty proceedings (TMA 1970 s 102).

Interest on penalties

Penalties under TMA 1970 Parts II (ss 7–12B), IV (ss 28A–43B), VA (ss 59A–59D) and X (ss 93–107) carry interest at the prescribed rate (see p 14): TMA 1970 s 103A. Surcharges on unpaid income tax and capital gains tax carry interest under TMA 1970 s 59C.

Time limits for claims and elections

Whenever possible, a claim or election must be made on the tax return or by an amendment to the return (TMA 1970 s 42 and FA 1998 Sch 18 paras 9, 10, 67 and 79). Exceptions to this general rule are dealt with in TMA 1970 Sch 1A. Except where another period is expressly prescribed, a claim for relief in respect of income tax and capital gains tax must be made within four years after the end of the tax year (for claims made before 1 April 2010 such claims had to be made within five years from the 31 January following the year of assessment to which it relates). (TMA 1970 s 43(1); FA 2008 Sch 39 para 12). The time limit for claims by companies is four years from the end of the accounting period to which it relates (six years for claims made before 1 April 2010) (FA 1998 Sch 18 para 55 and FA 2008 Sch 39 para 44).

The tables below set out some of the main exceptions to the general limits.

Income tax

Claim	*Time limit*
Trading losses: Loss sustained in a trade, profession or vocation to be set against other income of the year or the last preceding year. Extended to certain pre-trading expenditure by TA 1988 s 401 and ITTOIA 2005 s 57 (ITA 2007 s 64).	One year after 31 January next following tax year in which loss arose.
Unrelieved trading losses to be set against capital gains (TCGA 1992 ss 261B, 261C).	One year after 31 January next following tax year in which loss sustained.
Losses of new trade etc: Loss sustained in the first four years of a new trade, profession or vocation to be offset against other income arising in the three years immediately preceding the year of loss. Extended to certain pre-trading expenditure by TA 1988 s 401 and ITTOIA 2005 s 57 (ITA 2007 s 72).	One year after 31 January next following tax year in which loss sustained.
Property business losses: Claim for relief against total income (ITA 2007 s 124).	One year after 31 January next following tax year.
Loss on disposal of unlisted shares: Loss on disposal of shares in an EIS company or a qualifying trading company to be offset against other income of the year of loss or the last preceding year (ITA 2007 s 124).	One year after 31 January next following tax year in which loss incurred.
Gift aid: Election to treat donations to charity under gift aid made after 5 April 2003 as made in the previous tax year (ITA 2007 s 426).	On or before date on which donor delivers tax return for the previous tax year and not later than 31 January after that year.

Capital gains

Claim	*Time limit*
Assets of negligible value: Loss to be allowed where the value of an asset has become negligible (TCGA 1992 s 24(2)).	Two years after end of chargeable period of deemed sale (and reacquisition).
Assets held on 31 March 1982: Events occurring prior to 31 March 1982 to be ignored in computing gains arising after 5 April 1988 (TCGA 1992 s 35(5), (6) as amended).	One year after 31 January next following tax year in which first relevant disposal made after 5.4.88 (capital gains tax); two years after end of accounting period in which first relevant disposal made after 31.3.88 (corporation tax).
Main residence: Determination of main residence for principal private residence exemption (TCGA 1992 s 222(5)(*a*)).	Two years after acquisition of second residence.
Relief for loans to traders: Losses on certain loans to traders to be allowed as capital losses (TCGA 1992 s 253(3)).	Two years.
Relief for loans to traders (payments by guarantor): Losses arising from payments by guarantor of certain irrecoverable loans to traders to be allowed as capital losses at time of claim or 'earlier time' (TCGA 1992 s 253(4), (4A); FA 1996 s 135(2)).	Four years after the end of the tax year or accounting period in which payment made (for claims before 1 April 2010, five years after 31 January following tax year in which payment made (capital gains tax); six years after end of accounting period in which payment made (corporation tax)).
Election for valuation at 6 April 1965: Gain on a disposal of an asset held at 6 April 1965 to be computed as if the asset had been acquired on that date. An election once made is irrevocable (TCGA 1992 Sch 2 para 17).	One year after 31 January following tax year in which disposal made (capital gains tax); two years after end of accounting period in which disposal made (corporation tax); or such further time as HMRC may allow.

Corporation tax

Claim	*Time limit*
Trading losses: Loss sustained by a company in a trade in an accounting period to be offset against profits of that accounting period and profits of the preceding year. (CTA 2010 s 37(7); TA 1988 s 393A(1), (2A), (10)).	Two years or such further period as HMRC may allow.
Group relief: Group relief to be given for accounting periods ending after 30 June 1999. The surrendering company must consent to the claim (FA 1998 Sch 18 paras 66–77).	The last of: (*a*) one year from filing date of claimant company's return for accounting period for which claim is made; (*b*) 30 days after end of an enquiry into return; (*c*) if HMRC amend return after an enquiry, 30 days after issue of notice of amendment; (*d*) if an appeal is made against amendment, 30 days after determination of appeal; (or such later time as HMRC may allow).

Claim	Time limit
Non-trading deficit on loan relationship: Claim for non-trading deficits on loan relationships (including non-trading debits on derivative contracts) in an accounting period ending after 30 September 2002 to be:	
(*a*) offset against profits of same period or carried back (CTA 2009 s 460; FA 1996 s 83, Sch 8 paras 1, 3);	Two years after end of accounting period in which deficit arose (or such later time as HMRC may allow).
(*b*) treated as non-trading deficit of subsequent accounting period to be carried forward to succeeding accounting periods (CTA 2009 s 458; FA 1996 s 83, Sch 8).	Two years after end of that subsequent accounting period.
Intangible assets: Election to replace accounts depreciation with fixed writing-down allowance of 4% (CTA 2009 s 730; FA 2002 Sch 29 para 10).	Two years after end of the accounting period in which asset was created or acquired.
Research and development: Claim for tax relief to be made, amended or withdrawn in company tax return (or amended return) (FA 1998 Sch 18 paras 83E, 83LE).	One year from the filing date for return or such later time as HMRC may allow.
UITF 40 spreading adjustment: Election to treat it as arising and charged in an accounting period rather than spreading it over three to six years (FA 2006, Sch 15 para 13).	One year from filing date for return.

Capital allowances

Claim	Time limit
Corporation tax claims (accounting periods ending after 30 June 1999): Claims, amended claims and withdrawals of claims in respect of corporation tax capital allowances for accounting periods ending after 30 June 1999 (CAA 2001 s 3(2), (3)(*b*), FA 1998 Sch 18 para 82).	The last of: (*a*) one year after filing date of claimant company's return for accounting period for which claim is made; (*b*) 30 days after end of enquiry into return; (*c*) if HMRC amend the return after an enquiry, 30 days after issue of notice of amendment; (*d*) if appeal is made against amendment, 30 days after determination of appeal; (or such later time as HMRC may allow).
Short life assets: Plant or machinery to be treated as a short life asset (CAA 2001 s 85(2)).	One year after 31 January after tax year in which chargeable period ends (IT); two years after end of chargeable period (CT).
Connected persons: Succession to a trade between connected persons to be ignored in computing capital allowances (CAA 2001 s 266).	Two years after date of the succession.
Sales between persons under common control treated as made at the lower of open market value and tax written down value (CAA 2001 s 570(5)).	Two years after date of the disposal.

Exchanges

Recognised stock exchanges

The following is a list of countries with exchanges which have been designated as recognised stock exchanges under ITA 2007 s 1005; CTA 2010 s 1137; TA 1988 s 841. Unless otherwise specified, any stock exchange (or options exchange) in a country listed below is a recognised stock exchange provided it is recognised under the law of the country concerned relating to stock exchanges.

HMRC may make an order designating a market in the UK as a recognised stock exchange.

Country	*Date of recognition*
Australian Stock Exchange and its stock exchange subsidiaries	22 September 1988
Austria[3]	22 October 1970
Belgium[3]	22 October 1970
Bermuda	4 December 2007
Brazil	
Rio De Janeiro Stock Exchange	17 August 1995
São Paulo Stock Exchange	11 December 1995
Canada	
Any stock exchange prescribed for the purposes of the Canadian Income Tax Act	22 October 1970
Cayman Islands Stock Exchange	4 March 2004
China	
Hong Kong – Any stock exchange recognised under Section 2A(1) of the Hong Kong Companies Ordinance	26 February 1971
Cyprus	
Cyprus Stock Exchange	22 June 2009
Denmark	
Copenhagen Stock Exchange	22 October 1970
Finland	
Helsinki Stock Exchange	22 October 1970
France[3]	22 October 1970
Germany[3]	5 August 1971
Greece	
Athens Stock Exchange	14 June 1993
Guernsey[3]	10 December 2002
Iceland	31 March 2006
Irish Republic[3]	22 October 1970
Italy[3]	3 May 1972
Japan[3]	22 October 1970
Korea	10 October 1994
Luxembourg[3]	21 February 1972
Malaysia	
Kuala Lumpur Stock Exchange	10 October 1994
Malta Stock Exchange	29 December 2005
Mexico	10 October 1994
Netherlands[3]	22 October 1970
New Zealand	22 September 1988
Norway[3]	22 October 1970
Poland	
Warsaw Stock Exchange	25 February 2010
Portugal[3]	21 February 1972
Singapore	30 June 1977
South Africa	
Bond Exchange of South Africa	16 April 2008
Johannesburg Stock Exchange	22 October 1970
Spain[3]	5 August 1971
Sri Lanka	
Colombo Stock Exchange	21 February 1972
Sweden	
Stockholm Stock Exchange	16 July 1985
Swiss Stock Exchange	12 May 1997
Thailand	10 October 1994
United Kingdom	19 July 2007

Country	Date of recognition
United States	
Any stock exchange registered with the SEC as a national securities exchange[1]	22 October 1970
Nasdaq Stock Market[2]	10 March 1992

1 'National securities exchange' does not include any local exchanges registered with Securities and Exchange Commission.
2 As maintained through the facilities of the National Association of Securities Dealers Inc and its subsidiaries.
3 i.e., a stock exchange according to the law of the country concerned relating to stock exchanges.

Recognised futures exchanges

The following is a list of exchanges which have been designated as recognised futures exchanges under TCGA 1992 s 288(6). By concession, those exchanges were recognised futures exchanges for the tax year of recognition onwards.

Recognised futures exchanges	*Date of recognition*
International Petroleum Exchange of London	6.August 1985
London Metal Exchange	6 August 1985
London Gold Market	12 December 1985
London Silver Market	12 December 1985
CME Group (formerly Chicago Mercantile Exchange and Chicago Board of Trade)	19 December 1986
New York Mercantile Exchange	19 December 1986
Philadelphia Board of Trade	19 December 1986
Mid America Commodity Exchange	29 July 1987
Montreal Exchange	29 July 1987
Hong Kong Futures Exchange	15 December 1987
Commodity Exchange (Comex)	25 August 1988
Sydney Futures Exchange	13 October 1988
Euronext (London International Financial Futures and Options Exchange)	22 March 1992
OM Stockholm	18 March 1992
OM London	18 March 1992
New York Board of Trade	10 June 2004

Recognised investment exchanges and clearing houses

The following is a list of investment exchanges and clearing houses recognised as investment exchanges under the Financial Services and Markets Act 2000 and able to carry out investment business in the UK.

Recognised investment exchanges	*Date of recognition*
London Stock Exchange	22 November 2001
International Petroleum Exchange of London	5 April 1988
LIFFE Administration and Management	22 November 2001
London Metal Exchange	22 November 2001
Virt-x Exchange Ltd	23 November 2001
ICE Futures	22 November 2001
EDX London Ltd	1 July 2003
NYMEX Europe	7 September 2005

Recognised clearing houses	*Date of recognition*
CH Clearnet	23 November 2001
CRESTCo	23 November 2001

Recognised overseas investment exchanges and clearing houses

The following is a list of overseas investment exchanges and clearing houses recognised under the Financial Services and Markets Act 2000 and able to conduct investment business in the UK.

Recognised overseas investment exchange	*Date of recognition*
National Association of Securities Dealers Automated Quotations (NASDAQ)	23 November 2001

Recognised overseas investment exchange	*Date of recognition*
Sydney Futures Exchange	30 January 2002
Chicago Mercantile Exchange (CME)	23 November 2001
Chicago Board of Trade (CBOT)	23 November 2001
New York Mercantile Exchange (NYMEX)	23 November 2001
NQLX LLC	23 November 2001
Swiss Stock Exchange (SWX)	23 November 2001
Cantor Financial Futures Exchange (CFEE)	23 November 2001
EUREX Zurich	23 November 2001
Warenterminborse Hannover	23 November 2001
US Futures Exchange	21 May 2004

Recognised clearing house	*Date of recognition*
SIS x-clear AG	19 August 2004

Applications for clearances and approvals

Clearance application	*Address*
Transfer of long-term insurance business (TCGA 1992 s 211, TA 1988 s 444A)	Richard Thomas, CT & VAT (Insurance Group), 3rd (3C/10) Floor, 100 Parliament Street, London SW1A 2BQ
Demergers (TA 1988 s 215); Company purchase of own shares (TA 1988 s 225); Transactions in securities (TA 1988 s 707; ITA 2007 s 701); Enterprise Investment Scheme – acquisition of shares by new company (ITA 2007 s 247(1)(f)); Share exchanges (TCGA 1992 ss 138, 139, 140B, 140D); and Intangible fixed assets (FA 2002 Sch 29 para 88)	Clearance and Counteraction Team, Anti-Avoidance Group, First Floor, 22 Kingsway, London WC2B 6NR (Market sensitive applications to Team Leader– see note below)[1]
Company migration (FA 1988 s 130)	Neil Nagle, Business International, Transfer Pricing Team, 100 Parliament Street, London SW1A 2BQ
Advance pricing agreements (FA 1999 ss 85–87)	Ian Wood, CT & VAT (International CT), 100 Parliament Street, London SW1A 2BQ For APAs involving oil taxation: Susan New or Jo Wakeman, Large Business Service Oil & Gas (APAs), 2nd Floor, 22 Kingsway, London WC2B 6 NR
Controlled foreign companies (TA 1988 ss 747–756, Schs 24–26)	Mary Sharp/David Price/Des Hanna, CT & VAT (International CT), 100 Parliament Street, London SW1A 2BQ
Corporate Venturing Schemes (FA 2000 Sch 15)	Small Company Enterprise Centre, CRI, Ty Glas, Llanishen, Cardiff CF14 5ZG

Approval application	*Address*
Pensions (TA 1988 ss 590, 591)	HMRC, Pension Schemes Office, Fitzroy House, PO Box 62, Castle Meadow Road, Nottingham NG2 1BG
Employee share schemes (ITEPA 2003 Schs 2,3,4)	HMRC Employee Shares & Securities Unit, Room G52, 100 Parliament Street, London SW1A 2BQ
Qualifying life assurance policies (TA 1988 Sch 15)	Claire Ritchie, CT & VAT (Insurance Group), Third Floor, 100 Parliament Street, London SW1A 2BQ
Professional bodies (relief for subscriptions) (ITEPA 2003 s 343)	A list of approved professional bodies and learned societies is available on the HMRC website (at www.hmrc.gov.uk/list3/index.htm)

Confirmation or pre-transaction advice	*Address*
Funding issues (TA 1988 ss 209, 703)	Miles Nelson, CT & VAT (International CT), 100 Parliament Street, London SW1A 2BQ
Transactions in land (TA 1988 ss 35, 776)	Applications for clearance should be sent to the HMRC Officer who deals with the returns
Non-statutory clearances	Large businesses should contact their client relationship manager. All other businesses and their agents should sent applications to HMRC Clearances Team, Alexander House, 21 Victoria Avenue, Southend-on-Sea, Essex SS99 1BD.[2]

Application for treasury consent	*Address*
Transactions in shares or debentures (TA 1988, ss 590, 591)	Des Hanna/David Price/Ian Wright (s 765) Mark Bryan (s 765A), CT & VAT (International CT), 100 Parliament Street, London SW1A 2BQ.

1 Where clearance is sought under any one or more of the sections handled by the Clearance and Counteraction Team, clearance applications may be sent in a single letter to the above London address for clearances under those sections. The letter should make clear what clearance is required. E-mail applications can be sent to reconstructions@hmrc.gsi.gov.uk and fax applications to 020 7438 4409. For market sensitive information, call Team Leader on 020 7438 6585 before sending an e-mail or fax. A reply by e-mail should be requested if required. General enquiries can be made on 020 7438 7474.

2 Non-statutory clearances: Businesses may apply for a non-statutory clearance where there is material uncertainty and the issue is commercially significant.

Capital allowances

Rates

Agricultural buildings

	Expenditure incurred after	*% Rate*
Initial allowance	31 October 1992[1]	20
	31 October 1993	Nil
Writing-down allowance	**31 March 1986 and before 6 April 2011(1 April 2011 for companies)**	**4**[2,3]

1 Initial allowances were temporarily reintroduced for 1 year in respect of capital expenditure on agricultural buildings or works. The allowances applied to buildings or works constructed under a contract entered into between 1 November 1992 and 31 October 1993, and brought into use for the purposes of the farming trade by 31 December 1994. See CAA 1990 s 124A.

2 Agricultural buildings allowances are to be abolished for income tax purposes for 2011/12 onwards and for corporation tax purposes for the financial year beginning 1 April 2011 onwards. (FA 2008, s 84)

3 As a transitional measure, writing-down allowances are being stepped down over the three financial or tax years prior to abolition. For 2008/09 (for corporation tax, the financial year beginning 1 April 2008) only 75% of the allowance is given. For 2009/10 (or financial year beginning 1 April 2009) only 50% is given and for 2010/11 (or financial year beginning 1 April 2010) only 25%. Where a chargeable period falls in more than one tax or financial year, time apportionment applies to determine the amount of the allowance. (FA 2008, s 85)

Note: For balancing events on or after 21 March 2007, no election for a balancing adjustment can be made so that the new holder of the relevant interest will, in all cases, calculate writing-down allowances based on the previous owner's balance of qualifying expenditure (cost less allowances claimed).

Dredging

	Expenditure incurred after	*% Rate*
Writing-down allowance	**5 November 1962**	**4**

Industrial buildings and structures

Initial allowance	*Expenditure*[1] *incurred after*	*% Rate*
Generally:	31 October 1992	20
	31 October 1993	Nil
Exception: Enterprise zones	**within 10 years of site being included in zone**[2]	**100**
Writing-down allowance		
Generally:	**5 April 1946**	**2**
	5 November 1962[3] and before 6 April 2011 (1 April 2011 for companies)[5,6]	**4**
Exception: Enterprise zones	**within 10 years of site being included in zone**[2]	**25**

1 The amount qualifying for allowance is the price paid for the relevant interest *minus* (i) the value of the land element and (ii) any value attributable to elements over and above those which would feature in a normal commercial lease negotiated in the open market: FA 1995 s 100 confirming previous practice.

2 CAA 2001 s 306, 310. Includes expenditure on qualifying hotels. See p 27 for enterprise zones.

3 Includes expenditure on qualifying hotels (other than in an enterprise zone). Also includes expenditure on the construction of toll roads incurred for accounting periods or basis periods ending after 5 April 1991.

4 For balancing events on or after 21 March 2007, no balancing adjustment will arise and the new holder of the relevant interest will calculate writing-down allowances based on the previous owner's balance of qualifying expenditure (cost less allowances claimed).

5 Industrial buildings allowances and allowances for buildings in enterprise zones are to be abolished for income tax purposes for 2011/12 onwards and for corporation tax purposes for the financial year beginning 1 April 2011 onwards. (FA 2008, ss 84, 86)

6 As a transitional measure, writing-down allowances are being stepped down over the three financial or tax years prior to abolition. For 2008/09 (for corporation tax, the financial year beginning 1 April 2008) only 75% of the allowance was given. For 2009/10 (or financial year beginning 1 April 2009) only 50% is given and for 2010/11 (or financial year beginning 1 April 2010) only 25%. Where a chargeable period falls in more than one tax or financial year, time apportionment applies to determine the amount of the allowance. (FA 2008, ss 85, 87)

Flat conversions

Initial allowance	*Expenditure incurred after*	*% Rate*
	10 May 2001	**100**

Applies to expenditure incurred on renovating or converting vacant or storage space above commercial properties to provide low value flats for rent. A writing-down allowance is given at 25% (on a straight-line basis) on unrelieved expenditure. (CAA 2001 ss 393A–393W; FA 2001 s 67, Sch 19).

Know-how

Expenditure incurred after 31 March 1986: annual 25% writing-down allowance (reducing balance basis).

Plant and machinery

Expenditure incurred	*after*	*before*	*Up to pa*
Annual investment allowance[1]			
for income tax purposes	**5 April 2010**		**£100,000**
	5 April 2008	6 April 2010	£50,000
for corporation tax purposes	**31 March 2010**		**£100,000**
	31 March 2008	1 April 2010	£50,000
First-year allowance (FYA)			
General[12]			% Rate
for income tax purposes	6 April 2009	5 April 2010	40
for corporation tax purposes	1 April 2009	31 March 2010	40
Small and medium-sized businesses[2]			
for income tax purposes	1 July 1998	6 April 2008	40
for corporation tax purposes	1 July 1998	1 April 2008	40
	1 July 1997	2 July 1998	50
in Northern Ireland *only*	11 May 1998	12 May 2002	100
Small businesses[3]			
for income tax purposes	5 April 2006	6 April 2008	50
	5 April 2004	6 April 2005	50
for corporation tax purposes	31 March 2006	1 April 2008	50
	31 March 2004	1 April 2005	50
ICT	31 March 2000	1 April 2004	100
Energy-saving plant or machinery[4]	**31 March 2001**		**100**
New low-emission cars and refuelling equipment[5]	**16 April 2002**	**1 April 2013**	**100**
Environmentally beneficial plant or machinery[6]	**31 March 2003**		**100**
Zero-emissions goods vehicles[7]			
for income tax purposes	**5 April 2010**		**100**
for corporation tax purposes	**31 March 2010**		**100**
Writing-down allowance (WDA)[8]			
	Chargeable period starting after		
Long life assets[9]			
for income tax purposes	**5 April 2008**		**10**
for corporation tax purposes	**31 March 2008**		**10**
	Chargeable period ending before		
for income tax purposes	6 April 2008		6
for corporation tax purposes	1 April 2008		6
Integral features[10]	**Expenditure incurred on or after**		
for income tax purposes	**6 April 2008**		**10**
for corporation tax purposes	**1 April 2008**		**10**
Thermal insulation			
for income tax purposes	**6 April 2008**		**10**
for corporation tax purposes	**1 April 2008**		**10**
Cushion gas	**1 April 2010**		**10**
Foreign leased assets[11]	9 March 1982	1 April 2006	10
	Chargeable period ending before		
Generally	1 or 6 April 2008		25

	Chargeable periods starting after	
for income tax purposes	**5 April 2008**	**20**
for corporation tax	**31 March 2008**	**20**
	Chargeable periods straddling	
for income tax	6 April 2008	Hybrid rate[8]
for corporation tax	1 April 2008	Hybrid rate[8]

1 The first £100,000 (£50,000 for expenditure incurred before 6 April 2010 (income tax) or 1 April 2010 (corporation tax) of qualifying expenditure incurred in a chargeable period qualifies for the annual investment allowance at 100%. The limit is proportionately increased or decreased where the chargeable period is longer or shorter than a year. A group of companies (defined as for company law purposes) can only receive a single allowance. This restriction also applies to certain related businesses or companies. Expenditure on cars does not qualify. (CAA 2001 ss 38A, 38B, 51A–51N; FA 2008, s 74, Sch 24).

2 **Small and medium-sized businesses:** The allowance does not apply to certain expenditure including that on plant and machinery for leasing, motor cars, ships, railway assets or long-life assets. After the first year, allowances revert to the normal WDA. The rate of 50% applied only for expenditure incurred during the year ended 1 July 1998 when a 12% FYA applied to long-life assets. (See notes 4 and 11 below.) Small and medium-sized businesses are, broadly, those satisfying any two of the following conditions: (*a*) turnover £22,800,000 or less (*b*) assets £11,400,000 or less (*c*) not more than 250 employees (CAA 1990 ss 22(3C), (6B), 22A, 44, 46–49). For accounting periods ending before 30.01.04, the thresholds were: (*a*) turnover £11,200,000 or less (*b*) assets £5,600,000 or less.

3 **Small businesses:** See note 2 above for conditions for relief. Small businesses are, broadly, those satisfying any two of the following conditions: (*a*) turnover £5,600,000 or less (*b*) assets £2,800,000 or less (*c*) not more than 50 employees. For accounting periods ending before 30.01.04, the thresholds were: (*a*) turnover £2,800,000 or less (*b*) assets £1,400,000 or less. (FA 2004 s 142).

4 **Energy-saving plant or machinery:** The allowances are available for investment by *any* business in designated energy-saving plant and machinery in accordance with the Government's Energy Technology Product List (CAA 2001 ss 45A–45C, 46; FA 2001 s 65, Sch 17; SI 2001/2541; SI 2005/1114). The product lists are available at www.eca.gov.uk.

5 **Low-emission cars:** The allowance is given on (*a*) new cars which are either electrically propelled or emit not more than 110g/km of CO2(120g/km for expenditure incurred before 1 April 2008), registered after 16 April 2002 and (*b*) new plant and machinery to refuel vehicles in a gas refuelling station with natural gas, hydrogen fuels, or (for expenditure on or after 1 April 2008) biogas (CAA 2001 ss 45D, 45E, 46).

6 **Environmentally beneficial plant or machinery:** Allowances are available for expenditure by *any* business on new and unused designated technologies and products which satisfy the relevant environmental criteria in accordance with the Government's technologies or products lists (FA 2003 s 167, Sch 30). The product lists are available at www.eca.gov.uk.

7 **Zero-emissions goods vehicles:** The allowance is given on new (and not second hand) vehicles which cannot under any circumstances produce CO2 emissions when driven and which are of a design primarily suited to the conveyance of goods or burden. The expenditure must be incurred before 1 April 2015 (corporation tax) or 6 April 2015 (income tax).

8 **WDAs** are calculated on a reducing balance basis. For chargeable periods beginning before 6 April 2008 and ending on or after that date (or, for corporation tax purposes, beginning before 1 April 2008 and ending on or after that date) a hybrid rate of WDAs applies, calculated by time apportionment of the 25% and 20% rates, for the long-life asset pool, the 6% and 10% rates. For chargeable periods beginning on or after 6 April 2008 (1 April 2008 for corporation tax purposes), a WDA of up to £1,000 can be claimed in respect of the main pool and/or the special rate pool where the unrelieved expenditure in the pool concerned is £1,000 or less.

9 **Long-life assets:** Applies to plant or machinery with an expected working life, when new, of 25 years or more. Applies where expenditure on long-life assets in a year is £100,000 or more (in the case of companies the de minimis limit is £100,000 divided by one plus the number of associated companies). Transitional provisions apply to maintain a 25% allowance for expenditure incurred before 1 January 2001 under a contract entered into before 26 November 1996 and to expenditure on second-hand plant or machinery if old rules applied to vendor. It does not apply to plant or machinery in a building used wholly or mainly as, or for purposes ancillary to, a dwelling-house, retail shop, showroom, hotel or office, cars, or sea-going ships and railway assets acquired before 1 January 2011. Expenditure on or after 1 or 6 April 2008 qualifies, as special rate expenditure, for a writing down allowance of 10% reducing balance. The balance of the long-life asset pool at 1 or 6 April is also transferred into the special rate pool. (CAA 2001 ss 90–104, Sch 3 para 20).

10 Integral features of a building are electrical systems (including lighting systems); cold water systems; space or water heating systems, powered ventilation systems, air cooling or purification and any floor or ceiling comprised in such systems; lifts, escalators and moving walkways and external solar shading. They all fall into the special rate pool and qualify for a 10% writing down allowance. (CAA 2001, s 104E) Whenever possible, a claim or election must be made on the tax return or by an amendment to the return (TMA 1970 s 42 and FA 1998 Sch 18 paras 9, 10, 67 and 79). Exceptions to this general rule are dealt with in TMA 1970 Sch 1A. Except where another period is expressly prescribed, a claim for relief in respect of income tax and capital gains tax must be made within five years from the 31 January following the year of assessment to which it relates. From a date to be appointed, the time limit is to be changed to four years after the end of the tax year. (TMA 1970 s 43(1) as amended and FA 2008 Sch 39 para 12).

11 The relief applies only to leases finalised before 1.April.06 (CAA 2001 s 109; FA 2006 Sch 9 para 13).

12 First-year tax credits: For expenditure incurred on or after 1 April 2008, a company can surrender a tax loss attributable to first-year allowances for energy saving or environmentally friendly equipment in exchange for a cash payment from the Government. The cash payment is equal to 19% of the loss surrendered, subject to an upper limit of the greater of £250,000 and the company's PAYE and NIC liability for the period concerned. (CAA 2001 Sch A1)

13 First year allowance is available on expenditure over the annual investment allowance level or on which annual investment allowance has not been claimed,, which would otherwise qualify for writing down allowance at 20% in the general plant and machinery pool.

14 For expenditure on and after 1 April 2009 for companies, 6 April 2009 for unincorporated businesses, the regime for cars costing £12,000 is abolished. Cars with CO2 emissions exceeding 160gm/km will be allocated to the special rate pool. All other cars will go into the general pool.

Cars: Car hire p 69.

Mineral extraction

First-year allowance: 100% FYA is available for certain expenditure incurred after 16 April 2002 wholly for the purposes of a North Sea Oil ring-fence trade or on plant and machinery used in such a trade.

Writing-down allowance: for expenditure incurred after 31 March 1986, 10% for expenditure on the acquisition of a mineral asset and certain pre-trading expenditure, otherwise 25% (on reducing balance basis). (CA 2001 s 418)

Motor cars

Expenditure on or after 1 April 2009 (corporation tax) or 6 April 2009 (income tax) on cars is allocated to the special rate (10%) plant and machinery pool if the car's CO2 emissions exceed 160g/km and otherwise to the 20% main pool. (CAA 2001, ss 104AA, 104F, 208A, 268A-268D). The position for expenditure before 1 April 2009 (for companies) or 6 April 2009 (for unincorporated business) is as follows.

		% Rate[1]
Writing-down allowance (WDA)	Chargeable period ending before 1 April 2008 for corporation tax and 5 April 2008 for income tax	25%
	Chargeable period straddling 1 April 2008 for corporation tax and 5 April 2008 for income tax	hybrid rate
	Chargeable period beginning after 31 March 2008 for corporation tax or 5 April 2008 income tax	**20%**

1 Restricted to £3,000 for cars costing more than £12,000 and bought outright, on hire purchase or by way of a lease with an option to purchase (CAA 2001 ss 74, 75).

2 See also note 5, p 25 and Car hire, p 69.

3 Cars that have an element of non-business use will still be dealt with in a single asset pool, but the rate of WDA will depend on its emissions.

Patent rights

Writing-down allowance

Expenditure incurred after 31 March 1986: annual 25% writing-down allowance (reducing balance basis). (CA 2001 s 472)

Research and development (formerly scientific research)

	Expenditure incurred after	% Rate
Allowance in year 1	5 November 1962	**100**

Note: Land and houses are excluded from 1 April 1985.

Disadvantaged areas

Renovation of business premises

	Expenditure incurred on or after	% Rate
First-year allowance	11 April 2007	**100**

The expenditure must be incurred on renovating or converting vacant business properties in Northern Ireland or the designated disadvantaged areas in the UK that have been vacant for at least a year, to bring the property back into business use. (Premises refurbished by or used by businesses in the following trades are excluded from the scheme: fisheries and aquaculture, shipbuilding, the coal or steel industries, synthetic fibres, primary production of certain agricultural products and the manufacture of products which imitate or substitute for milk or milk products.) The enhanced rate will apply to any expenditure currently qualifying for plant and machinery, industrial buildings or agricultural buildings allowances and also to expenditure on commercial buildings (such as shops and offices). A writing-down allowance is given at 25% (on a straight-line basis) on unrelieved expenditure. (FA 2005 s 92, Sch 6).

Enterprise zones

Before 1 April 2011 (6 April 2011 for individuals) an initial allowance of 100% is available for expenditure on industrial or commercial building by businesses within enterprise zones. Where the initial allowance is not or is only partially claimed a 25% writing-down allowance on cost, on a straight-line basis, applies to the unclaimed balance. There is no phasing out of the allowance between 2008 and 2011.

Capital gains

Annual exemption

Individuals[a], personal representatives[b] and certain trusts[c]

[a] For 2008–09 onwards, an individual who claims to use the remittance basis for a tax year is not entitled to the capital gains tax annual exemption for that year. This does not apply if the individual's unremitted foreign income and gains for the year are less than £2,000.

[b] Year of death and following two years (maximum).

[c] Trusts for mentally disabled persons and those in receipt of attendance allowance or disability living allowance. Exemption divided by number of qualifying settlements created (after 9 March 1981) by one settlor, subject to a minimum of one-tenth.

Exempt amount of net gains	***2005–06***	***2006–07***	***2007–08***	***2008–09***	***2009–10***	***2010–11***
	£8,500	£8,800	£9,200	£9.600	£10,100	**£10,100**

Trusts[a] generally

Exempt amount of net gains	***2005–05***	***2006–07***	***2007–08***	***2008–09***	***2009–10***	***2010–11***
	£4,250	£4,400	£4,600	£4,800	£5,050	**£5,050**

[a] Exemption divided by number of qualifying settlements created (after 6 June 1978) by one settlor, subject to a minimum of one-fifth.

Chattel exemption

	Disposals exemption	*Marginal relief: Maximum chargeable gain*
From 1989–90 onwards	£6,000	$^5/_3$ excess over £6,000

Rates of tax

2008–09 to 2010/11	***Individuals, trusts and personal representatives***		**18%**
2007–08	*Individuals*	• to income tax starting rate limit £2,230	10%
		• from £2,231 to income tax basic rate limit £34,600	20%
		• above income tax basic rate limit £34,600	40%
	Trusts and personal representatives		40%
2006–07	*Individuals*	• to income tax starting rate limit £2,150	10%
		• from £2,151 to income tax basic rate limit £33,300	20%
		• above income tax basic rate limit £33,300	40%
	Trusts and personal representatives		40%
2004–05 to 2005–06	*Individuals*	• to income tax starting rate limit	10%
		• above starting rate limit to income tax basic rate limit	20%
		• above income tax basic rate limit	40%
	Trusts and personal representatives		40%
2000–01 to 2003–04	*Individuals*	• to income tax starting rate limit	10%
		• above starting rate limit to income tax basic rate limit	20%
		• above income tax basic rate limit	40%
	Trusts and personal representatives		34%
For 2007/08 and earlier years, gains are taxed on individuals as the top slice of income.			
Trusts for vulnerable persons: From 2004–05 onwards, gains taxed at beneficiary's rates (on beneficiary if UK resident or on trustees if beneficiary not UK-resident).			

Indexation allowance – individuals

(TCGA 1992 ss 53–57, 109)

Indexation allowance is abolished for disposals on or after 6 April 2008 by individuals, trustees and personal representatives (but not companies). For disposals before that date by such persons, an indexation allowance is given up to April 1998 and taper relief applies thereafter on disposals made after 5 April 1998 (see below). Indexation allowance is deducted before applying taper relief. The indexation allowance is calculated by multiplying each item of allowable expenditure by:

where:

RD is the retail prices index figure for month of disposal;
RI is the retail prices index for month of expenditure (or March 1982 if later).

See pp 37–53 for indexation allowances applicable for corporation tax and pp 54–55 for RPI values.

For disposals after 31 March 1998 of assets acquired on or before that date the factors below can be used to calculate the indexation allowance available to April 1998 for acquisitions in the month shown.

	Jan	*Feb*	*Mar*	*Apr*	*May*	*Jun*	*Jul*	*Aug*	*Sept*	*Oct*	*Nov*	*Dec*
1982	–	–	1·047	1·006	0·992	0·987	0·986	0·985	0·987	0·977	0·967	0·971
1983	0·968	0·960	0·956	0·929	0·921	0·917	0·906	0·898	0·889	0·883	0·876	0·871
1984	0·872	0·865	0·859	0·834	0·828	0·823	0·825	0·808	0·804	0·793	0·788	0·789
1985	0·783	0·769	0·752	0·716	0·708	0·704	0·707	0·703	0·704	0·701	0·695	0·693
1986	0·689	0·683	0·681	0·665	0·662	0·663	0·667	0·662	0·654	0·652	0·638	0·632
1987	0·626	0·620	0·616	0·597	0·596	0·596	0·597	0·593	0·588	0·580	0·573	0·574
1988	0·574	0·568	0·562	0·537	0·531	0·525	0·524	0·507	0·500	0·485	0·478	0·474
1989	0·465	0·454	0·448	0·423	0·414	0·409	0·408	0·404	0·395	0·384	0·372	0·369
1990	0·361	0·353	0·339	0·300	0·288	0·283	0·282	0·269	0·258	0·248	0·251	0·252
1991	0·249	0·242	0·237	0·222	0·218	0·213	0·215	0·213	0·208	0·204	0·199	0·198
1992	0·199	0·193	0·189	0·171	0·167	0·167	0·171	0·171	0·166	0·162	0·164	0·168
1993	0·179	0·171	0·167	0·156	0·152	0·153	0·156	0·151	0·146	0·147	0·148	0·146
1994	0·151	0·144	0·141	0·128	0·124	0·124	0·129	0·124	0·121	0·120	0·119	0·114
1995	0·114	0·107	0·102	0·091	0·087	0·085	0·091	0·085	0·080	0·085	0·085	0·079
1996	0·083	0·078	0·073	0·066	0·063	0·063	0·067	0·062	0·057	0·057	0·057	0·053
1997	0·053	0·049	0·046	0·040	0·036	0·032	0·032	0·026	0·021	0·019	0·019	0·016
1998	0·019	0·014	0·011	–	–	–	–	–	–	–	–	–

Losses. For disposals after 30 November 1993, indexation allowance can only be used to reduce or extinguish a gain. It cannot be used to create or increase a capital loss.

Share identification rules

(TCGA 1992 ss 104–106A; FA 2006 s 74)

For disposals on or after 6 April 2008 by individuals, trustees or personal representatives, shares and securities of the same class in the same company are identified with acquisitions in the following order:

- acquisitions on the same day as the disposal;
- acquisitions within 30 days after the day of disposal;
- shares comprised in a single pool incorporating all other shares of the same class, whenever acquired.

For acquisitions after 5 April 1998 and before 5 April 2008 for individuals, trustees and personal representatives, disposals are identified with acquisitions in the following order:

- same day acquisitions (subject to special rules distinguishing shares acquired after 5 April 2002 from approved employee share option schemes from other shares acquired on the same day);
- acquisitions within the following 30 days[1] (thus countering 'bed and breakfasting');
- previous acquisitions after 5 April 1998 on a last in/first out basis;
- shares acquired after 5 April 1982 in the pool at 5 April 1998 (the 'section 104 holding');
- shares acquired before 6 April 1982 (the '1982 holding');
- any shares acquired on or before 6 April 1965 on a last in/first out basis;
- if any shares disposed of are still not fully matched, shares acquired subsequent to the disposal (beyond the above mentioned 30-day period).

For the purposes of corporation tax on chargeable gains, disposals of shares etc are identified with acquisitions in the following order:

- same day acquisitions;
- acquisitions within the previous nine days on a first in/first out basis;
- the pool of shares acquired after 31 March 1982;
- any shares held at 31 March 1982;
- any shares acquired on or before 6 April 1965 on a last in/first out basis;
- (if shares disposed of still not fully matched) subsequent acquisitions.

These rules are modified for disposals of shares before 5 December 2005 if the company acquired shares of the same class within a short period and held not less than 2% of the number issued.

1 The 30-day matching rule does not apply in relation to acquisitions after 21 March 2006 where the individual making the disposal is not (or is not treated as) resident or ordinarily resident in the UK at the time of the acquisition.

Entrepreneur's relief

(TCGA 1992 ss 169H–169S; FA 2008, s 9, Sch 3)

Entrepreneur's relief applies to disposals by an individual on or after 6 April 2008 of:

- all or part of a trade carried on alone or in partnership;
- assets of such a trade following cessation; or
- shares or securities in the individual's 'personal trading company (as defined).

Where a disposal of shares or of an interest in the assets of a partnership qualifies for relief, an associated disposal of assets owned by the individual and used by the company or partnership also qualifies for relief.

Trustees can claim relief where a qualifying beneficiary has an interest in the business concerned.

The relief is available where the relevant conditions are met throughout a period of one year and operates by reducing the amount of qualifying gains by four-ninths (so that the gains are effectively charged to CGT at 10%). Relief is subject to a lifetime limit of gains of £2 million (£1 million for disposals before 6 April 2010), but disposals before 6 April 2008 do not count towards the limit. Relief given to trustees counts towards the limit of the qualifying beneficiary.

Transitional rules apply to allow relief to be claimed in certain circumstances where a gain made before 6 April 2008 is deferred and becomes chargeable on or after that date.

Taper relief

(TCGA 1992 s 2A, Sch A1; FA 2000 ss 66, 67; FA 2002 ss 46, 47, Sch 10; FA 2003 s 160)

Taper relief is abolished for gains accruing, or treated as accruing, on or after 6 April 2008. (FA 2008 Sch 2 para 25.) Taper relief was available for disposals made after 5 April 1998 by individuals, trustees and personal representatives. The chargeable gain is reduced according to the number of complete years for which the asset has been held (counting from 6 April 1998). Non-business assets acquired before 17 March 1998 qualify for an addition of one year to the period for which they are held after 5 April 1998. Business assets acquired before 17 March 1998 also qualify for the one-year addition but only if disposed of before 6 April 2000.

Taper relief applies to gains after all deductions and before the annual exemption. Losses are set against pre-tapered gains in the most beneficial way possible. Where applicable, the combined period of holding by spouses is taken into account.

Business assets			
Disposals from 6 April 2002 to 5 April 2008		*Disposals from 6 April 2000 to 5 April 2002*	
No of complete yrs from 6.4.98 for which asset held	*% of gain chargeable*	*No of complete yrs from 6.4.98 for which asset held*	*% of gain chargeable*
		0	100
0	100	1	87.5
1	50	2	75
2 or more	25	3	50
		4 or more	25

Non-business assets			
No of complete yrs from 6.4.98 for which asset held	*% of gain chargeable*	*No of complete yrs from 6.4.98 for which asset held*	*% of gain chargeable*
0	100	6	80
1	100	7	75
2	100	8	70
3	95	9	65
4	90	10 or more	60
5	85		

Business assets. A 'business asset' is one of the following:

- an asset used for the purposes of a trade carried on (alone or in partnership) by the taxpayer or, after 5 April 2004, any individual, trustee or personal representative; *or*
- an asset used for the purposes of a trade carried on by a 'qualifying company' (alone or, after 4 April 2004, in partnership); *or*
- shares or securities in a 'qualifying company'; *or*
- from 6 April 2000, an asset used for the purpose of any office or employment (full-time or part-time) held by the taxpayer with a person carrying on a trade; or
- before 6 April 2000, an asset held for the purposes of a qualifying office or employment to which the taxpayer is required to devote substantially the whole of his time.

Qualifying company. From 6 April 2000, a *'qualifying company'*, by reference to an individual, is a trading company (or holding company of a trading group), where one or more of the following conditions is met:

- the company is unlisted (including an AIM company); *or*
- the taxpayer is an employee (full-time or part-time) of the company or a fellow group company (in which case the requirement that the company be a trading company etc is dropped, provided the taxpayer's interest in the company, including connected person holdings, is no more than 10%); *or*
- the taxpayer can exercise at least 5% of the voting rights.

Leases

Depreciation table (TCGA 1992 Sch 8 para 1)

Yrs	%	*Yrs*	%	*Yrs*	%	*Yrs*	%
50 (or more)	100	37	93·497	24	79·622	11	50·038
49	99·657	36	92·761	23	78·055	10	46·695
48	99·289	35	91·981	22	76·399	9	43·154
47	98·902	34	91·156	21	74·635	8	39·399
46	98·490	33	90·280	20	72·770	7	35·414
45	98·059	32	89·354	19	70·791	6	31·195
44	97·595	31	88·371	18	68·697	5	26·722
43	97·107	30	87·330	17	66·470	4	21·983
42	96·593	29	86·226	16	64·116	3	16·959
41	96·041	28	85·053	15	61·617	2	11·629
40	95·457	27	83·816	14	58·971	1	5·983
39	94·842	26	82·496	13	56·167	0	0
38	94·189	25	81·100	12	53·191		

Formula: Fraction of expenditure disallowed—

Where:

AE is the percentage for duration of lease at acquisition or expenditure; and
D is the percentage for duration of lease at disposal.

Fractions of years: Add one-twelfth of the difference between the percentage for the whole year and the next higher percentage for each additional month. Odd days under 14 are not counted; 14 odd days or more count as a month.

Short leases: premiums treated as rent (TA 1988 s 34, TCGA 1992 Sch 8 para 5; ITTOIA 2005 ss 277–281) Part of premium for grant of a short lease which is chargeable to income tax as property income:

Where:

P is the amount of premium;
n is the number of complete years which lease has to run when granted.

Length of lease (complete years)	*Amount chargeable to CGT %*	*Income tax charge %*	*Length of lease (complete years)*	*Amount chargeable to CGT %*	*Income tax charge %*	*Length of lease (complete years)*	*Amount chargeable to CGT %*	*Income tax charge %*
Over 50	100	0	34	66	34	17	32	68
50	98	2	33	64	36	16	30	70
49	96	4	32	62	38	15	28	72
48	94	6	31	60	40	14	26	74
47	92	8	30	58	42	13	24	76
46	90	10	29	56	44	12	22	78
45	88	12	28	54	46	11	20	80
44	86	14	27	52	48	10	18	82
43	84	16	26	50	50	9	16	84
42	82	18	25	48	52	8	14	86
41	80	20	24	46	54	7	12	88
40	78	22	23	44	56	6	10	90
39	76	24	22	42	58	5	8	92
38	74	26	21	40	60	4	6	94
37	72	28	20	38	62	3	4	96
36	70	30	19	36	64	2	2	98
35	68	32	18	34	66	1 or less	0	100

Reliefs

The following is a summary of the other main capital gains tax reliefs and exemptions.

Charities

Gains accruing to charities which are both applicable and applied for charitable purposes are exempt. The exemption is extended from 6 April 2002 to donations to Community Amateur Sports Clubs (CASCs).

Individuals

Compensation (injury to person, profession or vocation)	Exempt.
Decorations for valour (acquired otherwise than for money or money's worth)	Gain exempt.
Enterprise Investment Scheme (see p 81)	Gain on disposal after relevant three-year period exempt to extent full relief given on shares.
Entrepreneurs relief (see p 32)	Five ninths of gains on specified assets chargeable at 18% (an effective rate of 10%) up to lifetime limit of £1 million.
Foreign currency acquired for personal expenditure	Gain exempt.
Gifts for public benefit, works of art, historic buildings etc	No chargeable gain/allowable loss.
Gilt-edged stock	No chargeable gain/allowable loss.
Hold-over relief for gifts	Restricted to: (1) gifts of business assets (including unquoted shares in trading companies and holding companies of trading groups). Relief is not available on the transfer of shares or securities to a company made after 8 November 1999 (other than transfers between 6.4.03 and 20.10.03); (2) gifts of heritage property; (3) gifts to heritage maintenance funds; (4) gifts to political parties; and (5) gifts which are chargeable transfers for inheritance tax. Where available, transferee's acquisition cost treated as reduced by held-over gain.
Married persons or civil partners living together	No chargeable gain/allowable loss on transfers between spouses or civil partners.
Motor vehicles	Gain exempt.
Principal private residence	Gain exempt.
If residence is partly let, exemption for the let part is limited to the smaller of–	(1) exemption on owner-occupied part; and (2) £40,000.
Qualifying corporate bonds	No chargeable gain (for loans made before 17 March 1998, allowable loss in certain cases if all or part of loss is irrecoverable).
Venture capital trusts (see p 81)	Gain on disposal of shares by original investor exempt if company still a venture capital trust. Exemption applies only to shares acquired up to the permitted maximum of £200,000 per year of assessment (£100,000 for shares acquired before 6 April 2004). Deferral relief is available on gains on assets where the disposal proceeds are reinvested in VCT shares issued before 6 April 2004 and within one year before or after the disposal. This relief is withdrawn for shares issued after that date.

Businesses

Roll-over relief for replacement of business assets

Qualifying assets:

- Buildings and land both occupied and used for the purposes of the trade.
- Fixed plant and machinery.
- Ships, aircraft and hovercraft.
- Satellites, space stations and spacecraft.
- Goodwill*.
- Milk and potato quotas*.
- Ewe and suckler cow premium quotas*.
- Fish quotas (from 29 March 1999)*.
- UK oil licences (from 1 July 1999).
- Payment entitlement under farmers' single payment scheme (from 22 March 2005).

The 'replacement' assets must be acquired within 12 months before or three years after the disposal of the old asset. Both assets must be within any of the above classes. Holdover relief is available where the new asset is a depreciating asset (having a predictable useful life not exceeding 60 years).

* From 1 April 2002 onwards, subject to transitional rules, these items are removed from the list for companies only (as they fall within the intangible assets regime from that date (FA 2002 Sch 29 para 132(5))).

Personal representatives

Allowable expenses

Expenses allowable for the costs of establishing title in computing chargeable gains on disposal of assets in a deceased person's estate: deaths occurring after 5 April 2004 (SP 2/04). (HMRC accepts computations based either on the scale or on the actual allowable expenditure incurred.)

Gross value of estate	*Allowable expenditure*
Up to £50,000	1.8% of the probate value of the assets sold by the personal representatives
Between £50,001 and £90,000	£900, to be divided between all the assets of the estate in proportion to the probate values and allowed in those proportions on assets sold by the personal representatives
Between £90,001 and £400,000	1% of the probate value of the assets sold
Between £400,001 and £500,000	£4,000, to be divided between all the assets of the estate in proportion to the probate values and allowed in those proportions on assets sold by the personal representatives
Between £500,001 and £1,000,000	0.8% of the probate value of the assets sold
Between £1,000,001 and £5,000,000	£8,000 to be divided between all the assets of the estate in proportion to the probate values and allowed in those proportions on assets sold by the personal representatives
Exceeding £5,000,000	0.16% of the probate value of the assets sold subject to a maximum of £10,000

Trustees

Allowable expenses

Expenses allowable in computing chargeable gains of corporate trustees in the administration of trusts and estates: acquisition, disposals and deemed disposals after 5 April 2004 (SP 2/04). (HMRC accepts computations based either on the scale or on the actual allowable expenditure incurred.)

Transfers of assets to beneficiaries etc	
(*a*) Quoted stocks and shares	
(i) One beneficiary	£25 per holding
(ii) More than one beneficiary	£25 per holding, divided equally between the beneficiaries
(*b*) Unquoted shares	As (*a*) above, plus any exceptional expenditure
(*c*) Other assets	As (*a*) above, plus any exceptional expenditure
Actual disposals and acquisitions	
(*a*) Quoted stocks and shares	Investment fee as charged by the trustees (where a comprehensive annual management fee is charged, the investment fee is taken to be £0.25 per £100 of the sale or purchase moneys)
(*b*) Unquoted shares	As (*a*) above, plus actual valuation costs
(*c*) Other assets	Investment fee (as (*a*) above), subject to a maximum of £75, plus actual valuation costs
Deemed disposals by trustees	
(*a*) Quoted stocks and shares	£8 per holding
(*b*) Unquoted shares	Actual valuation costs
(*c*) Other assets	Actual valuation costs

Indexation allowance – corporation tax on capital gains

For corporation tax purposes, an indexation allowance is given as a deduction in calculating gains on disposals from the amount realised (or deemed to be realised) on disposal. The indexation allowance is calculated by multiplying each item of allowable expenditure by:

Where:

RD is the retail prices index figure for month of disposal;
RI is the retail prices index for month of expenditure (or March 1982 if later).

See p 31for indexation allowances up to April 1998 and p 33 taper relief which applies thereafter on disposals made after 5 April 1998 and before 6 April 2008 by individuals, trustees and personal representatives. See p 54–55 for RPI values. The factors below can be used to calculate the indexation allowance for corporation tax purposes.

MONTH OF DISPOSAL

	2007				**2008**										
1982	Sept	Oct	Nov	Dec	Jan	Feb	Mar	Apr	May	June	July	Aug	Sept	Oct	Nov
Mar	1·618	1·630	1·640	1·655	1·641	1·661	1·670	1·694	1·708	1·729	1·725	1·734	1·749	1·740	1·719
Apr	1·567	1·578	1·588	1·602	1·589	1·609	1·617	1·641	1·654	1·675	1·672	1·680	1·695	1·686	1·665
May	1·548	1·559	1·569	1·584	1·570	1·590	1·599	1·622	1·635	1·656	1·652	1·661	1·676	1·667	1·646
June	1·541	1·552	1·562	1·577	1·563	1·583	1·591	1·615	1·628	1·649	1·645	1·654	1·668	1·660	1·639
July	1·540	1·551	1·561	1·576	1·562	1·582	1·591	1·614	1·627	1·648	1·648	1·653	1·667	1·659	1·638
Aug	1·540	1·551	1·560	1·575	1·562	1·581	1·590	1·613	1·626	1·647	1·647	1·652	1·667	1·658	1·637
Sept	1·541	1·552	1·562	1·577	1·563	1·583	1·591	1·615	1·628	1·649	1·645	1·654	1·668	1·660	1·639
Oct	1·529	1·540	1·549	1·564	1·551	1·570	1·579	1·602	1·615	1·636	1·632	1·641	1·655	1·647	1·626
Nov	1·516	1·527	1·537	1·551	1·538	1·557	1·566	1·589	1·602	1·623	1·619	1·628	1·642	1·634	1·613
Dec	1·521	1·532	1·542	1·556	1·543	1·562	1·571	1·594	1·607	1·628	1·624	1·632	1·647	1·638	1·618
1983	Sept	Oct	Nov	Dec	Jan	Feb	Mar	Apr	May	June	July	Aug	Sept	Oct	Nov
Jan	1·518	1·529	1·538	1·553	1·540	1·559	1·567	1·590	1·604	1·624	1·621	1·629	1·644	1·635	1·615
Feb	1·507	1·518	1·528	1·542	1·529	1·548	1·556	1·579	1·593	1·613	1·610	1·618	1·632	1·624	1·603
Mar	1·502	1·513	1·523	1·537	1·524	1·543	1·552	1·575	1·588	1·608	1·605	1·613	1·628	1·619	1·599
Apr	1·468	1·479	1·488	1·502	1·489	1·508	1·516	1·539	1·552	1·572	1·569	1·577	1·591	1·583	1·563
May	1·458	1·468	1·478	1·492	1·479	1·498	1·506	1·528	1·541	1·561	1·558	1·566	1·580	1·572	1·552
June	1·452	1·462	1·472	1·486	1·473	1·492	1·500	1·522	1·535	1·555	1·552	1·560	1·574	1·566	1·546
July	1·439	1·449	1·458	1·473	1·460	1·478	1·487	1·509	1·522	1·542	1·542	1·546	1·560	1·552	1·532
Aug	1·428	1·438	1·448	1·462	1·449	1·467	1·476	1·498	1·511	1·530	1·530	1·535	1·549	1·541	1·521
Sept	1·417	1·427	1·437	1·451	1·438	1·456	1·465	1·487	1·499	1·519	1·516	1·524	1·538	1·530	1·510
Oct	1·408	1·419	1·428	1·442	1·429	1·448	1·456	1·478	1·491	1·510	1·507	1·515	1·529	1·521	1·501
Nov	1·400	1·410	1·420	1·433	1·421	1·469	1·447	1·469	1·482	1·502	1·498	1·506	1·520	1·512	1·492
Dec	1·394	1·404	1·413	1·427	1·414	1·433	1·441	1·463	1·475	1·495	1·492	1·500	1·513	1·505	1·486
1984	Sept	Oct	Nov	Dec	Jan	Feb	Mar	Apr	May	June	July	Aug	Sept	Oct	Nov
Jan	1·395	1·405	1·415	1·428	1·416	1·434	1·442	1·464	1·477	1·496	1·493	1·501	1·515	1·507	1·487
Feb	1·385	1·396	1·405	1·419	1·406	1·424	1·432	1·454	1·467	1·486	1·483	1·491	1·505	1·497	1·477
Mar	1·378	1·388	1·397	1·411	1·398	1·417	1·425	1·446	1·459	1·478	1·475	1·483	1·497	1·489	1·469
Apr	1·346	1·357	1·366	1·379	1·367	1·385	1·393	1·414	1·427	1·446	1·442	1·450	1·464	1·456	1·437
May	1·338	1·348	1·357	1·370	1·358	1·376	1·384	1·405	1·418	1·437	1·433	1·441	1·455	1·447	1·428
June	1·332	1·342	1·351	1·364	1·352	1·370	1·378	1·399	1·411	1·430	1·427	1·435	1·448	1·441	1·421
July	1·334	1·345	1·354	1·367	1·355	1·373	1·380	1·402	1·414	1·433	1·433	1·438	1·451	1·443	1·424
Aug	1·313	1·323	1·332	1·345	1·333	1·351	1·358	1·379	1·392	1·411	1·411	1·415	1·428	1·421	1·402
Sept	1·308	1·318	1·327	1·340	1·328	1·346	1·354	1·375	1·387	1·406	1·403	1·410	1·424	1·416	1·397
Oct	1·294	1·304	1·313	1·326	1·314	1·331	1·339	1·360	1·372	1·391	1·388	1·395	1·409	1·401	1·382
Nov	1·287	1·297	1·306	1·319	1·307	1·324	1·332	1·353	1·365	1·384	1·380	1·388	1·401	1·394	1·375
Dec	1·289	1·299	1·308	1·321	1·309	1·326	1·334	1·355	1·367	1·386	1·382	1·390	1·403	1·396	1·377
1985	Sept	Oct	Nov	Dec	Jan	Feb	Mar	Apr	May	June	July	Aug	Sept	Oct	Nov
Jan	1·281	1·290	1·299	1·312	1·300	1·318	1·326	1·346	1·358	1·377	1·374	1·381	1·395	1·387	1·368
Feb	1·262	1·272	1·281	1·294	1·282	1·299	1·307	1·328	1·340	1·358	1·355	1·362	1·375	1·368	1·349
Mar	1·241	1·251	1·260	1·273	1·261	1·278	1·286	1·306	1·318	1·336	1·333	1·340	1·353	1·346	1·328
Apr	1·195	1·204	1·213	1·225	1·214	1·230	1·238	1·258	1·270	1·287	1·284	1·292	1·304	1·297	1·279
May	1·185	1·194	1·203	1·215	1·204	1·220	1·228	1·248	1·259	1·277	1·274	1·281	1·294	1·287	1·269
June	1·180	1·189	1·198	1·210	1·199	1·216	1·223	1·243	1·254	1·272	1·269	1·276	1·289	1·282	1·264
July	1·184	1·194	1·202	1·215	1·203	1·220	1·227	1·247	1·259	1·276	1·276	1·281	1·293	1·286	1·268
Aug	1·178	1·188	1·196	1·209	1·197	1·214	1·221	1·241	1·253	1·270	1·270	1·275	1·287	1·280	1·262
Sept	1·179	1·189	1·197	1·210	1·198	1·215	1·222	1·242	1·254	1·272	1·269	1·276	1·288	1·281	1·263
Oct	1·176	1·185	1·194	1·206	1·195	1·212	1·219	1·239	1·250	1·268	1·265	1·272	1·285	1·277	1·260
Nov	1·168	1·178	1·186	1·199	1·187	1·204	1·211	1·231	1·243	1·260	1·257	1·264	1·277	1·270	1·252
Dec	1·166	1·175	1·183	1·196	1·184	1·201	1·208	1·228	1·240	1·257	1·254	1·261	1·274	1·267	1·249

MONTH OF DISPOSAL

	2008	**2009**												**2010**	
1982	Dec	Jan	Feb	Mar	Apr	May	June	July	Aug	Sept	Oct	Nov	Dec	Jan	Feb
Mar	1·680	1·645	1·661	1·660	1·662	1·679	1·686	1·686	1·699	1·710	1·719	1·727	1·744	1·743	1·759
Apr	1·627	1·593	1·609	1·607	1·610	1·626	1·633	1·633	1·646	1·657	1·665	1·673	1·690	1·689	1·705
May	1·608	1·574	1·590	1·589	1·591	1·607	1·614	1·614	1·627	1·638	1·646	1·654	1·671	1·670	1·686
June	1·601	1·567	1·583	1·582	1·584	1·600	1·607	1·607	1·619	1·630	1·639	1·646	1·663	1·662	1·678
July	1·600	1·566	1·582	1·581	1·583	1·599	1·606	1·606	1·619	1·630	1·638	1·645	1·663	1·661	1·677
Aug	1·599	1·565	1·581	1·580	1·582	1·598	1·606	1·606	1·618	1·629	1·637	1·645	1·662	1·661	1·676
Sept	1·601	1·567	1·583	1·582	1·584	1·600	1·607	1·607	1·619	1·630	1·639	1·646	1·663	1·662	1·678
Oct	1·588	1·554	1·570	1·569	1·571	1·587	1·594	1·594	1·606	1·617	1·626	1·633	1·650	1·649	1·665
Nov	1·576	1·542	1·557	1·556	1·559	1·574	1·582	1·582	1·594	1·605	1·613	1·620	1·637	1·636	1·652
Dec	1·580	1·546	1·562	1·561	1·563	1·579	1·586	1·586	1·598	1·609	1·618	1·625	1·642	1·641	1·657
1983	Dec	Jan	Feb	Mar	Apr	May	June	July	Aug	Sept	Oct	Nov	Dec	Jan	Feb
Jan	1·577	1·543	1·559	1·558	1·560	1·576	1·583	1·583	1·595	1·606	1·615	1·622	1·639	1·638	1·653
Feb	1·566	1·532	1·548	1·547	1·549	1·565	1·572	1·572	1·584	1·595	1·603	1·611	1·628	1·626	1·642
Mar	1·561	1·528	1·543	1·542	1·545	1·560	1·567	1·567	1·579	1·590	1·599	1·606	1·623	1·622	1·637
Apr	1·526	1·493	1·508	1·507	1·509	1·525	1·532	1·532	1·544	1·554	1·563	1·570	1·586	1·585	1·601
May	1·515	1·482	1·498	1·496	1·499	1·514	1·521	1·521	1·533	1·544	1·552	1·559	1·576	1·574	1·590
June	1·509	1·547	1·492	1·491	1·493	1·508	1·515	1·515	1·527	1·538	1·546	1·553	1·569	1·568	1·584
July	1·496	1·463	1·478	1·477	1·480	1·495	1·502	1·502	1·514	1·524	1·532	1·539	1·556	1·555	1·570
Aug	1·485	1·452	1·467	1·466	1·469	1·484	1·491	1·491	1·502	1·513	1·521	1·528	1·544	1·543	1·558
Sept	1·474	1·441	1·456	1·455	1·458	1·473	1·480	1·480	1·491	1·502	1·510	1·517	1·533	1·532	1·547
Oct	1·465	1·433	1·448	1·447	1·449	1·464	1·471	1·471	1·483	1·493	1·501	1·508	1·524	1·523	1·538
Nov	1·457	1·424	1·439	1·438	1·440	1·455	1·462	1·462	1·474	1·484	1·492	1·499	1·515	1·514	1·529
Dec	1·450	1·418	1·433	1·432	1·434	1·449	1·456	1·456	1·467	1·478	1·486	1·493	1·509	1·508	1·523
1984	Dec	Jan	Feb	Mar	Apr	May	June	July	Aug	Sept	Oct	Nov	Dec	Jan	Feb
Jan	1·452	1·419	1·434	1·433	1·435	1·450	1·457	1·457	1·469	1·479	1·487	1·494	1·510	1·509	1·524
Feb	1·442	1·409	1·424	1·423	1·425	1·440	1·447	1·447	1·459	1·469	1·477	1·484	1·500	1·499	1·514
Mar	1·434	1·402	1·417	1·415	1·418	1·433	1·439	1·439	1·451	1·461	1·469	1·476	1·492	1·491	1·506
Apr	1·402	1·372	1·385	1·384	1·386	1·401	1·407	1·407	1·419	1·429	1·437	1·443	1·459	1·459	1·473
May	1·393	1·361	1·376	1·375	1·377	1·392	1·398	1·398	1·410	1·420	1·428	1·434	1·450	1·449	1·464
June	1·387	1·355	1·370	1·369	1·371	1·386	1·392	1·392	1·404	1·414	1·421	1·428	1·444	1·443	1·457
July	1·389	1·358	1·373	1·371	1·374	1·388	1·395	1·395	1·406	1·414	1·424	1·431	1·447	1·446	1·460
Aug	1·367	1·336	1·351	1·349	1·352	1·366	1·373	1·373	1·384	1·394	1·402	1·408	1·424	1·423	1·437
Sept	1·363	1·331	1·346	1·345	1·347	1·361	1·368	1·368	1·379	1·389	1·397	1·404	1·419	1·418	1·432
Oct	1·348	1·317	1·331	1·330	1·333	1·347	1·354	1·354	1·365	1·374	1·382	1·389	1·404	1·403	1·418
Nov	1·341	1·311	1·324	1·323	1·325	1·340	1·346	1·346	1·357	1·367	1·375	1·382	1·397	1·396	1·410
Dec	1·343	1·312	1·326	1·325	1·327	1·342	1·348	1·348	1·359	1·369	1·377	1·384	1·399	1·398	1·412
1985	Dec	Jan	Feb	Mar	Apr	May	June	July	Aug	Sept	Oct	Nov	Dec	Jan	Feb
Jan	1·334	1·304	1·318	1·317	1·319	1·333	1·340	1·340	1·351	1·361	1·368	1·375	1·390	1·389	1·403
Feb	1·316	1·328	1·299	1·298	1·300	1·315	1·321	1·321	1·332	1·342	1·349	1·356	1·371	1·370	1·384
Mar	1·294	1·264	1·278	1·277	1·279	1·293	1·300	1·300	1·310	1·320	1·328	1·334	1·349	1·348	1·362
Apr	1·246	1·217	1·230	1·229	1·232	1·245	1·252	1·252	1·262	1·272	1·279	1·285	1·300	1·299	1·313
May	1·236	1·207	1·220	1·219	1·221	1·235	1·241	1·241	1·252	1·261	1·269	1·275	1·290	1·289	1·302
June	1·231	1·202	1·216	1·215	1·217	1·230	1·237	1·237	1·247	1·257	1·264	1·270	1·285	1·284	1·297
July	1·236	1·206	1·220	1·219	1·221	1·234	1·241	1·241	1·251	1·261	1·268	1·274	1·289	1·288	1·302
Aug	1·230	1·201	1·214	1·213	1·215	1·229	1·235	1·235	1·245	1·255	1·262	1·268	1·283	1·282	1·296
Sept	1·231	1·201	1·215	1·214	1·216	1·230	1·236	1·236	1·247	1·256	1·256	1·270	1·284	1·283	1·297
Oct	1·227	1·198	1·212	1·210	1·213	1·226	1·232	1·232	1·243	1·252	1·260	1·266	1·281	1·280	1·293
Nov	1·220	1·190	1·204	1·203	1·205	1·219	1·225	1·225	1·235	1·245	1·252	1·258	1·273	1·272	1·285
Dec	1·217	1·188	1·201	1·200	1·202	1·216	1·222	1·222	1·232	1·242	1·249	1·255	1·270	1·269	1·282

MONTH OF DISPOSAL

	2007				***2008***										
1986	Sept	Oct	Nov	Dec	Jan	Feb	Mar	Apr	May	June	July	Aug	Sept	Oct	Nov
Jan	1·161	1·170	1·179	1·191	1·180	1·196	1·204	1·223	1·235	1·253	1·249	1·257	1·269	1·262	1·244
Feb	1·153	1·162	1·171	1·183	1·172	1·188	1·196	1·215	1·227	1·244	1·241	1·248	1·261	1·254	1·236
Mar	1·150	1·160	1·168	1·180	1·169	1·185	1·193	1·212	1·224	1·241	1·238	1·245	1·258	1·251	1·233
Apr	1·130	1·139	1·147	1·159	1·148	1·164	1·172	1·191	1·202	1·220	1·217	1·224	1·236	1·229	1·212
May	1·126	1·135	1·143	1·155	1·144	1·161	1·168	1·187	1·198	1·216	1·213	1·220	1·232	1·225	1·208
June	1·127	1·136	1·144	1·157	1·145	1·162	1·169	1·188	1·200	1·217	1·214	1·221	1·233	1·226	1·209
July	1·133	1·142	1·150	1·163	1·151	1·168	1·175	1·195	1·206	1·223	1·223	1·227	1·240	1·232	1·215
Aug	1·126	1·136	1·144	1·156	1·145	1·161	1·168	1·188	1·199	1·216	1·216	1·220	1·233	1·226	1·208
Sept	1·116	1·125	1·133	1·145	1·134	1·151	1·158	1·177	1·188	1·205	1·202	1·210	1·222	1·215	1·197
Oct	1·113	1·122	1·130	1·142	1·131	1·147	1·154	1·174	1·185	1·202	1·199	1·206	1·218	1·211	1·194
Nov	1·095	1·104	1·112	1·124	1·113	1·129	1·136	1·155	1·166	1·183	1·180	1·188	1·200	1·193	1·175
Dec	1·088	1·097	1·105	1·117	1·106	1·122	1·129	1·148	1·159	1·176	1·173	1·180	1·192	1·185	1·168
1987	Sept	Oct	Nov	Dec	Jan	Feb	Mar	Apr	May	June	July	Aug	Sept	Oct	Nov
Jan	1·080	1·089	1·097	1·109	1·098	1·114	1·121	1·140	1·151	1·168	1·165	1·172	1·184	1·177	1·160
Feb	1·072	1·081	1·089	1·101	1·090	1·106	1·113	1·131	1·142	1·159	1·156	1·163	1·175	1·168	1·151
Mar	1·068	1·077	1·084	1·096	1·085	1·101	1·108	1·127	1·138	1·155	1·152	1·159	1·171	1·164	1·147
Apr	1·043	1·052	1·060	1·072	1·061	1·077	1·083	1·102	1·113	1·130	1·127	1·134	1·145	1·139	1·122
May	1·041	1·050	1·058	1·070	1·059	1·075	1·081	1·100	1·111	1·128	1·125	1·132	1·143	1·136	1·120
June	1·041	1·050	1·058	1·070	1·059	1·075	1·081	1·100	1·111	1·128	1·125	1·132	1·143	1·136	1·120
July	1·043	1·052	1·060	1·072	1·061	1·077	1·083	1·102	1·113	1·130	1·130	1·134	1·145	1·139	1·122
Aug	1·037	1·046	1·054	1·066	1·055	1·071	1·077	1·096	1·107	1·123	1·123	1·127	1·139	1·132	1·116
Sept	1·031	1·040	1·048	1·060	1·049	1·064	1·071	1·090	1·101	1·117	1·114	1·121	1·133	1·126	1·109
Oct	1·021	1·030	1·038	1·050	1·039	1·054	1·061	1·080	1·090	1·107	1·104	1·111	1·122	1·116	1·099
Nov	1·012	1·020	1·028	1·040	1·029	1·044	1·051	1·070	1·080	1·097	1·094	1·101	1·112	1·105	1·089
Dec	1·014	1·022	1·030	1·042	1·031	1·046	1·053	1·072	1·082	1·099	1·096	1·103	1·114	1·107	1·091
1988	Sept	Oct	Nov	Dec	Jan	Feb	Mar	Apr	May	June	July	Aug	Sept	Oct	Nov
Jan	1·014	1·022	1·030	1·042	1·031	1·046	1·053	1·072	1·082	1·099	1·096	1·103	1·114	1·107	1·091
Feb	1·006	1·014	1·022	1·034	1·023	1·039	1·045	1·064	1·074	1·091	1·088	1·095	1·106	1·099	1·083
Mar	·998	1·007	1·014	1·026	1·015	1·031	1·037	1·056	1·066	1·083	1·080	1·086	1·098	1·091	1·075
Apr	·966	·974	·982	·993	·983	·998	1·005	1·023	1·033	1·049	1·046	1·053	1·064	1·058	1·042
May	·959	·967	·975	·986	·976	·991	·997	1·015	1·025	1·041	1·039	1·045	1·056	1·050	1·034
June	·951	·960	·967	·978	·968	·983	·990	1·008	1·018	1·034	1·031	1·038	1·049	1·042	1·026
July	·949	·958	·965	·977	·966	·981	·988	1·006	1·016	1·032	1·032	1·036	1·047	1·040	1·024
Aug	·928	·936	·943	·955	·944	·959	·966	·983	·994	1·009	1·009	1·013	1·024	1·018	1·002
Sept	·919	·927	·935	·946	·935	·950	·957	·974	·984	1·000	·997	1·004	1·015	1·008	·993
Oct	·900	·908	·915	·926	·916	·931	·937	·954	·964	·980	·977	·984	·995	·988	·973
Nov	·891	·899	·906	·917	·907	·922	·928	·945	·955	·971	·968	·975	·985	·979	·964
Dec	·886	·894	·901	·912	·902	·917	·923	·940	·950	·966	·963	·969	·980	·974	·958
1989	Sept	Oct	Nov	Dec	Jan	Feb	Mar	Apr	May	June	July	Aug	Sept	Oct	Nov
Jan	·874	·882	·889	·900	·890	·905	·911	·928	·938	·953	·950	·957	·968	·961	·946
Feb	·860	·869	·876	·886	·877	·891	·897	·914	·924	·939	·936	·943	·953	·947	·932
Mar	·852	·860	·867	·878	·868	·882	·889	·906	·915	·931	·928	·934	·945	·939	·923
Apr	·820	·828	·835	·845	·836	·850	·856	·872	·882	·897	·894	·900	·911	·905	·890
May	·809	·817	·823	·834	·824	·838	·844	·861	·870	·885	·883	·889	·899	·893	·878
June	·802	·810	·817	·828	·818	·832	·838	·854	·864	·879	·876	·882	·893	·886	·872
July	·801	·809	·816	·826	·816	·830	·836	·853	·862	·877	·874	·881	·891	·885	·870
Aug	·796	·804	·811	·821	·812	·826	·832	·848	·858	·872	·870	·876	·886	·880	·865
Sept	·784	·792	·798	·809	·799	·813	·819	·835	·845	·859	·857	·863	·873	·867	·852
Oct	·770	·778	·785	·795	·786	·799	·805	·821	·831	·845	·843	·849	·859	·853	·838
Nov	·755	·763	·770	·780	·770	·784	·790	·806	·815	·830	·827	·833	·843	·837	·823
Dec	·751	·758	·765	·775	·766	·779	·785	·801	·811	·825	·822	·828	·838	·832	·818

MONTH OF DISPOSAL

	2008	**2009**												**2010**	
1986	Dec	Jan	Feb	Mar	Apr	May	June	July	Aug	Sept	Oct	Nov	Dec	Jan	Feb
Jan	1·212	1·183	1·196	1·195	1·197	1·211	1·217	1·217	1·228	1·237	1·244	1·250	1·265	1·264	1·277
Feb	1·204	1·175	1·188	1·187	1·189	1·203	1·209	1·209	1·219	1·229	1·236	1·242	1·257	1·256	1·269
Mar	1·201	1·172	1·185	1·184	1·186	1·200	1·206	1·206	1·216	1·226	1·233	1·239	1·254	1·253	1·266
Apr	1·180	1·151	1·164	1·163	1·166	1·179	1·185	1·185	1·195	1·204	1·212	1·218	1·232	1·231	1·244
May	1·176	1·147	1·161	1·160	1·162	1·175	1·181	1·181	1·191	1·200	1·208	1·214	1·228	1·227	1·240
June	1·177	1·148	1·162	1·161	1·163	1·176	1·182	1·182	1·192	1·202	1·209	1·215	1·229	1·228	1·241
July	1·183	1·155	1·168	1·167	1·169	1·182	1·188	1·188	1·199	1·208	1·215	1·221	1·236	1·235	1·248
Aug	1·176	1·148	1·161	1·160	1·162	1·175	1·182	1·182	1·192	1·201	1·208	1·214	1·229	1·228	1·241
Sept	1·166	1·137	1·151	1·150	1·152	1·165	1·171	1·171	1·181	1·190	1·197	1·203	1·218	1·217	1·230
Oct	1·162	1·134	1·147	1·146	1·148	1·161	1·168	1·168	1·178	1·187	1·194	1·200	1·214	1·213	1·226
Nov	1·144	1·116	1·129	1·128	1·130	1·143	1·149	1·149	1·159	1·168	1·175	1·181	1·196	1·195	1·208
Dec	1·137	1·109	1·122	1·121	1·123	1·136	1·142	1·142	1·152	1·161	1·168	1·174	1·188	1·187	1·200
1987	Dec	Jan	Feb	Mar	Apr	May	June	July	Aug	Sept	Oct	Nov	Dec	Jan	Feb
Jan	1·129	1·101	1·114	1·113	1·115	1·128	1·134	1·134	1·144	1·153	1·160	1·166	1·180	1·179	1·192
Feb	1·121	1·093	1·106	1·105	1·107	1·120	1·125	1·125	1·135	1·144	1·151	1·157	1·171	1·170	1·183
Mar	1·116	1·088	1·101	1·100	1·102	1·115	1·121	1·121	1·131	1·140	1·147	1·153	1·167	1·166	1·179
Apr	1·091	1·064	1·077	1·076	1·078	1·090	1·096	1·096	1·106	1·115	1·122	1·128	1·141	1·140	1·153
May	1·089	1·062	1·075	1·074	1·076	1·088	1·094	1·094	1·104	1·113	1·120	1·126	1·139	1·138	1·151
June	1·089	1·062	1·075	1·074	1·076	1·088	1·094	1·094	1·104	1·113	1·120	1·126	1·139	1·138	1·151
July	1·091	1·064	1·077	1·076	1·078	1·090	1·096	1·096	1·106	1·115	1·122	1·128	1·141	1·140	1·153
Aug	1·085	1·058	1·071	1·070	1·071	1·084	1·090	1·090	1·100	1·109	1·116	1·121	1·135	1·134	1·147
Sept	1·079	1·052	1·064	1·063	1·065	1·078	1·084	1·084	1·094	1·103	1·109	1·115	1·129	1·128	1·141
Oct	1·069	1·042	1·054	1·053	1·055	1·068	1·074	1·074	1·084	1·092	1·099	1·105	1·119	1·118	1·130
Nov	1·059	1·032	1·044	1·044	1·045	1·058	1·064	1·064	1·074	1·082	1·089	1·095	1·108	1·107	1·120
Dec	1·061	1·034	1·046	1·045	1·047	1·060	1·066	1·066	1·076	1·084	1·091	1·097	1·110	1·109	1·122
1988	Dec	Jan	Feb	Mar	Apr	May	June	July	Aug	Sept	Oct	Nov	Dec	Jan	Feb
Jan	1·061	1·034	1·046	1·045	1·047	1·060	1·066	1·066	1·076	1·084	1·091	1·097	1·110	1·109	1·122
Feb	1·053	1·026	1·039	1·038	1·040	1·052	1·058	1·058	1·068	1·076	1·083	1·089	1·102	1·101	1·114
Mar	1·045	1·018	1·031	1·030	1·032	1·044	1·050	1·050	1·060	1·068	1·075	1·081	1·094	1·093	1·106
Apr	1·012	·986	·998	·997	·999	1.011	1.017	1.017	1.026	1.035	1.042	1.047	1.060	1.060	1.072
May	1·005	·978	·991	·990	·992	1.004	1.009	1.009	1.019	1.027	1.034	1.040	1.053	1.052	1.064
June	·997	·971	·983	·982	·984	·996	1.002	1.002	1.011	1.020	1.026	1.032	1.045	1.044	1.056
July	·995	·969	·981	·980	·982	·994	1.000	1.000	1.009	1.018	1.024	1.030	1.043	1.042	1.054
Aug	·973	·947	·959	·958	·960	·972	·978	·978	·987	·995	1.002	1.007	1.020	1.019	1.032
Sept	·964	·938	·950	·949	·951	·963	·969	·969	·978	·986	·993	·998	1.011	1.010	1.022
Oct	·944	·919	·931	·930	·932	·943	·949	·949	·958	·966	·973	·978	·991	·990	1.002
Nov	·935	·909	·922	·921	·923	·935	·940	·940	·949	·957	·964	·969	·982	·981	·993
Dec	·930	·905	·917	·916	·917	·929	·935	·935	·944	·952	·958	·964	·976	·976	·987
1989	Dec	Jan	Feb	Mar	Apr	May	June	July	Aug	Sept	Oct	Nov	Dec	Jan	Feb
Jan	·918	·893	·905	·904	·905	·917	·923	·923	·932	·940	·946	·951	·964	·963	·975
Feb	·904	·879	·891	·890	·892	·903	·909	·909	·918	·926	·932	·937	·950	·949	·961
Mar	·896	·871	·882	·882	·883	·895	·900	·900	·909	·917	·923	·929	·941	·940	·952
Apr	·863	·838	·850	·849	·850	·862	·867	·867	·876	·884	·890	·895	·907	·906	·918
May	·851	·827	·838	·837	·839	·850	·856	·856	·864	·872	·878	·883	·896	·895	·906
June	·845	·821	·832	·831	·833	·844	·849	·849	·858	·866	·872	·877	·889	·888	·899
July	·843	·819	·830	·829	·831	·842	·848	·848	·856	·864	·870	·875	·887	·887	·898
Aug	·839	·814	·826	·825	·826	·838	·843	·843	·851	·859	·865	·870	·883	·882	·893
Sept	·826	·802	·813	·812	·814	·825	·830	·830	·839	·846	·852	·858	·870	·869	·880
Oct	·812	·788	·799	·798	·800	·811	·816	·816	·825	·832	·838	·843	·855	·854	·866
Nov	·797	·773	·784	·783	·785	·796	·801	·801	·809	·817	·823	·828	·840	·839	·850
Dec	·792	·769	·779	·779	·780	·791	·796	·796	·805	·812	·818	·823	·835	·834	·845

MONTH OF DISPOSAL

	2007				***2008***										
1990	Sept	Oct	Nov	Dec	Jan	Feb	Mar	Apr	May	June	July	Aug	Sept	Oct	Nov
Jan	·741	·748	·755	·765	·756	·769	·775	·791	·800	·814	·812	·818	·828	·822	·808
Feb	·730	·738	·745	·755	·745	·759	·765	·780	·790	·804	·801	·807	·817	·811	·797
Mar	·713	·721	·727	·737	·728	·741	·747	·763	·772	·786	·783	·789	·799	·793	·779
Apr	·663	·670	·676	·686	·677	·690	·695	·711	·719	·733	·731	·736	·746	·740	·727
May	·648	·655	·662	·671	·662	·675	·681	·696	·704	·718	·716	·721	·731	·725	·712
June	·642	·649	·655	·665	·656	·669	·674	·689	·698	·711	·709	·714	·724	·718	·705
July	·640	·647	·654	·663	·655	·667	·673	·688	·696	·710	·707	·713	·722	·717	·703
Aug	·624	·631	·637	·646	·638	·650	·656	·671	·679	·692	·690	·696	·705	·699	·686
Sept	·609	·616	·622	·631	·623	·635	·640	·655	·664	·677	·674	·680	·689	·684	·671
Oct	·596	·603	·609	·619	·610	·622	·628	·642	·651	·664	·662	·667	·676	·671	·658
Nov	·600	·607	·613	·622	·614	·626	·632	·646	·655	·668	·664	·671	·680	·675	·662
Dec	·601	·608	·614	·624	·615	·627	·633	·647	·656	·669	·667	·672	·681	·676	·663
1991	Sept	Oct	Nov	Dec	Jan	Feb	Mar	Apr	May	June	July	Aug	Sept	Oct	Nov
Jan	·598	·604	·611	·620	·611	·624	·629	·644	·652	·665	·663	·668	·677	·672	·659
Feb	·589	·596	·602	·611	·603	·615	·620	·635	·643	·656	·654	·659	·668	·663	·650
Mar	·583	·590	·596	·605	·597	·609	·614	·629	·637	·650	·648	·653	·662	·657	·644
Apr	·563	·569	·576	·585	·576	·588	·594	·608	·616	·629	·627	·632	·641	·636	·623
May	·558	·565	·571	·580	·572	·584	·589	·603	·611	·624	·622	·627	·636	·631	·618
June	·551	·558	·564	·573	·565	·576	·582	·596	·604	·617	·614	·620	·629	·623	·611
July	·5655	·561	·567	·576	·568	·580	·585	·599	·608	·620	·618	·623	·632	·627	·614
Aug	·551	·558	·564	·573	·565	·576	·582	·596	·604	·617	·614	·620	·629	·623	·611
Sept	·545	·552	·558	·567	·559	·571	·576	·590	·598	·611	·608	·614	·623	·617	·605
Oct	·540	·546	·552	·561	·553	·565	·570	·584	·592	·605	·603	·608	·617	·611	·599
Nov	·534	·541	·546	·555	·547	·559	·564	·578	·586	·599	·597	·602	·611	·605	·593
Dec	·533	·539	·545	·554	·546	·558	·563	·577	·585	·598	·595	·601	·609	·604	·592
1992	Sept	Oct	Nov	Dec	Jan	Feb	Mar	Apr	May	June	July	Aug	Sept	Oct	Nov
Jan	·534	·541	·546	·555	·547	·559	·564	·578	·586	·599	·597	·602	·611	·605	·593
Feb	·526	·533	·539	·547	·539	·551	·556	·570	·578	·591	·585	·594	·602	·597	·585
Mar	·522	·528	·534	·543	·535	·546	·552	·565	·574	·586	·584	·589	·598	·593	·580
Apr	·499	·505	·511	·519	·512	·523	·528	·542	·550	·562	·560	·565	·573	·568	·556
May	·493	·500	·505	·514	·506	·518	·523	·536	·544	·556	·554	·559	·568	·563	·551
June	·493	·500	·505	·514	·506	·518	·523	·536	·544	·556	·554	·559	·568	·563	·551
July	·499	·505	·511	·519	·512	·523	·528	·542	·550	·562	·560	·565	·573	·568	·556
Aug	·497	·504	·510	·518	·510	·522	·527	·541	·549	·561	·559	·564	·572	·567	·555
Sept	·492	·499	·504	·513	·505	·516	·522	·535	·543	·555	·553	·558	·567	·562	·549
Oct	·488	·493	·499	·508	·500	·511	·516	·530	·538	·550	·548	·553	·561	·556	·544
Nov	·489	·495	·501	·510	·502	·513	·518	·532	·540	·552	·550	·555	·563	·558	·546
Dec	·494	·501	·506	·515	·507	·519	·524	·537	·545	·557	·555	·560	·569	·564	·552
1993	Sept	Oct	Nov	Dec	Jan	Feb	Mar	Apr	May	June	July	Aug	Sept	Oct	Nov
Jan	·508	·515	·521	·529	·521	·533	·538	·552	·560	·572	·570	·575	·584	·579	·566
Feb	·499	·505	·511	·519	·512	·523	·528	·542	·550	·562	·560	·565	·573	·568	·556
Mar	·493	·500	·505	·514	·506	·518	·523	·536	·544	·556	·554	·559	·568	·563	·551
Apr	·479	·486	·491	·500	·492	·504	·509	·522	·530	·542	·540	·545	·553	·548	·536
May	·474	·481	·486	·495	·487	·498	·503	·517	·524	·536	·534	·539	·548	·543	·531
June	·475	·482	·487	·496	·488	·499	·504	·518	·526	·538	·635	·540	·549	·544	·532
July	·478	·485	·490	·499	·491	·502	·507	·521	·529	·541	·539	·544	·552	·547	·535
Aug	·472	·478	·484	·493	·485	·496	·501	·515	·522	·534	·532	·537	·546	·541	·529
Sept	·466	·472	·478	·486	·479	·490	·495	·508	·516	·528	·526	·531	·539	·534	·522
Oct	·467	·473	·479	·487	·480	·491	·496	·509	·517	·529	·527	·532	·540	·535	·523
Nov	·469	·475	·481	·489	·482	·493	·498	·511	·519	·531	·529	·534	·542	·537	·525
Dec	·466	·472	·478	·486	·479	·490	·495	·508	·516	·528	·526	·531	·539	·534	·522

MONTH OF DISPOSAL

	2008	**2009**											**2010**	
1990	Dec	Jan	Feb	Mar	Apr	May	June	July	Aug	Sept	Oct	Nov	Dec	Jan	Feb
Jan	·782	·758	·769	·768	·770	·781	·786	·786	·794	·802	·808	·813	·824	·823	·834
Feb	·771	·748	·759	·758	·760	·770	·775	·775	·784	·791	·797	·802	·814	·813	·824
Mar	·754	·731	·741	·741	·742	·753	·758	·758	·766	·773	·779	·784	·796	·795	·806
Apr	·702	·679	·690	·689	·691	·701	·706	·706	·714	·721	·727	·731	·743	·742	·752
May	·687	·665	·675	·674	·676	·686	·691	·691	·699	·706	·712	·716	·727	·727	·737
June	·680	·658	·669	·668	·669	·680	·684	·684	·692	·699	·705	·710	·721	·720	·730
July	·679	·657	·667	·666	·668	·678	·683	·683	·691	·698	·703	·708	·719	·718	·729
Aug	·662	·640	·650	·649	·651	·661	·666	·666	·674	·681	·686	·691	·702	·701	·711
Sept	·647	·625	·635	·634	·636	·646	·650	·650	·658	·665	·665	·675	·686	·685	·695
Oct	·634	·612	·622	·622	·623	·633	·638	·638	·645	·652	·658	·662	·673	·672	·682
Nov	·638	·616	·626	·625	·627	·637	·642	·642	·649	·656	·662	·666	·677	·676	·686
Dec	·639	·617	·627	·627	·628	·638	·643	·643	·651	·657	·663	·667	·678	·677	·687
1991	Dec	Jan	Feb	Mar	Apr	May	June	July	Aug	Sept	Oct	Nov	Dec	Jan	Feb
Jan	·635	·614	·624	·623	·624	·634	·639	·639	·647	·654	·659	·664	·674	·674	·684
Feb	·626	·605	·615	·614	·616	·626	·630	·630	·638	·645	·650	·655	·665	·665	·675
Mar	·620	·599	·609	·608	·610	·619	·624	·624	·632	·639	·644	·648	·659	·658	·668
Apr	·600	·579	·588	·588	·589	·599	·603	·603	·611	·618	·623	·627	·638	·637	·647
May	·595	·574	·584	·583	·584	·594	·599	·599	·606	·613	·618	·622	·633	·632	·642
June	·588	·567	·576	·576	·577	·587	·591	·591	·599	·599	·611	·615	·626	·625	·635
July	·591	·570	·580	·579	·581	·590	·595	·595	·602	·606	·614	·619	·629	·629	·638
Aug	·588	·567	·576	·576	·577	·587	·591	·591	·599	·609	·611	·615	·626	·625	·635
Sept	·582	·561	·571	·570	·571	·581	·585	·585	·593	·600	·605	·609	·620	·619	·629
Oct	·576	·555	·565	·564	·566	·575	·580	·580	·587	·594	·599	·603	·614	·613	·623
Nov	·570	·549	·559	·558	·560	·569	·574	·574	·581	·588	·593	·597	·608	·607	·617
Dec	·569	·548	·558	·557	·559	·568	·573	·573	·580	·587	·592	·596	·606	·606	·615
1992	Dec	Jan	Feb	Mar	Apr	May	June	July	Aug	Sept	Oct	Nov	Dec	Jan	Feb
Jan	·570	·549	·559	·558	·560	·569	·574	·574	·581	·588	·593	·597	·608	·607	·617
Feb	·562	·541	·551	·550	·552	·561	·566	·566	·573	·580	·585	·589	·599	·599	·608
Mar	·557	·537	·546	·546	·547	·557	·561	·561	·568	·575	·580	·584	·595	·594	·604
Apr	·534	·514	·523	·522	·524	·533	·537	·537	·545	·551	·556	·561	·571	·570	·579
May	·528	·508	·518	·517	·518	·528	·532	·532	·539	·539	·551	·555	·565	·564	·574
June	·528	·508	·518	·517	·518	·528	·532	·532	·539	·546	·551	·555	·565	·564	·574
July	·534	·514	·523	·522	·524	·533	·537	·537	·545	·546	·556	·561	·571	·570	·579
Aug	·533	·513	·522	·521	·523	·532	·536	·536	·544	·550	·555	·559	·569	·569	·578
Sept	·527	·507	·516	·516	·517	·527	·531	·531	·538	·544	·549	·554	·564	·563	·572
Oct	·522	·502	·511	·510	·512	·521	·525	·525	·533	·539	·544	·548	·558	·558	·567
Nov	·524	·504	·513	·513	·514	·523	·528	·528	·535	·541	·546	·550	·560	·560	·569
Dec	·529	·509	·519	·518	·519	·529	·533	·533	·540	·547	·552	·556	·566	·565	·575
1993	Dec	Jan	Feb	Mar	Apr	May	June	July	Aug	Sept	Oct	Nov	Dec	Jan	Feb
Jan	·544	·524	·533	·532	·534	·543	·547	·547	·555	·561	·566	·571	·581	·580	·590
Feb	·534	·514	·523	·522	·524	·533	·537	·537	·545	·551	·556	·561	·571	·570	·579
Mar	·528	·508	·518	·517	·518	·528	·532	·532	·539	·546	·551	·555	·565	·564	·574
Apr	·514	·494	·504	·503	·504	·514	·518	·518	·525	·531	·536	·541	·550	·550	·559
May	·509	·489	·498	·498	·499	·508	·512	·512	·519	·526	·531	·535	·545	·544	·554
June	·510	·490	·499	·499	·500	·509	·513	·513	·521	·527	·532	·536	·546	·545	·555
July	·513	·493	·502	·502	·503	·512	·517	·517	·524	·530	·535	·539	·549	·549	·558
Aug	·507	·487	·496	·495	·497	·506	·510	·510	·517	·524	·529	·533	·543	·542	·551
Sept	·500	·481	·490	·489	·490	·500	·504	·504	·511	·517	·522	·526	·536	·536	·545
Oct	·501	·482	·491	·490	·492	·501	·505	·505	·512	·518	·523	·528	·537	·537	·546
Nov	·504	·484	·493	·492	·494	·503	·507	·507	·514	·520	·525	·530	·540	·539	·548
Dec	·500	·481	·490	·489	·490	·500	·504	·504	·511	·517	·522	·526	·536	·536	·545

MONTH OF DISPOSAL

	2007				***2008***										
1994	Sept	Oct	Nov	Dec	Jan	Feb	Mar	Apr	May	June	July	Aug	Sept	Oct	Nov
Jan	·472	·478	·484	·493	·485	·496	·501	·515	·522	·534	·532	·537	·546	·541	·529
Feb	·464	·470	·476	·484	·476	·488	·493	·506	·514	·526	·524	·529	·537	·532	·520
Mar	·460	·466	·472	·480	·472	·484	·488	·502	·509	·521	·519	·524	·533	·528	·516
Apr	·442	·449	·454	·463	·455	·466	·471	·484	·492	·503	·501	·506	·515	·510	·498
May	·437	·444	·449	·457	·450	·461	·466	·479	·487	·498	·496	·501	·509	·504	·493
June	·437	·444	·449	·457	·450	·461	·466	·479	·487	·498	·496	·501	·509	·504	·493
July	·444	·451	·456	·465	·457	·468	·473	·486	·494	·506	·503	·508	·517	·512	·500
Aug	·437	·444	·449	·457	·450	·461	·466	·479	·487	·498	·496	·501	·509	·504	·493
Sept	·434	·441	·446	·454	·447	·458	·463	·476	·483	·495	·493	·498	·506	·501	·490
Oct	·433	·439	·444	·452	·445	·456	·461	·474	·481	·493	·491	·496	·504	·499	·488
Nov	·432	·438	·443	·451	·444	·455	·460	·473	·480	·492	·490	·495	·503	·498	·487
Dec	·425	·431	·436	·445	·437	·448	·453	·466	·473	·485	·483	·488	·496	·491	·479
1995	Sept	Oct	Nov	Dec	Jan	Feb	Mar	Apr	May	June	July	Aug	Sept	Oct	Nov
Jan	·425	·431	·436	·445	·437	·448	·453	·466	·473	·485	·483	·488	·496	·491	·479
Feb	·416	·422	·428	·436	·428	·439	·444	·457	·464	·476	·474	·479	·487	·482	·470
Mar	·410	·416	·422	·430	·422	·433	·438	·451	·458	·470	·468	·473	·481	·476	·464
Apr	·396	·402	·407	·415	·408	·419	·423	·436	·444	·455	·453	·458	·466	·461	·450
May	·390	·396	·402	·410	·402	·413	·418	·430	·438	·449	·447	·452	·460	·455	·444
June	·389	·395	·400	·408	·401	·411	·416	·429	·436	·447	·445	·450	·458	·453	·442
July	·395	·401	·406	·414	·407	·418	·423	·435	·443	·454	·452	·457	·465	·460	·449
Aug	·388	·394	·399	·407	·400	·410	·415	·428	·435	·446	·444	·449	·457	·452	·441
Sept	·381	·387	·392	·400	·393	·404	·408	·421	·428	·440	·438	·442	·450	·446	·434
Oct	·389	·395	·400	·408	·401	·411	·416	·429	·436	·447	·445	·450	·458	·453	·442
Nov	·389	·395	·400	·408	·401	·411	·416	·429	·436	·447	·445	·450	·458	·453	·442
Dec	·380	·386	·392	·399	·392	·403	·407	·420	·427	·439	·437	·441	·449	·445	·433
1996	Sept	Oct	Nov	Dec	Jan	Feb	Mar	Apr	May	June	July	Aug	Sept	Oct	Nov
Jan	·385	·391	·396	·404	·397	·407	·412	·425	·432	·443	·441	·446	·454	·449	·438
Feb	·378	·384	·390	·398	·390	·401	·406	·418	·425	·437	·435	·439	·447	·443	·431
Mar	·373	·379	·384	·392	·385	·395	·400	·413	·420	·431	·429	·434	·442	·437	·426
Apr	·363	·369	·374	·382	·375	·385	·390	·402	·410	·421	·419	·423	·431	·427	·415
May	·360	·366	·371	·379	·372	·383	·387	·400	·407	·418	·416	·421	·428	·424	·413
June	·359	·365	·371	·378	·371	·382	·386	·399	·406	·417	·415	·420	·427	·423	·412
July	·365	·371	·376	·384	·377	·387	·392	·404	·411	·423	·421	·425	·433	·428	·417
Aug	·359	·364	·370	·378	·370	·381	·385	·398	·405	·416	·414	·419	·427	·422	·411
Sept	·352	·358	·363	·371	·364	·375	·379	·391	·399	·410	·408	·412	·420	·415	·404
Oct	·352	·358	·363	·371	·364	·375	·379	·391	·399	·410	·408	·412	·420	·415	·404
Nov	·352	·357	·363	·370	·363	·374	·378	·391	·398	·409	·407	·411	·419	·415	·404
Dec	·347	·353	·358	·366	·359	·369	·374	·386	·393	·404	·402	·407	·415	·410	·399
1997	Sept	Oct	Nov	Dec	Jan	Feb	Mar	Apr	May	June	July	Aug	Sept	Oct	Nov
Jan	·347	·353	·358	·366	·359	·369	·374	·386	·393	·404	·402	·407	·415	·410	·399
Feb	·342	·348	·353	·361	·354	·364	·368	·381	·388	·399	·397	·401	·409	·405	·394
Mar	·338	·344	·349	·357	·350	·360	·365	·377	·384	·395	·393	·398	·405	·401	·390
Apr	·331	·337	·342	·349	·342	·353	·357	·369	·376	·387	·385	·390	·397	·393	·382
May	·326	·331	·337	·344	·337	·347	·352	·364	·371	·382	·380	·384	·392	·388	·377
June	·321	·326	·331	·339	·332	·342	·347	·359	·366	·377	·375	·379	·387	·382	·371
July	·321	·326	·331	·339	·332	·342	·347	·359	·366	·377	·375	·379	·387	·382	·371
Aug	·312	·318	·323	·331	·324	·334	·338	·350	·357	·368	·366	·370	·378	·374	·363
Sept	·306	·311	·316	·324	·317	·327	·331	·343	·350	·361	·359	·363	·371	·367	·356
Oct	·304	·310	·315	·322	·315	·325	·330	·342	·349	·359	·357	·362	·369	·365	·354
Nov	·303	·309	·314	·321	·315	·325	·329	·341	·348	·358	·357	·361	·368	·364	·353
Dec	·300	·306	·311	·318	·311	·321	·326	·338	·344	·355	·353	·358	·365	·361	·350

MONTH OF DISPOSAL

	2008	**2009**											**2010**	
1994	Dec	Jan	Feb	Mar	Apr	May	June	July	Aug	Sept	Oct	Nov	Dec	Jan	Feb
Jan	·507	·487	·496	·495	·497	·506	·510	·510	·517	·524	·529	·533	·543	·542	·551
Feb	·498	·479	·488	·487	·488	·498	·502	·502	·509	·515	·520	·524	·534	·533	·543
Mar	·494	·474	·484	·483	·484	·493	·498	·498	·505	·511	·516	·520	·530	·529	·538
Apr	·476	·457	·466	·465	·467	·476	·480	·480	·487	·493	·498	·502	·512	·511	·520
May	·471	·452	·461	·460	·462	·471	·475	·475	·482	·488	·493	·497	·507	·506	·515
June	·471	·452	·461	·460	·462	·471	·475	·475	·482	·488	·493	·497	·507	·506	·515
July	·478	·459	·468	·467	·469	·478	·482	·482	·489	·495	·500	·504	·514	·513	·522
Aug	·471	·452	·461	·460	·462	·471	·475	·475	·482	·488	·493	·497	·507	·506	·515
Sept	·468	·449	·458	·457	·459	·468	·472	·472	·479	·485	·490	·494	·503	·503	·512
Oct	·466	·447	·456	·455	·457	·466	·470	·470	·477	·483	·488	·492	·501	·501	·510
Nov	·465	·446	·455	·454	·456	·465	·469	·469	·476	·482	·487	·491	·500	·500	·509
Dec	·458	·439	·448	·447	·449	·458	·462	·462	·468	·475	·479	·484	·493	·492	·501
1995	Dec	Jan	Feb	Mar	Apr	May	June	July	Aug	Sept	Oct	Nov	Dec	Jan	Feb
Jan	·458	·439	·448	·447	·449	·458	·462	·462	·468	·475	·479	·484	·493	·492	·501
Feb	·449	·430	·439	·438	·440	·449	·453	·453	·459	·466	·470	·474	·484	·483	·492
Mar	·443	·424	·433	·433	·434	·443	·447	·447	·454	·460	·464	·468	·478	·477	·486
Apr	·429	·410	·419	·418	·419	·428	·432	·432	·439	·445	·450	·454	·463	·462	·471
May	·423	·404	·413	·412	·414	·422	·426	·426	·433	·439	·444	·448	·457	·457	·465
June	·421	·403	·411	·411	·412	·421	·425	·425	·431	·437	·442	·446	·455	·455	·463
July	·428	·409	·418	·417	·419	·427	·431	·431	·438	·444	·449	·453	·462	·461	·470
Aug	·420	·402	·410	·410	·411	·420	·424	·424	·430	·436	·441	·445	·454	·454	·462
Sept	·414	·395	·404	·403	·404	·413	·417	·417	·424	·430	·434	·438	·448	·447	·456
Oct	·421	·403	·411	·411	·412	·421	·425	·425	·431	·437	·442	·446	·455	·455	·463
Nov	·421	·403	·411	·411	·412	·421	·425	·425	·431	·437	·442	·446	·455	·455	·463
Dec	·413	·394	·403	·402	·403	·412	·416	·416	·423	·429	·433	·437	·447	·446	·455
1996	Dec	Jan	Feb	Mar	Apr	May	June	July	Aug	Sept	Oct	Nov	Dec	Jan	Feb
Jan	·417	·399	·407	·407	·408	·417	·421	·421	·427	·433	·438	·442	·451	·451	·459
Feb	·411	·392	·401	·400	·402	·410	·414	·414	·421	·427	·431	·435	·445	·444	·453
Mar	·405	·387	·395	·395	·396	·405	·409	·409	·415	·421	·426	·430	·439	·438	·447
Apr	·395	·377	·385	·385	·386	·394	·398	·398	·405	·411	·415	·419	·429	·428	·436
May	·392	·374	·383	·382	·383	·392	·396	·396	·402	·408	·413	·417	·426	·425	·434
June	·392	·373	·382	·381	·382	·391	·395	·395	·401	·407	·412	·416	·425	·424	·433
July	·397	·379	·387	·386	·388	·396	·400	·400	·407	·413	·417	·421	·430	·430	·438
Aug	·391	·372	·381	·380	·381	·390	·394	·394	·400	·406	·411	·415	·424	·423	·432
Sept	·384	·366	·375	·374	·375	·384	·388	·388	·394	·400	·404	·408	·417	·417	·425
Oct	·384	·366	·375	·374	·375	·384	·388	·388	·394	·400	·404	·408	·417	·417	·425
Nov	·383	·365	·374	·373	·374	·383	·387	·387	·393	·399	·404	·407	·417	·416	·424
Dec	·379	·361	·369	·369	·370	·378	·382	·382	·389	·394	·399	·403	·412	·411	·420
1997	Dec	Jan	Feb	Mar	Apr	May	June	July	Aug	Sept	Oct	Nov	Dec	Jan	Feb
Jan	·379	·361	·369	·369	·370	·378	·382	·382	·389	·394	·399	·403	·412	·411	·420
Feb	·374	·355	·364	·363	·365	·373	·377	·377	·383	·389	·394	·397	·406	·406	·414
Mar	·370	·352	·360	·360	·361	·369	·373	·373	·380	·385	·390	·394	·403	·402	·411
Apr	·362	·344	·353	·352	·353	·361	·365	·365	·372	·377	·382	·386	·395	·394	·402
May	·357	·339	·347	·347	·348	·356	·360	·360	·366	·372	·377	·380	·389	·389	·397
June	·352	·334	·342	·342	·343	·351	·355	·355	·361	·367	·371	·375	·384	·383	·392
July	·352	·334	·342	·342	·343	·351	·355	·355	·361	·367	·371	·375	·384	·383	·392
Aug	·343	·326	·334	·333	·334	·343	·346	·346	·353	·358	·363	·367	·375	·375	·383
Sept	·336	·319	·327	·326	·328	·336	·340	·340	·346	·352	·356	·360	·368	·368	·376
Oct	·335	·317	·325	·325	·326	·334	·338	·338	·344	·350	·354	·358	·367	·366	·374
Nov	·334	·316	·325	·324	·325	·333	·337	·337	·343	·349	·353	·357	·366	·365	·373
Dec	·331	·313	·321	·321	·322	·330	·334	·334	·340	·346	·350	·354	·363	·362	·370

MONTH OF DISPOSAL

	2007				***2008***										
1998	Sept	Oct	Nov	Dec	Jan	Feb	Mar	Apr	May	June	July	Aug	Sept	Oct	Nov
Jan	·304	·310	·315	·322	·315	·325	·330	·342	·349	·359	·357	·362	·369	·365	·354
Feb	·298	·303	·308	·316	·309	·319	·323	·335	·342	·352	·351	·355	·362	·358	·347
Mar	·294	·299	·304	·312	·305	·315	·319	·331	·338	·348	·346	·351	·358	·354	·343
Apr	·279	·285	·290	·297	·290	·300	·304	·316	·323	·333	·331	·336	·343	·339	·328
May	·272	·278	·283	·290	·283	·293	·297	·309	·316	·326	·324	·328	·336	·331	·321
June	·273	·278	·283	·291	·284	·294	·298	·310	·316	·327	·325	·329	·337	·332	·322
July	·276	·282	·287	·294	·287	·297	·301	·313	·320	·330	·328	·333	·340	·336	·325
Aug	·271	·276	·281	·288	·282	·291	·296	·307	·314	·324	·323	·327	·334	·330	·319
Sept	·265	·271	·276	·283	·276	·286	·290	·302	·308	·319	·317	·321	·328	·324	·314
Oct	·264	·270	·275	·282	·275	·285	·289	·301	·308	·318	·316	·320	·328	·323	·313
Nov	·265	·271	·276	·283	·276	·286	·290	·302	·308	·319	·317	·321	·328	·324	·314
Dec	·265	·271	·276	·283	·276	·286	·290	·302	·308	·319	·317	·321	·328	·324	·314
1999	Sept	Oct	Nov	Dec	Jan	Feb	Mar	Apr	May	June	July	Aug	Sept	Oct	Nov
Jan	·273	·278	·283	·291	·284	·294	·298	·310	·316	·327	·325	·329	·337	·332	·322
Feb	·271	·276	·281	·288	·282	·291	·296	·307	·314	·324	·323	·327	·334	·330	·319
Mar	·268	·273	·278	·285	·278	·288	·293	·304	·311	·321	·319	·324	·331	·327	·316
Apr	·259	·265	·269	·277	·270	·280	·284	·295	·302	·312	·311	·315	·322	·318	·308
May	·256	·261	·266	·274	·267	·277	·281	·292	·299	·309	·307	·312	·319	·315	·304
June	·256	·261	·266	·274	·267	·277	·281	·292	·299	·309	·307	·312	·319	·315	·304
July	·260	·265	·270	·277	·271	·280	·285	·296	·303	·313	·311	·316	·323	·319	·308
Aug	·257	·262	·267	·274	·268	·277	·282	·293	·300	·310	·308	·312	·320	·315	·305
Sept	·252	·257	·262	·269	·262	·272	·276	·288	·294	·304	·303	·307	·314	·310	·300
Oct	·249	·255	·259	·267	·260	·270	·274	·285	·292	·302	·300	·305	·312	·308	·297
Nov	·248	·253	·258	·265	·259	·268	·272	·284	·290	·301	·299	·303	·310	·306	·296
Dec	·243	·249	·253	·261	·254	·264	·268	·279	·286	·296	·294	·298	·305	·301	·291
2000	Sept	Oct	Nov	Dec	Jan	Feb	Mar	Apr	May	June	July	Aug	Sept	Oct	Nov
Jan	·248	·254	·259	·266	·259	·269	·273	·285	·291	·301	·300	·304	·311	·307	·297
Feb	·242	·247	·252	·259	·253	·262	·266	·278	·284	·294	·293	·297	·304	·300	·290
Mar	·235	·240	·245	·252	·246	·255	·260	·271	·277	·287	·286	·290	·297	·293	·283
Apr	·223	·228	·233	·240	·233	·243	·247	·258	·265	·275	·273	·277	·284	·280	·270
May	·219	·224	·228	·236	·229	·238	·243	·254	·260	·270	·268	·272	·279	·275	·265
June	·216	·221	·226	·233	·226	·236	·240	·251	·257	·267	·265	·269	·276	·272	·262
July	·220	·225	·230	·237	·230	·240	·244	·255	·262	·272	·270	·274	·281	·277	·267
Aug	·220	·225	·230	·237	·230	·240	·244	·255	·262	·272	·270	·274	·281	·277	·267
Sept	·211	·217	·221	·228	·222	·231	·235	·246	·253	·263	·261	·265	·272	·268	·258
Oct	·212	·217	·222	·229	·223	·232	·236	·247	·253	·263	·262	·266	·273	·269	·259
Nov	·209	·214	·218	·225	·219	·228	·232	·243	·250	·260	·258	·262	·269	·265	·255
Dec	·208	·213	·218	·225	·218	·228	·232	·243	·249	·259	·257	·261	·268	·264	·254
2001	Sept	Oct	Nov	Dec	Jan	Feb	Mar	Apr	May	June	July	Aug	Sept	Oct	Nov
Jan	·216	·221	·226	·233	·226	·236	·240	·251	·257	·267	·265	·269	·276	·272	·262
Feb	·209	·215	·219	·226	·220	·229	·233	·244	·251	·260	·259	·263	·270	·266	·256
Mar	·208	·213	·218	·225	·218	·228	·232	·243	·249	·259	·257	·261	·268	·264	·254
Apr	·202	·207	·211	·218	·212	·221	·225	·236	·243	·252	·251	·255	·262	·258	·248
May	·194	·199	·204	·211	·204	·214	·218	·228	·235	·245	·243	·247	·254	·250	·240
June	·193	·198	·202	·209	·203	·212	·216	·227	·233	·243	·241	·245	·252	·248	·239
July	·200	·205	·210	·217	·211	·220	·224	·235	·241	·251	·249	·253	·260	·256	·246
Aug	·195	·201	·205	·212	·206	·215	·219	·230	·236	·246	·244	·248	·255	·251	·241
Sept	·191	·196	·201	·208	·202	·211	·215	·226	·232	·242	·240	·244	·251	·247	·237
Oct	·193	·199	·203	·290	·204	·213	·217	·228	·234	·244	·242	·26	·253	·249	·239
Nov	·198	·203	·208	·215	·209	·218	·222	·233	·239	·249	·247	·251	·258	·254	·244
Dec	·200	·205	·209	·216	·210	·219	·223	·234	·240	·250	·249	·253	·260	·255	·246

MONTH OF DISPOSAL

	2008	***2009***												***2010***	
1998	Dec	Jan	Feb	Mar	Apr	May	June	July	Aug	Sept	Oct	Nov	Dec	Jan	Feb
Jan	·335	·317	·325	·325	·326	·334	·338	·338	·344	·350	·354	·358	·367	·366	·374
Feb	·328	·311	·319	·318	·319	·328	·331	·331	·337	·343	·347	·351	·360	·359	·367
Mar	·324	·307	·315	·314	·315	·323	·327	·327	·333	·339	·343	·347	·356	·355	·363
Apr	·309	·292	·300	·300	·301	·309	·312	·312	·319	·324	·328	·332	·341	·340	·348
May	·302	·285	·293	·292	·294	·302	·305	·305	·311	·317	·321	·325	·333	·333	·341
June	·303	·286	·294	·293	·294	·302	·306	·306	·312	·318	·322	·326	·334	·334	·341
July	·306	·289	·297	·296	·298	·306	·309	·309	·315	·321	·325	·329	·337	·337	·345
Aug	·301	·283	·291	·291	·292	·300	·304	·304	·310	·315	·319	·323	·332	·331	·339
Sept	·295	·278	·286	·285	·286	·294	·298	·298	·304	·310	·314	·318	·326	·325	·333
Oct	·294	·277	·285	·284	·286	·294	·297	·297	·303	·309	·313	·317	·325	·325	·333
Nov	·295	·278	·286	·285	·286	·294	·298	·298	·304	·310	·314	·318	·326	·325	·333
Dec	·295	·278	·286	·285	·286	·294	·298	·298	·304	·310	·314	·318	·326	·325	·333
1999	Dec	Jan	Feb	Mar	Apr	May	June	July	Aug	Sept	Oct	Nov	Dec	Jan	Feb
Jan	·303	·286	·294	·293	·294	·302	·306	·306	·312	·318	·322	·326	·334	·334	·341
Feb	·301	·283	·291	·291	·292	·300	·304	·304	·310	·315	·319	·323	·332	·331	·339
Mar	·297	·280	·288	·288	·289	·297	·300	·300	·307	·312	·316	·320	·328	·328	·336
Apr	·289	·272	·280	·279	·280	·288	·292	·292	·298	·303	·308	·311	·320	·319	·327
May	·286	·269	·277	·276	·277	·285	·289	·289	·295	·300	·304	·308	·316	·316	·324
June	·286	·269	·277	·276	·277	·285	·289	·289	·295	·300	·304	·308	·316	·316	·324
July	·290	·273	·280	·280	·281	·289	·293	·293	·299	·304	·308	·312	·320	·320	·328
Aug	·286	·269	·277	·277	·278	·286	·289	·289	·295	·301	·305	·309	·317	·317	·324
Sept	·281	·264	·272	·271	·273	·280	·284	·284	·290	·295	·300	·303	·312	·311	·319
Oct	·279	·262	·270	·269	·270	·278	·282	·282	·288	·293	·297	·301	·309	·309	·317
Nov	·277	·260	·268	·268	·269	·277	·280	·280	·286	·251	·296	·299	·308	·307	·315
Dec	·273	·256	·264	·263	·264	·272	·276	·276	·282	·250	·291	·295	·303	·302	·310
2000	Dec	Jan	Feb	Mar	Apr	May	June	July	Aug	Sept	Oct	Nov	Dec	Jan	Feb
Jan	·278	·261	·269	·268	·270	·277	·281	·281	·287	·292	·297	·300	·309	·308	·316
Feb	·271	·254	·262	·261	·263	·270	·274	·274	·280	·285	·290	·293	·301	·301	·309
Mar	·264	·248	·255	·255	·256	·264	·267	·267	·273	·279	·283	·286	·295	·294	·302
Apr	·252	·235	·243	·242	·243	·251	·255	·255	·260	·266	·270	·273	·282	·281	·289
May	·247	·231	·238	·238	·239	·247	·250	·250	·256	·261	·265	·269	·277	·277	·284
June	·244	·228	·236	·235	·236	·244	·247	·247	·253	·258	·262	·266	·274	·274	·281
July	·249	·232	·240	·239	·240	·248	·252	·252	·257	·263	·267	·270	·279	·278	·286
Aug	·249	·232	·240	·239	·240	·248	·252	·252	·257	·263	·267	·270	·279	·278	·286
Sept	·240	·224	·231	·231	·232	·239	·243	·243	·249	·254	·258	·262	·270	·269	·277
Oct	·241	·224	·232	·231	·233	·240	·244	·244	·249	·255	·259	·262	·270	·270	·277
Nov	·237	·221	·228	·228	·229	·236	·240	·240	·246	·251	·255	·259	·267	·266	·274
Dec	·236	·220	·228	·227	·228	·236	·239	·239	·245	·250	·254	·258	·266	·265	·273
2001	Dec	Jan	Feb	Mar	Apr	May	June	July	Aug	Sept	Oct	Nov	Dec	Jan	Feb
Jan	·244	·228	·236	·235	·236	·244	·247	·247	·253	·258	·262	·266	·274	·274	·281
Feb	·238	·222	·229	·228	·230	·237	·241	·241	·247	·252	·256	·259	·267	·267	·274
Mar	·236	·220	·228	·227	·228	·236	·239	·239	·245	·250	·254	·258	·266	·265	·273
Apr	·230	·214	·221	·221	·222	·229	·233	·233	·239	·244	·248	·251	·259	·259	·266
May	·222	·206	·214	·213	·214	·222	·225	·225	·231	·236	·240	·243	·251	·251	·258
June	·221	·205	·212	·212	·213	·220	·224	·224	·229	·235	·239	·242	·250	·249	·257
July	·229	·212	·220	·219	·220	·228	·231	·231	·237	·242	·246	·250	·258	·257	·265
Aug	·224	·207	·215	·214	·216	·223	·226	·226	·232	·237	·241	·245	·253	·252	·260
Sept	·219	·203	·211	·210	·211	·219	·222	·222	·228	·233	·237	·241	·249	·248	·255
Oct	·221	·205	·213	·212	·213	·221	·224	·224	·230	·235	·239	·243	·251	·250	·258
Nov	·226	·210	·218	·217	·218	·226	·229	·229	·235	·240	·244	·248	·256	·255	·263
Dec	·228	·212	·219	·219	·220	·227	·231	·231	·236	·242	·246	·249	·257	·257	·264

MONTH OF DISPOSAL

	2007				***2008***										
2002	Sept	Oct	Nov	Dec	Jan	Feb	Mar	Apr	May	June	July	Aug	Sept	Oct	Nov
Jan	·200	·205	·210	·217	·211	·220	·224	·235	·241	·251	·249	·253	·260	·256	·246
Feb	·197	·202	·207	·213	·207	·216	·220	·231	·238	·247	·246	·250	·257	·253	·243
Mar	·192	·197	·202	·209	·202	·211	·215	·226	·233	·242	·241	·245	·252	·248	·238
Apr	·184	·189	·194	·200	·194	·203	·207	·218	·224	·234	·232	·236	·243	·239	·229
May	·180	·186	·190	·197	·191	·200	·204	·215	·221	·230	·229	·233	·240	·236	·226
June	·180	·186	·190	·197	·191	·200	·204	·215	·221	·230	·229	·233	·240	·236	·226
July	·182	·188	·192	·199	·193	·202	·206	·217	·223	·233	·231	·235	·242	·238	·228
Aug	·179	·184	·189	·196	·189	·198	·202	·213	·219	·229	·227	·231	·238	·234	·224
Sept	·171	·176	·181	·188	·181	·190	·194	·205	·211	·221	·219	·223	·230	·226	·216
Oct	·169	·174	·179	·185	·179	·188	·192	·203	·209	·219	·217	·221	·228	·224	·214
Nov	·167	·172	·177	·184	·177	·186	·190	·201	·207	·217	·215	·219	·226	·222	·212
Dec	·165	·170	·175	·182	·175	·184	·188	·199	·205	·215	·213	·217	·224	·220	·210
2003	Sept	Oct	Nov	Dec	Jan	Feb	Mar	Apr	May	June	July	Aug	Sept	Oct	Nov
Jan	·166	·171	·175	·182	·176	·185	·189	·200	·206	·215	·214	·217	·224	·220	·211
Feb	·160	·165	·170	·176	·170	·179	·183	·194	·200	·209	·207	·211	·218	·214	·205
Mar	·156	·161	·166	·172	·166	·175	·179	·190	·196	·205	·203	·207	·214	·210	·201
Apr	·148	·153	·157	·164	·158	·167	·171	·181	·187	·196	·195	·199	·205	·201	·192
May	·146	·151	·155	·162	·156	·165	·169	·179	·185	·194	·193	·197	·203	·199	·190
June	·147	·152	·157	·163	·157	·166	·170	·180	·186	·196	·194	·198	·205	·201	·191
July	·147	·152	·157	·163	·157	·166	·170	·180	·186	·196	·194	·198	·205	·201	·191
Aug	·145	·150	·155	·161	·155	·164	·168	·178	·184	·194	·192	·196	·203	·199	·189
Sept	·140	·145	·149	·156	·150	·158	·162	·173	·179	·188	·186	·190	·197	·193	·184
Oct	·139	·144	·148	·155	·149	·158	·162	·172	·178	·187	·186	·189	·196	·192	·183
Nov	·138	·1438	·148	·154	·148	·157	·161	·171	·177	·187	·185	·189	·195	·192	·182
Dec	·134	·138	·143	·149	·143	·152	·156	·166	·172	·181	·180	·184	·190	·186	·177
2004	Sept	Oct	Nov	Dec	Jan	Feb	Mar	Apr	May	June	July	Aug	Sept	Oct	Nov
Jan	·136	·141	·145	·152	·146	·155	·158	·169	·175	·184	·182	·186	·193	·189	·180
Feb	·132	·137	·141	·147	·141	·150	·154	·164	·170	·180	·178	·182	·188	·184	·175
Mar	·127	·132	·136	·142	·137	·145	·149	·159	·165	·174	·173	·177	·183	·179	·170
Apr	·120	·125	·129	·136	·130	·138	·142	·152	·158	·167	·166	·170	·176	·172	·163
May	·115	·120	·124	·131	·125	·134	·137	·147	·153	·162	·161	·165	·171	·167	·158
June	·113	·118	·123	·129	·123	·132	·135	·146	·151	·161	·159	·163	·169	·165	·156
July	·113	·118	·123	·129	·123	·132	·135	·146	·151	·161	·159	·163	·169	·165	·156
Aug	·110	·115	·119	·125	·120	·123	·132	·142	·148	·157	·155	·159	·165	·162	·153
Sept	·106	·111	·115	·121	·115	·124	·128	·138	·144	·153	·151	·155	·161	·157	·148
Oct	·103	·108	·112	·118	·112	·121	·125	·135	·141	·150	·148	·152	·158	·154	·145
Nov	·101	·105	·110	·116	·110	·119	·122	·132	·138	·147	·146	·149	·156	·152	·143
Dec	·095	·100	·104	·111	·105	·113	·117	·127	·133	·142	·140	·144	·150	·146	·137
2005	Sept	Oct	Nov	Dec	Jan	Feb	Mar	Apr	May	June	July	Aug	Sept	Oct	Nov
Jan	·101	·106	·110	·116	·111	·119	·123	·133	·139	·148	·146	·150	·156	·152	·143
Feb	·097	·102	·106	·112	·107	·115	·119	·129	·134	·143	·142	·146	·152	·148	·139
Mar	·092	·097	·101	·107	·101	·110	·113	·123	·129	·138	·136	·140	·146	·143	·134
Apr	·086	·090	·094	·101	·095	·103	·107	·117	·123	·132	·130	·134	·140	·136	·127
May	·083	·088	·092	·098	·093	·101	·105	·115	·120	·129	·128	·131	·138	·134	·125
June	·082	·087	·091	·097	·092	·100	·104	·113	·119	·128	·126	·130	·136	·133	·124
July	·082	·087	·091	·097	·092	·100	·104	·113	·119	·128	·126	·130	·136	·133	·124
Aug	·080	·085	·089	·095	·089	·098	·101	·111	·117	·126	·124	·128	·134	·130	·121
Sept	·077	·082	·086	·092	·086	·095	·098	·108	·114	·123	·121	·125	·131	·127	·119
Oct	·076	·081	·085	·091	·085	·094	·097	·107	·113	·122	·120	·124	·130	·126	·117
Nov	·074	·079	·083	·089	·084	·092	·096	·105	·111	·120	·118	·122	·128	·124	·116
Dec	·072	·076	·080	·087	·081	·089	·093	·103	·108	·117	·115	·119	·125	·122	·113

MONTH OF DISPOSAL

	2008	2009												2010	
2002	Dec	Jan	Feb	Mar	Apr	May	June	July	Aug	Sept	Oct	Nov	Dec	Jan	Feb
Jan	·229	·212	·220	·219	·220	·228	·231	·231	·237	·242	·246	·250	·258	·257	·265
Feb	·225	·209	·216	·216	·217	·224	·228	·228	·234	·239	·243	·246	·254	·254	·261
Mar	·220	·204	·211	·211	·212	·219	·223	·223	·229	·234	·238	·241	·249	·249	·256
Apr	·212	·196	·203	·203	·204	·211	·215	·215	·220	·225	·229	·233	·241	·240	·248
May	·208	·192	·200	·199	·200	·208	·211	·211	·217	·222	·226	·229	·237	·237	·244
June	·208	·192	·200	·199	·200	·208	·211	·211	·217	·222	·226	·229	·237	·237	·244
July	·210	·194	·202	·201	·202	·210	.213	.213	.219	.224	.228	.231	.239	.239	.246
Aug	·207	·191	·198	·198	·199	·206	·210	·210	·215	·221	·224	·228	·236	·235	·243
Sept	·199	·183	·190	·190	·191	·198	·202	·202	·207	·212	·216	·220	·227	·227	·234
Oct	·197	·181	·188	·188	·189	·196	·200	·200	·205	·210	·214	·218	·225	·225	·232
Nov	·195	·179	·186	·186	·187	·194	·198	·198	·203	·208	·212	·215	·223	·223	·230
Dec	·193	·177	·184	·184	·185	·192	·196	·196	·201	·206	·210	·213	·221	·221	·228
2003	Dec	Jan	Feb	Mar	Apr	May	June	July	Aug	Sept	Oct	Nov	Dec	Jan	Feb
Jan	·193	·178	·185	·184	·186	·193	·196	·196	·202	·207	·211	·214	·222	·221	·229
Feb	·187	·172	·179	·178	·180	·187	·190	·190	·196	·201	·205	·208	·216	·215	·223
Mar	·183	·168	·175	·175	·176	·183	·186	·186	·192	·197	·201	·204	·212	·211	·218
Apr	·175	·159	·167	·166	·167	·174	·178	·178	·183	·188	·192	·195	·203	·203	·210
May	·173	·158	·165	·164	·165	·172	·176	·176	·181	·186	·190	·193	·201	·201	·208
June	·174	·159	·166	·165	·167	·174	·177	·177	·183	·188	·191	·195	·202	·202	·209
July	·174	·159	·166	·165	·167	·174	·177	·177	·183	·188	·191	·195	·202	·202	·209
Aug	·172	·157	·164	·164	·165	·172	·175	·175	·181	·186	·189	·193	·200	·200	·207
Sept	·167	·151	·158	·158	·159	·166	·169	·169	·175	·180	·184	·187	·195	·194	·201
Oct	·166	·151	·158	·157	·158	·165	·169	·169	·174	·179	·183	·186	·194	·193	·200
Nov	·165	·150	·157	·157	·158	·165	·168	·168	·174	·178	·182	·186	·193	·193	·200
Dec	·160	·145	·152	·151	·153	·160	·163	·163	·168	·173	·177	·180	·188	·187	·195
2004	Dec	Jan	Feb	Mar	Apr	May	June	July	Aug	Sept	Oct	Nov	Dec	Jan	Feb
Jan	·163	·147	·155	·154	·155	·162	·165	·165	·171	·176	·180	·183	·191	·190	·197
Feb	·158	·143	·150	·150	·151	·158	·161	·161	·166	·171	·175	·178	·186	·186	·193
Mar	·153	·138	·145	·145	·146	·153	·156	·156	·161	·166	·170	·173	·181	·180	·187
Apr	·146	·131	·138	·138	·139	·146	·149	·149	·155	·159	·163	·166	·174	·173	·180
May	·142	·127	·134	·133	·134	·141	·144	·144	·150	·154	·158	·161	·169	·168	·175
June	·140	·125	·132	·131	·132	·139	·142	·142	·148	·153	·156	·160	·167	·168	·173
July	·140	·125	·132	·131	·132	·139	·142	·142	·148	·153	·156	·160	·167	·168	·173
Aug	·136	·121	·128	·128	·129	·136	·139	·139	·144	·149	·153	·156	·163	·163	·170
Sept	·132	·117	·124	·123	·124	·131	·135	·135	·140	·145	·148	·152	·159	·158	·165
Oct	·129	·114	·121	·120	·121	·128	·131	·131	·137	·142	·145	·148	·156	·155	·162
Nov	·126	·112	·119	·118	·119	·126	·129	·129	·134	·139	·143	·146	·153	·153	·160
Dec	·121	·106	·113	·113	·114	·121	·124	·124	·129	·134	·137	·141	·148	·147	·154
2005	Dec	Jan	Feb	Mar	Apr	May	June	July	Aug	Sept	Oct	Nov	Dec	Jan	Feb
Jan	·127	·112	·119	·119	·120	·127	·130	·130	·135	·140	·143	·147	·154	·154	·160
Feb	·123	·108	·115	·114	·116	·122	·126	·126	·131	·136	·139	·142	·150	·149	·156
Mar	·118	·103	·110	·109	·110	·117	·120	·120	·125	·130	·134	·137	·144	·144	·151
Apr	·111	·097	·103	·103	·104	·111	·114	·114	·119	·124	·127	·130	·138	·137	·144
May	·109	·094	·101	·101	·102	·108	·111	·111	·117	·121	·125	·128	·135	·135	·142
June	·108	·093	·100	·099	·100	·107	·110	·110	·116	·120	·124	·127	·134	·134	·140
July	·108	·093	·100	·099	·100	·107	·110	·110	·116	·120	·124	·127	·134	·134	·140
Aug	·105	·091	·098	·097	·098	·105	·108	·108	·113	·118	·121	·125	·132	·131	·138
Sept	·103	·088	·095	·094	·095	·102	·105	·105	·110	·115	·119	·122	·129	·128	·135
Oct	·101	·087	·094	·093	·094	·101	·104	·104	·109	·114	·117	·121	·128	·127	·134
Nov	·100	·085	·092	·091	·092	·099	·102	·102	·107	·112	·116	·119	·126	·126	·132
Dec	·097	·082	·089	·089	·090	·096	·099	·099	·105	·109	·113	·116	·123	·123	·129

MONTH OF DISPOSAL

	2007				***2008***										
2006	Sept	Oct	Nov	Dec	Jan	Feb	Mar	Apr	May	June	July	Aug	Sept	Oct	Nov
Jan	·075	·080	·084	·090	·085	·093	·097	·107	·112	·121	·119	·123	·129	·126	·117
Feb	·071	·076	·080	·086	·080	·089	·092	·102	·108	·116	·115	·118	·125	·121	·112
Mar	·067	·071	·075	·082	·076	·084	·088	·097	·103	·112	·110	·114	·120	·116	·108
Apr	·059	·063	·067	·073	·068	·076	·079	·089	·095	·103	·102	·105	·111	·108	·099
May	·052	·057	·061	·067	·061	·069	·073	·082	·088	·097	·095	·099	·105	·101	·093
June	·048	·052	·056	·062	·057	·065	·069	·078	·084	·092	·091	·094	·100	·097	·088
July	·048	·052	·056	·062	·057	·065	·069	·078	·084	·092	·091	·094	·100	·097	·088
Aug	·044	·049	·053	·059	·053	·061	·065	·074	·080	·088	·087	·090	·096	·093	·084
Sept	·039	·044	·048	·054	·048	·056	·060	·069	·075	·083	·082	·085	·091	·088	·079
Oct	·038	·042	·046	·052	·047	·055	·058	·068	·073	·082	·080	·084	·090	·086	·078
Nov	·034	·039	·043	·049	·043	·051	·055	·064	·070	·078	·077	·080	·086	·083	·074
Dec	·026	·031	·035	·040	·035	·043	·046	·056	·061	·070	·068	·072	·077	·074	·066
2007	Sept	Oct	Nov	Dec	Jan	Feb	Mar	Apr	May	June	July	Aug	Sept	Oct	Nov
Jan	·032	·036	·040	·046	·041	·049	·052	·062	·067	·075	·074	·077	·083	·080	·071
Feb	·024	·029	·032	·038	·033	·041	·044	·054	·059	·067	·066	·069	·075	·072	·064
Mar	·018	·022	·026	·032	·026	·034	·038	·047	·052	·061	·059	·063	·068	·065	·057
Apr	·013	·017	·021	·027	·021	·029	·033	·042	·047	·056	·054	·057	·063	·060	·052
May	·009	·013	·017	·023	·017	·025	·029	·038	·043	·051	·050	·053	·059	·056	·048
June	·003	·008	·012	·017	·012	·020	·023	·032	·038	·046	·044	·048	·054	·050	·042
July	·009	·014	·017	·023	·018	·026	·029	·038	·044	·052	·050	·054	·060	·056	·048
Aug	·003	·008	·012	·017	·012	·020	·023	·032	·038	·046	·044	·048	·054	·050	·042
Sept	·000	·004	·008	·014	·009	·016	·020	·029	·034	·042	·041	·044	·050	·047	·038
Oct	—	·000	·004	·010	·004	·012	·015	·024	·030	·038	·036	·040	·045	·042	·034
Nov	—	—	·000	·006	·000	·008	·011	·021	·026	·034	·032	·036	·041	·038	·030
Dec	—	—	—	·000	·000	·002	·006	·015	·020	·028	·027	·030	·036	·032	·024
2008	Sept	Oct	Nov	Dec	Jan	Feb	Mar	Apr	May	June	July	Aug	Sept	Oct	Nov
Jan	—	—	—	—	·000	·008	·011	·020	·025	·033	·032	·035	·041	·038	·030
Feb	—	—	—	—	—	·000	·003	·012	·018	·026	·024	·027	·033	·030	·022
Mar	—	—	—	—	—	—	·000	·009	·014	·022	·021	·024	·030	·026	·018
Apr	—	—	—	—	—	—	—	·000	·005	·013	·012	·015	·021	·017	·009
May	—	—	—	—	—	—	—	—	·000	·008	·007	·010	·015	·012	·004
June	—	—	—	—	—	—	—	—	—	·000	·000	·002	·007	·004	·000
July	—	—	—	—	—	—	—	—	—	—	·000	·003	·009	·006	·000
Aug	—	—	—	—	—	—	—	—	—	—	—	·000	·006	·002	·000
Sept	—	—	—	—	—	—	—	—	—	—	—	—	·000	·000	·000
Oct	—	—	—	—	—	—	—	—	—	—	—	—	—	·000	·000
Nov	—	—	—	—	—	—	—	—	—	—	—	—	—	—	·000
Dec	—	—	—	—	—	—	—	—	—	—	—	—	—	—	—
2009	Sept	Oct	Nov	Dec	Jan	Feb	Mar	Apr	May	June	July	Aug	Sept	Oct	Nov
Jan	—	—	—	—	—	—	—	—	—	—	—	—	—	—	—
Feb	—	—	—	—	—	—	—	—	—	—	—	—	—	—	—
Mar	—	—	—	—	—	—	—	—	—	—	—	—	—	—	—
Apr	—	—	—	—	—	—	—	—	—	—	—	—	—	—	—
May	—	—	—	—	—	—	—	—	—	—	—	—	—	—	—
June	—	—	—	—	—	—	—	—	—	—	—	—	—	—	—
July	—	—	—	—	—	—	—	—	—	—	—	—	—	—	—
Aug	—	—	—	—	—	—	—	—	—	—	—	—	—	—	—
Sept	—	—	—	—	—	—	—	—	—	—	—	—	—	—	—
Oct	—	—	—	—	—	—	—	—	—	—	—	—	—	—	—
Nov	—	—	—	—	—	—	—	—	—	—	—	—	—	—	—
Dec	—	—	—	—	—	—	—	—	—	—	—	—	—	—	—

MONTH OF DISPOSAL

	2008	*2009*												*2010*	
2006	Dec	Jan	Feb	Mar	Apr	May	June	July	Aug	Sept	Oct	Nov	Dec	Jan	Feb
Jan	·101	·086	·093	·093	·094	·100	·103	·103	·109	·113	·117	·120	·127	·127	·133
Feb	·096	·082	·089	·088	·089	·096	·099	·099	·104	·109	·112	·115	·123	·122	·129
Mar	·092	·077	·084	·084	·085	·091	·094	·094	·099	·104	·108	·111	·118	·117	·124
Apr	·083	·069	·076	·075	·076	·083	·086	·086	·091	·096	·099	·102	·109	·109	·116
May	·077	·063	·069	·069	·070	·076	·079	·079	·084	·089	·093	·096	·103	·102	·109
June	·073	·058	·065	·064	·065	·072	·075	·075	·080	·085	·088	·091	·098	·098	·104
July	·073	·058	·065	·064	·065	·072	·075	·075	·080	·085	·088	·091	·098	·098	·104
Aug	·069	·055	·061	·061	·062	·068	·071	·071	·076	·081	·084	·087	·094	·094	·100
Sept	·064	·050	·056	·056	·057	·063	·066	·066	·071	·076	·079	·082	·089	·089	·095
Oct	·062	·048	·055	·054	·055	·062	·065	·065	·070	·074	·078	·081	·088	·087	·094
Nov	·059	·045	·051	·051	·052	·058	·061	·061	·066	·071	·074	·077	·084	·084	·090
Dec	·050	·037	·043	·042	·043	·050	·053	·053	·058	·062	·066	·069	·075	·075	·081
2007	Dec	Jan	Feb	Mar	Apr	May	June	July	Aug	Sept	Oct	Nov	Dec	Jan	Feb
Jan	·056	·042	·049	·048	·049	·056	·059	·059	·063	·068	·071	·074	·081	·081	·087
Feb	·048	·034	·041	·040	·041	·048	·051	·051	·056	·060	·064	·066	·073	·073	·079
Mar	·042	·028	·034	·034	·035	·041	·044	·044	·049	·053	·057	·060	·067	·066	·072
Apr	·037	·023	·029	·029	·030	·036	·039	·039	·044	·048	·052	·055	·061	·061	·067
May	·032	·019	·025	·025	·026	·032	·035	·035	·040	·044	·048	·050	·057	·057	·063
June	·027	·014	·020	·019	·020	·027	·029	·029	·034	·039	·042	·045	·052	·051	·057
July	·033	·019	·026	·025	·026	·033	·035	·035	·040	·045	·048	·051	·058	·057	·064
Aug	·027	·014	·020	·019	·020	·027	·029	·029	·034	·039	·042	·045	·052	·051	·057
Sept	·024	·010	·016	·016	·017	·023	·026	·026	·031	·035	·038	·041	·048	·048	·054
Oct	·019	·006	·012	·011	·012	·019	·022	·022	·026	·031	·034	·037	·044	·043	·049
Nov	·015	·002	·008	·008	·009	·015	·018	·018	·022	·027	·030	·033	·040	·039	·045
Dec	·009	·000	·002	·002	·003	·009	·012	·012	·017	·021	·024	·027	·034	·033	·039
2008	Dec	Jan	Feb	Mar	Apr	May	June	July	Aug	Sept	Oct	Nov	Dec	Jan	Feb
Jan	·015	·001	·008	·007	·008	·014	·017	·017	·022	·026	·030	·032	·039	·039	·045
Feb	·007	·000	·000	·000	·000	·007	·009	·009	·014	·018	·022	·025	·031	·031	·037
Mar	·004	·000	·000	·000	·000	·003	·006	·006	·011	·015	·018	·021	·028	·027	·033
Apr	·000	·000	·000	·000	·000	·000	·000	·000	·002	·006	·009	·012	·019	·018	·024
May	·000	·000	·000	·000	·000	·000	·000	·000	·000	·001	·004	·007	·013	·013	·019
June	·000	·000	·000	·000	·000	·000	·000	·000	·000	·000	·000	·000	·006	·005	·011
July	·000	·000	·000	·000	·000	·000	·000	·000	·000	·000	·000	·000	·007	·006	·012
Aug	·000	·000	·000	·000	·000	·000	·000	·000	·000	·000	·000	·000	·004	·003	·009
Sept	·000	·000	·000	·000	·000	·000	·000	·000	·000	·000	·000	·000	·000	·000	·004
Oct	·000	·000	·000	·000	·000	·000	·000	·000	·000	·000	·000	·000	·001	·001	·007
Nov	·000	·000	·000	·000	·000	·000	·000	·000	·000	·000	·000	·003	·009	·009	·015
Dec	·000	·000	·000	·000	·000	·000	·002	·002	·007	·011	·015	·017	·024	·023	·030
2009	Dec	Jan	Feb	Mar	Apr	May	June	July	Aug	Sept	Oct	Nov	Dec	Jan	Feb
Jan	—	·000	·006	·006	·007	·013	·016	·016	·020	·025	·028	·031	·038	·037	·043
Feb	—	—	·000	·000	·000	·007	·009	·009	·014	·018	·022	·025	·031	·031	·037
Mar	—	—	—	·000	·001	·007	·010	·010	·015	·019	·022	·025	·032	·031	·037
Apr	—	—	—	—	·000	·006	·009	·009	·014	·018	·021	·024	·031	·030	·036
May	—	—	—	—	—	·000	.003	.003	.008	.012	.015	.018	.024	.024	.030
June	—	—	—	—	—	—	.000	.000	.005	.009	.012	.015	.022	.021	.027
July	—	—	—	—	—	—	—	.000	.005	.009	.012	.015	.022	.021	.027
Aug	—	—	—	—	—	—	—	—	.000	.004	.007	.010	.017	.016	.022
Sept	—	—	—	—	—	—	—	—	—	.000	.003	.006	.013	.012	.018
Oct	—	—	—	—	—	—	—	—	—	—	—	.003	.009	.009	.015
Nov	—	—	—	—	—	—	—	—	—	—	—	—	.006	.006	.012
Dec	—	—	—	—	—	—	—	—	—	—	—	—	—	—	.006

MONTH OF DISPOSAL

	2007				2008										
2010	Sept	Oct	Nov	Dec	Jan	Feb	Mar	Apr	May	June	July	Aug	Sept	Oct	Nov
Jan	—	—	—	—	—	—	—	—	—	—	—	—	—	—	—
Feb	—	—	—	—	—	—	—	—	—	—	—	—	—	—	—

MONTH OF DISPOSAL

	2008	2009												2010	
2010	Dec	Jan	Feb	Mar	Apr	May	June	July	Aug	Sept	Oct	Nov	Dec	Jan	Feb
Jan	—	·000	·006	·006	·007	·013	·016	·016	·020	·025	·028	·031	·038	·000	·006
Feb	—	—	·000	·000	·000	·007	·009	·009	·014	·018	·022	·025	·031	—	·000

Retail prices index

	Jan	Feb	Mar	Apr	May	Jun
1982	78·73	78·76	79·44	81·04	81·62	81·85
1983	82·61	82·97	83·12	84·28	84·64	84·84
1984	86·84	87·20	87·48	88·64	88·97	89·20
1985	91·20	91·94	92·80	94·78	95·21	95·41
1986	96·25	96·60	96·73	97·67	97·85	97·79
1987	100·00	100·40	100·60	101·80	101·90	101·90
1988	103·30	103·70	104·10	105·80	106·20	106·60
1989	111·00	111·80	112·30	114·30	115·00	115·40
1990	119·50	120·20	121·40	125·10	126·20	126·70
1991	130·20	130·90	131·40	133·10	133·50	134·10
1992	135·60	136·30	136·70	138·80	139·30	139·30
1993	137·90	138·80	139·30	140·60	141·10	141·00
1994	141·30	142·10	142·50	144·20	144·70	144·70
1995	146·00	146·90	147·50	149·00	149·60	149·80
1996	150·20	150·90	151·50	152·60	152·90	153·00
1997	154·40	155·00	155·40	156·30	156·90	157·50
1998	159·50	160·30	160·80	162·60	163·50	163·40
1999	163·40	163·70	164·10	165·20	165·60	165·60
2000	166·60	167·50	168·40	170·10	170·70	171·10
2001	171·10	172·00	172·20	173·10	174·20	174·40
2002	173·30	173·80	174·50	175·70	176·20	176·20
2003	178·40	179·30	179·90	181·20	181·50	181·30
2004	183·10	183·80	184·60	185·70	186·50	186·80
2005	188·90	189·60	190·50	191·60	192·00	192·20
2006	193·40	194·20	195·00	196·50	197·70	198·50
2007	201·60	203·10	204·40	205·40	206·20	207·30
2008	209·80	211·40	212·10	214·00	215·10	216·80
2009	210·10	211·40	211·30	211·50	212·80	213·40
2010	218.00	219.20				

	Jul	Aug	Sept	Oct	Nov	Dec
1982	81·88	81·90	81·85	82·26	82·66	82·51
1983	85·30	85·68	86·06	86·36	86·67	86·89
1984	89·10	89·94	90·11	90·67	90·95	90·87
1985	95·23	95·49	95·44	95·59	95·92	96·05
1986	97·52	97·82	98·30	98·45	99·29	99·62
1987	101·80	102·10	102·40	102·90	103·40	103·30
1988	106·70	107·90	108·40	109·50	110·00	110·30
1989	115·50	115·80	116·60	117·50	118·50	118·80
1990	126·80	128·10	129·30	130·30	130·00	129·90
1991	133·80	134·10	134·60	135·10	135·60	135·70
1992	138·80	138·90	139·40	139·90	139·70	139·20
1993	140·70	141·30	141·90	141·80	141·60	141·90
1994	144·00	144·70	145·00	145·20	145·30	146·00
1995	149·10	149·90	150·60	149·80	149·80	150·70
1996	152·40	153·10	153·80	153·80	153·90	154·40
1997	157·50	158·50	159·30	159·50	159·60	160·00
1998	163·00	163·70	164·40	164·50	164·40	164·40
1999	165·10	165·50	166·20	166·50	166·70	167·30
2000	170·50	170·50	171·70	171·60	172·10	172·20
2001	173·30	174·00	174·60	174·30	173·60	173·40
2002	175·90	176·40	177·60	177·90	178·20	178·50
2003	181·30	181·60	182·50	182·60	182·70	183·50
2004	186·80	187·40	188·10	188·60	189·00	189·90
2005	192·20	192·60	193·10	193·30	193·60	194·10
2006	198·50	199·20	200·10	200·40	201·10	202·70
2007	206·10	207·30	208·00	208·90	209·70	210·90
2008	216·50	217·20	218·40	217·70	216·00	212·90
2009	213·40	214.40	215.30	216.00	216·60	218·00

Corporation tax

Rates

Financial year	***2005***	***2006***	***2007***	***2008***	***2009***	***2010***
Full rate	30%	30%	30%	28%	28%	28%
Starting rate	0%	–	–	–	–	–
first relevant amount[1]	£10,000	–	–	–	–	–
second relevant amount[1]	£50,000	–	–	–	–	–
marginal relief fraction	$^{19}/_{400}$	–	–	–	–	–
effective marginal rate	23.75%	–	–	–	–	–
Small companies' rate[3]	19%	19%	20%	21%	21%	21%
lower relevant amount[1]	£300,000	£300,000	£300,000	£300,000	£300,000	£300,000
upper relevant amount[1]	£1.5m	£1.5m	£1.5m	£1.5m	£1.5m	£1.5m
marginal relief fraction	$^{11}/_{400}$	$^{11}/_{400}$	$^{1}/_{40}$	$^{7}/_{400}$	$^{7}/_{400}$	$^{7}/_{400}$
effective marginal rate	32.75%	32.75%	32.50%	29.75%	29.75%	29.75%
Non-corporate distribution rate[2]	19%	–	–	–	–	–
Tax credit: from 6 April[3]	10%	10%	10%	10%	10%	10%

1 Reduced proportionally for accounting periods of less than 12 months. The limits are divided by the number of associated companies (including the company in question).

2 Applies where the underlying corporation tax rate is lower than 19% (TA 1988 s 13AB, Sch A2).

3 For ring fenced trades, the small companies rate remains at 19% for financial years 2007 to 2010 and the main rate of corporation tax remains at 30% for those years.

Marginal relief. The starting and small companies' rate apply to *basic profits* ('I') where *profits* ('P') do not exceed the first or lower relevant amounts. Where *profits* ('P') exceed those amounts but not the second or upper relevant amounts, corporation tax on *basic profits* ('I') is reduced by (marginal relief upper profit limit – P) × $^{I}/_{P}$ × fraction,

where 'P' is profits as finally computed for corporation tax purposes plus franked investment income, from UK companies excluding such income from UK companies in the same group or consortium of which the recipient is a member.

'I' is profits on which corporation tax is finally borne (income plus chargeable gains).

Reliefs

Corporate Venturing Scheme

(FA 2000 s 63, Schs 15, 16; FA 2001 s 64, Sch 16; FA 2004 s 95, Sch 20; FA 2006 s 91, Sch 14)

In relation to shares issued between 1 April 2000 and 31 March 2010, an investing company can obtain 20% CT relief on amounts subscribed for ordinary shares in small higher-risk unquoted trading companies which are held for at least three years. The investor must not own or be entitled to acquire more than 30% of the ordinary shares in the investee company. At least 20% must be owned by independent individuals. Chargeable gains on share disposals can be deferred by reinvestment in another shareholding. Allowable losses (net of 20% relief) can be set against income if not deducted from chargeable gains.

Research and development

(CTA 2009, ss 1039–1142; FA 2000 ss 68, 69, Schs 19–21; FA 2002 s 53, Sch 12; FA 2003 s 168, Sch 31; FA 2007 s 50)

From 1 August 2008, an 'SME' incurring R&D expenditure of at least £10,000 (£25,000 for accounting periods beginning before 27 September 2003) in a 12-month accounting period can obtain relief for 175% of that expenditure. From 1 April 2008, large companies incurring R&D expenditure of at least £10,000 (£25,000 for accounting periods beginning before 9 April 2003) can obtain relief for 130% of that expenditure. Companies not yet in profit or which have not yet started to trade can claim relief upfront as a cash payment.

An 'SME' is a company with less than 500 employees (250 before 1 August 2008) and either annual turnover of €100m or less (€50m before 1 August 2008; €40m for accounting periods ending before 1 January 2005) or annual balance sheet total of €86m or less (€43m before 1 August 2008; €27m for accounting periods ending before 1 January 2005). From 1 April 2002, large companies incurring R&D expenditure of at least £10,000 (£25,000 for accounting periods beginning before 9 April 2003) can generally deduct 125% of the expenditure for SMEs .

Real Estate Investment Trusts (REITs)

(CTA 2010 ss 518–609; FA 2006 ss 103–145, Schs 16, 17)

From 1 January 2007, qualifying rental income from and gains on disposals of investment properties by UK companies within the REIT scheme will be exempt from corporation tax.

Environmental taxes and other levies

Aggregates levy

(FA 2001 ss 16–49, Schs 4–10; SI 2004/1959)

Levy on commercial exploitation of aggregates including rock, gravel or sand together with any other substance incorporated or naturally occurring with it. Applies to all aggregate (not recycled) extracted in the UK or territorial waters unless exempt. It does not apply to quarried or mined products such as clay, shale, slate, metal and metal ores, gemstones, semi-precious gemstones and industrial minerals. It is charged at 20% of the full rate for aggregate processed in Northern Ireland until 31.3.2021. The full rate will increase to £2.10 with effect from 1 April 2011.

From 1 April 2009 onwards	**£2.00 per tonne**
1 April 2008 to 31 March 2009	£1.95 per tonne
1 April 2002 to 31 March 2008	£1.60 per tonne

Air passenger duty

(FA 1994, s 30)

Any carriage of a passenger which begins on or after 1 November 2009, irrespective of when the ticket was booked or paid for) will be taxed at the new rate of APD applicable to that journey.

Band and distance of capital city of destination country from UK in miles	Reduced rate (lowest class of travel)		Standard rate (all classes other than lowest class)	
	On and after 1.11.09	On and after 1.11.10	On and after 1.11.09	On and after 1.11.10
Band A (0–2,000)	£11	£12	£22	£24
Band B (2,001–4,000)	£45	£60	£90	£120
Band C (4,001–6,000)	£50	£75	£100	£150
Band D (over 6,000)	£55	£85	£110	£170

From 1 February to 31 October 2009	Standard class	Reduced class
Specified European destinations	£20	£10
All other destinations	£80	£40

The following specifies which countries come into which bands.

Band A territories — 0–2.000 miles from London		
Albania	Guernsey	Morocco
Algeria	Hungary	Netherlands
Andorra	Iceland	Norway (including Svalbard)
Austria	Republic of Ireland	Poland
Azores	Isle of Man	Portugal (including Madeira)
Belarus	Italy (including Sicily and Sardinia)	Russian Federation (west of the Urals)
Belgium	Jersey	Romania
Bosnia and Herzegovina	Republic of Kosovo	San Marino
Bulgaria	Latvia	Serbia
Croatia	Libya	Slovak Republic
Cyprus	Liechtenstein	Slovenia
Czech Republic	Lithuania	Spain (including the Balearic Islands and the Canary Islands)
Denmark (including the Faroe Islands)	Luxembourg	Sweden
Estonia	former Yugoslav Republic of Macedonia	Switzerland
Finland	Malta	Tunisia
France (including Corsica)	Moldova	Turkey
Germany	Malta	Ukraine

Gibraltar	Moldova	Western Sahara
Greece	Monaco	
Greenland	Montenegro	

Band B territories — 2,001–4,000 miles from London		
Afghanistan	Gambia	Oman
Armenia	Georgia	Pakistan
Azerbaijan	Ghana	Qatar
Bahrain	Guinea	Russian Federation (east of the Urals)
Benin	Guinea-Bissau	Saint Pierre and Miquelon
Bermuda	Iran	Sao Tome and Principe
Burkina Faso	Iraq	Saudi Arabia
Cameroon	Israel and the Occupied Palestinian Territories	Senegal
Canada	Ivory Coast	Sierra Leone
Cape Verde	Jordan	Sudan
Central African Republic	Kazakhstan	Syria
Chad	Kuwait	Tajikistan
Democratic Republic of Congo	Kyrgyzstan	Togo
Republic of Congo	Lebanon	Turkmenistan
Djibouti	Liberia	Uganda
Egypt	Mali	United Arab Emirates
Equatorial Guinea	Mauritania	United States of America
Ethiopia	Niger	Uzbekistan
Gabon	Nigeria	Yemen

Band C territories — 4,001–6,000 miles from London		
Angola	Grenada	Nepal
Anguilla	Guadelope	Netherlands Antilles
Antigua and Barbuda	Guatemala	Nicaragua
Aruba	Guyana	Panama
Ascension Island	Haiti	Puerto Rico
Bahamas	Honduras	Reunion
Bangladesh	Hong Kong SAR	Rwanda
Barbados	India	Saint Barthelemy
Belize	Jamaica	Saint Christopher and Nevis (St Kitts and Nevis)
Bhutan	Japan	Saint Helena
Botswana	Kenya	Saint Lucia
Brazil	North Korea	Saint Martin
British Indian Ocean Territory	South Korea	Saint Vincent and the Grenadines
British Virgin Islands	Laos	Seychelles
Burma	Lesotho	Somalia
Burundi	Macao SAR	South Africa
Cayman Islands	Madagascar	Sri Lanka
China	Malawi	Suriname
Columbia	Maldives	Swaziland
Comoros	Martinique	Tanzania
Costa Rica	Mauritius	Thailand
Cuba	Mayotte	Trinidad and Tobago
Dominica	Mexico	Turks and Caicos Islands
Dominican Republic	Mongolia	Venezuela
Ecuador	Montserrat	Vietnam
El Salvador	Mozambique	Virgin Islands
French Guiana	Namibia	Zambia

Band D — journey ends in any other place.

Climate change levy

(FA 2000 s 30, Sch 6; FA 2006 ss 171, 172; FA 2007 s 13; FA 2008 s 19)

Levy on supply for industrial or commercial purposes of energy, from 1.4.01, in the form of electricity, gas, petroleum and hydrocarbon gas supplied in a liquid state, coal and lignite, coke and semi-coke of coal or lignite and petroleum coke.

Taxable commodity supplied	*Rate*[1]			
	1.4.01–31.3.07	1.4.07–31.3.08	1.4.08–31.3.09	**From 1.4.09**
Electricity	0.43p per kWh	0.441p per kWh	0.456p per kWh	**0.47p per kWh**
Gas supplied by a gas utility or any gas supplied in a gaseous state that is of a kind supplied by a gas utility	0.15p per kWh	0.154p per kWh	0.159p per kWh	**0.164p per kWh**
Any petroleum gas, or other gaseous hydrocarbon supplied in a liquid state	0.96p per kg	0.985p per kg	1.018p per kg	**1.05p per kg**
Any other taxable commodity	1.17p per kg	1.201p per kg	1.242p per kg	**1.281 per kg**

1 Rate at which payable if supply is neither a half-rate supply nor a reduced-rate supply. The levy is charged at 20% of the full rate for energy-intensive users. It is charged at half the full rate for horticultural producers until 31.3.06. Horticultural businesses which sign climate change agreements can benefit from an 80% reduction in the levy in exchange for meeting specific energy efficiency targets.

Fuel duty

(FA 2009, ss 15, 16)

	Petrol/diesel	Biodiesel or bioethonal	LPG used as road fuel	Natural gas used as road fuel	Red diesel	Fuel oil
from 1 January 2011	58.95p per litre	58.95p per litre	33.04p per kg	26.15p per kg	11.33p per litre	10.88p per litre
from 1 October 2010 to 31 December 2010	58.19p per litre	58.19p per litre	31.95p per kg	25.05p per kg	11.18p per litre	10.74p per litre
from 1 April 2010 to 30 September 2010	57.19p per litre	57.19p per litre	30.53p per kg	23.60p per kg	10.99p per litre	10.55p per litre
from 1 September 2009 to 31 March 2010	56.19p per litre	36.19p per litre	27.67p per kg	22.16p per kg	10.80p per litre	10.37p per litre
from 1 April 2009 to 31 August 2009	54.19p per litre	34.19p per litre	24.82p per kg	19.26p per kg	10.42p per litre	10.00p per litre
from 1 December 2008 to 31 March 2009	52.35p per litre	32.35 per litre	20.77p per kg	16.60p per kg	10.07p per litre	9.66p per litre
from 1 October 2007 to 30 November 2008	50.35 per litre	30.35 per litre	16.49p per kg	13.70p per kg	9.69p per litre	9.29p per litre

Insurance premium tax

(FA 1994 ss 48–74, Schs 6A, 7, 7A)

IPT is a tax on premiums received under insurance contracts other than those which are specifically exempt.

	Standard rate	*Higher rate*[1]
From 1.7.99	**5.0%**	**17.5%**
1.4.97–30.6.99	4.0%	17.5%
1.10.94–31.3.97	2.5%	–

[1] The higher rate applies to sales of motor cars, light vans and motorcycles, electrical or mechanical domestic appliances, and travel insurance.

Landfill tax

(FA 1996 ss 39–71, 197, Sch 5; SI 1996/1527; SI 1996/1528)

Tax on disposal of waste imposed on operators of landfill sites calculated by reference to the weight and type of waste deposited. Exemption applies to mining and quarrying waste, dredging waste, pet cemeteries, waste from reclamation of contaminated land and inert waste used to restore licensed landfill sites. The standard rate will be increased to £56 per tonne after 31.3.11.

Period	*Active waste per tonne*	*Inert waste per tonne*	*Maximum credit*[1]
1.4.10–31.3.11	**£48**	**£2.50**	**5.5%**
1.4.09–31.3.10	£40	£2.50	6%
1.4.08–31.3.09	£32	£2.50	6%
1.4.07–31.3.08	£24	£2	6.6%
1.4.06–31.3.07	£21	£2	6.7%
1.4.05–31.3.06	£18	£2	6.0%
1.4.04–31.3.05	£15	£2	6.8%
1.4.03–31.3.04	£14	£2	6.5%
1.4.02–31.3.03	£13	£2	20.0%
1.4.01–31.3.02	£12	£2	20.0%

[1] Tax credits are available to operators who make donations to environmental trusts of 90% of the donation to the maximum percentage above of the tax payable in a 12-month period.

Vehicle excise duty

(FA 2009, ss 13, 14)

Vehicle tax, or 'road tax' is charged according to CO_2 emissions, as follows:

Band	CO_2(g/km)	2008–09	2009–10	2010–11
A	Up to 100	£0	£0	£0
B	101–110	£35	£35	£20
C	111–120	£35	£35	£30
D	121–130	£120	£120	£90
E	131–140	£120	£120	£110
F	141–150	£120	£125	£125
G	151–165	£145	£150	£155
H	166–175	£170	£175	£180
I	176–185	£170	£175	£200
J	186–200	£210	£215	£235
K	201–225	£210	£215	£245
L	226–255	£400	£405	£425
M	Over 255	£400	£405	£425

There are alternative tables for use when a car is powered by alternative fuel such as electricity or gas. From April 2010, a different rate of tax applies in the year of purchase of a new vehicle. In later years, the standard rate applies. The first-year rates are:

Band	CO_2(g/km)	2010–11 first-year rate
A	Up to 100	£0
B	101–110	£0
C	111–120	£0
D	121–130	£0
E	131–140	£110
F	141–150	£125
G	151–165	£155
H	166–175	£250
I	176–185	£300
J	186–200	£425
K	201–225	£550
L	226–255	£750
M	Over 255	£950

Heavy goods vehicle rates are frozen at the 2008/09 level. Light goods vehicle rates are as follows:

Tax class	2008–09	2009–10	2010–11
Light goods vehicle	£180	£185	£200
Euro 4 & 5 LGV	£120	£125	£125

VED band	2008–09 to 2009–10	2010–11
Up to 150 cc	£15	£15
151–400 cc	£33	£33
401–600 cc	£48	£50
Over 600 cc	£66	£70

Income tax

Starting, basic and higher rates

Band of taxable income £	***Band*** £	***Rate*** %	***Tax*** £	***Cumulative tax*** £
2010–11				
0–37,400	**37,400**	**20**	**7,480**	
37,401–150,000	**112,600**	**40**	**45,040**	**52,520**
Over 150,000	**–**	**50**	**–**	
2009–10				
0–37,400	37,400	20	7,480	7,480
Over 37,400	–	40	–	–
2008–09				
0–34,800	34,800	20	6,960.00	6,960.00
Over £34,800	–	40	–	–
2007–08				
0–2,230	2,230	10	223.00	223.00
2,231–34,600	32,370	22	7,121.40	7,344.40
over 34,600	–	40	–	–
2006–07				
0–2,150	2,150	10	215.00	215.00
2,151–33,300	31,150	22	6,853.00	7,068.00
over 33,300	–	40	–	–
2005–06				
0–2,090	2,090	10	209.00	209.00
2,091–32,400	30,310	22	6,668.20	6,877.20
over 32,400	–	40	–	–

Taxation of savings: For 2007–08 and earlier years, savings income is chargeable at the rates of 10% (if within the starting rate band), 20% and/or 40% (TA 1988 s 1A; FA 2000 s 32). From 2008–09 onwards the starting rate band is abolished. A new starting rate for savings band for individuals is introduced. For 2008–09 the band is £2,320 and for 2009–10 and 2010–11 it is £2,440. Where an individual's non-savings income is less than the starting rate limit for savings, the savings income is taxable at the 10% starting rate for savings up to the limit. Where non-savings income exceeds the limit, the starting rate for savings does not apply. Savings income includes interest from banks and building societies, interest distributions from authorised unit trusts, interest on gilts and other securities including corporate bonds, purchased life annuities and discounts. Where income does not exceed the basic rate limit, there will be no further tax to pay on savings income from which the 20% tax rate has been deducted, and any tax over-deducted is repayable. Higher rate taxpayers are liable to pay tax at 40% on that part of their savings income falling above the higher rate limit. For 2010/11, additional rate taxpayers are liable to pay tax at 50% on that part of their savings income falling above the additional rate limit. Savings income is generally treated as the second top slice of income behind dividends. Non-taxpayers may apply to have interest paid without deduction of tax where their total income is expected to be covered by personal allowances. Taxpayers who are entitled to a refund of tax deducted from interest can claim the refund using form R40. HMRC have a *Taxback* website page to simplify repayments: www.hmrc.gov.uk/taxback.

Taxation of dividends: UK and foreign dividends (except those foreign dividends taxed under the remittance basis) form the top slice of taxable income. Where income does not exceed the basic rate limit the rate is 10% (applied to the dividend grossed-up by a tax credit of ¹/₉) so that the liability is met by the tax credit. Higher rate taxpayers are liable to pay tax at 32.5% on that part of their dividend income falling above the higher rate limit. For 2010/11, additional rate taxpayers are liable to pay tax at 42.5% on that part of their dividend income falling above the additional rate limit. See ITA 2007 s 13. A non-payable tax credit of one-ninth of the dividend was extended to individuals in receipt of dividends from non-UK resident companies where they had a holding of less than 10% and the company is not an offshore fund, by ITTOIA 2005 s 397A on or after 6 April 2008. The tax credit is extended to taxpayers with a holding of 10% or more and to distributions from offshore funds with effect on or after 22 April 2009.

Construction industry sub-contractors rate of deduction at source (from 6 April 2007): (SI 2007 No 46)

Registered sub-contractors	20%	Unregistered sub-contractors	30%

Taxation of trusts

	Rate applicable to trusts	*Dividend trust rate*
From 2010–11 onwards	**50%**	**42.5%**
From 2004–05 to 2009–10	40%	32.5%
1999–2000 to 2003–04	34%	25%

From 2005–06 onwards: The first £1,000 for 2006–07 onwards and £500 for 2005–06 of income arising to a trust chargeable at the rate applicable to trusts or the dividend trust rate is instead chargeable at the basic, savings or dividend rate.
Vulnerable beneficiaries: From 2004–05 onwards, trustees can be taxed (on election) on trust income as if it were income of the vulnerable beneficiary taking into account the beneficiary's personal allowances, starting and basic rate bands (FA 2005 ss 23–45).

Table of income tax reliefs

	2010–11	**2009–10**
	£	**£**
Personal allowance[5](age under 65)	**6,475**	6,475
Age allowance[1]		
Total income limit	**22,900**	22,900
Personal allowance age 65–74	**9,490**	9,490
Not beneficial if individual's		
total income exceeds	**28,930**	28,930
Personal allowance age 75 and over	**9,640**	9,640
Not beneficial if individual's		
total income exceeds	**29,230**	29,230
Married couple's allowance[2,4]		
Elder partner 65 before 6.4.2000		
Basic allowance	**2,670**	2,670
Age allowance[3,4]		
Total income limit	**22,900**	22,900
Neither partner aged 75 or over	**N/A**	N/A
Not beneficial if relevant partner[3]		
under 65 and his total income exceeds	**N/A**	N/A
65–74 and his total income exceeds	**N/A**	N/A
Either partner aged 75 and over	**6,965**	6,965
Not beneficial if relevant partner[3]		
under 65 and his total income exceeds	**31,490**	31,490
65–74 and his total income exceeds	**37,520**	37,520
75 or over and his total income exceeds	**37,820**	37,820
Blind person's allowance[6]	**1,890**	1,890

1 The higher age allowances are available if the claimant's total income does not exceed the statutory income limit.
Where the total income exceeds the statutory limit, the maximum allowance is reduced by one-half of the excess until it is reduced to the ordinary personal allowance.

2 The universal married couple's allowance was withdrawn for 2000–01 onwards but continues to be available to any married couple or, from 2005–06, civil partnership where at least one spouse or partner was born before 6 April 1935.
The relief is given as a reduction in income tax liability restricted to the lower of 10% of the amount of the allowance or the claimant's total income tax liability.

3 The higher age allowances are available if the claimant's total income does not exceed the statutory income limit (subject to relief given as a reduction in tax liability as in note 2 above).
Where the total income exceeds the statutory limit, the maximum allowance is reduced by one-half of the excess (less any reduction made in the personal age allowance as in note 1 above) but it cannot be reduced to less than the basic couple's allowance.

National insurance contributions – self employed

Class 2	Flat rate per week	**£2.40**	£2.40
	Small earnings exception	**5,075**	5,075
Class 4	Band	**5,715–43,875**	5,715–43,875
	Rate	**38,160@ 8%**	38,160@ 8%
	Amount payable to upper limit	**3,052.80**	3,052.80
	Charge on profits above the limit	**1%**	1%

Table of income tax reliefs (cont.)

2008–09	*2007–08*	*2006–07*	*2005–06*	*2004–05*
£	£	£	£	£
6,035	5,225	5,035	4,895	4,745
21,800	20,900	20,100	19,500	18,900
9,030	7,550	7,280	7,090	6,830
27,790	25,550	24,590	23,890	23,070
9,180	7,690	7,420	7,220	6,950
28,090	25,830	24,870	24,150	23,310
2,540	2,440	2,350	2,280	2,210
21,800	20,900	20,100	19,500	18,900
6,535	6,285	6,065	5,905	5,725
29,790	28,590	27,530	26,750	25,930
35,780	33,240	32,020	31,140	30,100
6,625	6,365	6,135	5,975	5,795
29,790	28,750	27,670	26,890	26,070
35,960	33,400	32,160	31,280	30,240
36,260	33,680	32,440	31,540	30,480
1,800	1,730	1,660	1,610	1,560

4 For marriages entered into before 5 December 2005, married couple's allowance is given to the husband (subject to right of transfer to the wife), the amount of the allowance being determined by the level of the husband's income. For marriages and civil partnerships entered into on or after that date, the allowance is given to whichever of the two partners has the higher total income for the tax year in question, the amount of the allowance being determined by the level of that partner's income (subject to the right to transfer half or all of the basic allowance or excess allowances to the partner). Couples married before 5 December 2005 may make a joint election to be brought within the above rules for couples marrying on or after that date. The election must be made before the start of the first tax year for which it is to have effect. It will continue to have effect for all subsequent tax years and is irrevocable.

5 From 2010–11, the basic personal allowance for income tax is gradually reduced to nil for individuals with adjusted net incomes in excess of £100,000. The reduction is £1 for every £2 of income over the limit.

6 The allowance is available for persons who are registered blind but not for persons registered partially-sighted.

National insurance contributions – self employed (cont.)

£2.30	£2.20	£2.10	£2.10	£2.05
4,825	4,635	4,465	4,345	4,215
5,435–40,040	5,225–34,840	5,035–33,540	4,895–32,760	4,745–31,720
34,605@8%	29,615@8%	28,505@8%	27,865@8%	25,975@8%
2,768.40	2,369.20	2,280.40	2,229.20	2,158.00
1%	1%	1%	1%	1%

Cars, vans and related benefits

Cars

From 6 April 2002: The income tax charge is based on a percentage of the car's price graduated according to the level of the car's carbon dioxide measured in grams per kilometre (g/km) and rounded down to the nearest 5g/km. (ITEPA 2003 ss 114–148, 169; FA 2003 s 138).

CO_2 emissions in grams per kilometre					*% of list price*	
2003–04	***2004–05***	***2005–06–2007–08***	***2008–09–2009–10***	***2010–11***	*Petrol*	*Diesel*[1]
N/A	N/A	N/A	120	**120**	10%	13%
155	145	140	135	**130**	15%	18%
160	150	145	140	**135**	16%	19%
165	155	150	145	**140**	17%	20%
170	160	155	150	**145**	18%	21%
175	165	160	155	**150**	19%	22%
180	170	165	160	**155**	20%	23%
185	175	170	165	**160**	21%	24%
190	180	175	170	**165**	22%	25%
195	185	180	175	**170**	23%	26%
200	190	185	180	**175**	24%	27%
205	195	190	185	**180**	25%	28%
210	200	195	190	**185**	26%	29%
215	205	200	195	**190**	27%	30%
220	210	205	200	**195**	28%	31%
225	215	210	205	**200**	29%	32%
230	220	215	210	**205**	30%	33%
235	225	220	215	**210**	31%	34%
240	230	225	220	**215**	32%	35%
245	235	230	225	**220**	33%	35%
250	240	235	230	**225**	34%	35%
255	245	240	235	**230**	35%	35%

For 2008–09 onwards: For cars registered on or after 1.1.08 which are constructed to be capable of being propelled by bioethanol or E85 fuel, the percentage chargeable is reduced by 2%.

For 2010–11 to 2014–15: No benefit applies to cars which are incapable of producing carbon dioxide when driven. A 5% charge applies to cars with a CO_2 figure of 75 g/km or less.

Where a car's CO_2 figure is not a multiple of 5, it is rounded down to the nearest 5. For 2008–09 onwards, however, a car's emissions figure must be exactly 120g/km or less to qualify for the 10%/13% rate.

Cars registered after 28 February 2001

For cars registered on or after 1.3.01, the definitive CO_2 emissions figure is recorded on the vehicle registration document. For cars first registered between 1.1.98 and 28.2.01, the Vehicle Certification Agency supply relevant information on their website at www.vcacarfueldata.org.uk and in their free, twice-yearly edition of the 'New Car Fuel Consumption & Emission Figures' booklet.

Cars registered on or after 1 January 1998 with no CO_2 emission figures

Cylinder capacity of car	*Appropriate percentage*[1]
1,400cc or less	15%
Over 1,400cc up to 2,000cc	25%
Over 2,000cc	35%
Electrically propelled vehicle	15%

1 **Diesel cars:** A 3% supplement applies to diesel cars up to a maximum of 35%. The supplement does not apply to diesel cars meeting the Euro IV emissions standards until 5 April 2006 after which time it will apply to such cars registered on or after 1.1.06.

2 **Discounts:** Special discounts apply to cars, with or without CO_2 emission figures, registered on or after 1.1.98: 6% for electrically propelled vehicles (before 2010/11 only), 3% for hybrid electric vehicles (2% before 2006–07) and 2% for gas or bi-fuel cars with CO_2 emission figures for gas (1% before 2006–07).

Cars registered before 1.1.98 with no CO_2 emission figures: Tax is charged on 15% of the list price for engines to 1,400cc, 22% for engines of 1,401 to 2,000cc and 32% for engines above 2,000cc. Cars without a cylinder capacity are taxed on 32% of the list price (15% for electric cars).

Automatic cars for disabled drivers: CO_2 figure reduced to equivalent for manual car (ITEPA 2003 s 138).

Car unavailable for part of year: Value of the benefit is reduced proportionately (ITEPA 2003 s 143).

National Insurance: Also used to calculate the national insurance contributions payable by employers on the benefit of cars they provide for the private use of their employees, see p 97.

The cash equivalent is reduced proportionately where the car is not available for the whole tax year. The amount (as so reduced) is reduced by any payments made by the employee for private use.

List price of car:

(1) Includes qualifying accessories, excluding accessories provided after car made available if its list price was less than £100. Accessories designed for use only by disabled people also excluded. Where a car is manufactured so as to be capable of running on road fuel gas, its price is proportionately reduced by so much of that price as is reasonably attributable to it being manufactured in that way. Where a new car is converted to run on road fuel gas, the equipment is not regarded as an accessory.

(2) Reduced by capital contributions made by employee up to £5,000.

(3) List price as adjusted capped at £80,000.

(4) Classic cars (aged 15 years or more and with a market value of £15,000 or more at end of tax year): substitute market value at end of tax year if higher than adjusted list price. £80,000 cap and reduction for capital contributions apply.

(5) Mileage figures are reduced proportionately where car is not available for whole year.

(6) For second and subsequent cars there is no reduction if business mileage is under 18,000 miles; **from 1999–2000** reduce basic cash equivalent to 25% if business mileage is 18,000 miles or more.

Vans and fuel for vans

(ITEPA 2003 ss 114–118, 154–166, 168, 169A, 170)

	Van's age at end of tax year	
	Under 4 years	*4 years or more*
2007–08 to 2010–11		
Vehicle weight up to 3,500kg	**£3,000**	**£3,000**
1993–94 to 2006–07		
Vehicle weight up to 3,500kg	£500	£350

From 6 April 2005 no charge applies to employees who have to take their van home and private use is restricted other than for ordinary commuting (insignificant use is disregarded).
From 6 April 2007: an additional fuel charge of £550 (£500 before 2010–11) also applies for unrestricted private use (FA 2004 s 80, Sch 14).
For 2010–11 to 2014–15: No benefit applies to vans which are incapable of producing carbon dioxide when driven.

Related benefits

Parking facilities: No taxable benefit for work place provision of car parking spaces, or parking for bicycles or motorcycles or, from 6 April 2005, vans (ITEPA 2003 s 237).

Cycles and cyclist's safety equipment: No taxable benefit in respect of the provision to employees of bicycles or cycling safety equipment for travel to and from work (ITEPA 2003 s 244) nor, from 6 April 2005, for subsequent transfer to the employee at market value (ITEPA 2003 s 206).

On-call emergency vehicles: From 6 April 2004 onwards no tax or NIC charge where emergency service workers have private use of their emergency vehicle when on call (ITEPA 2003 s 248A).

Bus services: From 6 April 2002 onwards no taxable benefit in respect of the provision of works buses with a seating capacity of nine or more provided to employees (or their children) to travel to and from work (ITEPA 2003 s 242).

Car and motorcycle hire: restricted allowances

(TA 1988 ss 578A, 578B; ITTOIA 2005 ss 48–50)

Before April 2009, if a car with a retail price when new of more than £12,000 is acquired under a rental lease the maximum allowable deduction in computing trading profits is restricted to:

From April 2009, the disallowance is a flat rate of 15%. This applies only to cars with CO_2 emissions exceeding 160g/km.

P = retail price of car when new. R = annual rental.

Capital allowances see p 26.

Car fuel: company cars

(ITEPA 2003 ss 149–153; TA 1988 s 158)

For 2003–04 onwards, the same percentage figures on p 50 used to calculate the car benefit charge for the company car, which are directly linked to the car's CO_2 emissions, are used to calculate the benefit charge for fuel provided for private motoring. The relevant percentage figure is multiplied by £14,400 for 2003–04 to 2007–08, by £16,900 for 2008–09 and 2009–10 and by £18,000 for 2010–11.

CO_2 emissions grams per kilometre	*Petrol*	*Diesel*
2010–11	**£**	**£**
120	1,800	2,340
130	2,700	3,240
135	2,880	3,420
140	3,060	3,600
145	3,240	3,780
150	3,420	3,960
155	3,600	4,140
160	3,780	4,320
165	3,960	4,500
170	4,140	4,680
175	4,320	4,860
180	4,500	5,040
185	4,680	5,220
190	4,860	5,400
195	5,040	5,580
200	5,220	5,760
205	5,400	5,940
210	5,580	6,120
215	5,760	6,300
220	5,940	6,300
225	6,120	6,300
230	6,300	6,300

CO_2 emissions grams per kilometre	Petrol	Diesel
2008–09–2009–2010	**£**	**£**
120	1,690	2,197
135	2,535	3,042
140	2,704	3,211
145	2,873	3,380
150	3,042	3,549
155	3,211	3,718
160	3,380	3,887
165	3,549	4,056
170	3,718	4,225
175	3,887	4,394
180	4,056	4,563
185	4,225	4,732
190	4,394	4,901
195	4,563	5,070
200	4,732	5,239
205	4,901	5,408
210	5,070	5,577
215	5,239	5,746
220	5,408	5,915
225	5,577	5,915
230	5,746	5,915
235	5,915	5,915

CO_2 emissions grams per kilometre			Petrol	Diesel
2003–04	***2004–05***	***2005–06–2007–08***	**£**	**£**
155	145	**140**	2,160	2,592
160	150	**145**	2,304	2,736
165	155	**150**	2,448	2,880
170	160	**155**	2,592	3,024
175	165	**160**	2,736	3,168
180	170	**165**	2,880	3,312
185	175	**170**	3,024	3,456
190	180	**175**	3,168	3,600
195	185	**180**	3,312	3,744
200	190	**185**	3,456	3,888
205	195	**190**	3,600	4,032
210	200	**195**	3,744	4,176
215	205	**200**	3,888	4,320
220	210	**205**	4,032	4,464
225	215	**210**	4,176	4,608
230	220	**215**	4,320	4,752
235	225	**220**	4,464	4,896
240	230	**225**	4,608	5,040
245	235	**230**	4,752	5,040
250	240	**235**	4,896	5,040
255	245	**240**	5,040	5,040

The benefit is reduced to nil if the employee is required to, and does, make good all fuel provided for private use. There is no taxable benefit where the employer only provides fuel for business travel. The charge is proportionately reduced where the employee stops receiving free fuel part way through the tax year, but where free fuel is subsequently provided in the same tax year, the full year's charge is payable. The benefit is proportionately reduced where a car is not available or is incapable of being used for part of a year (being at least 30 days).

Mileage allowances

Advisory fuel rates for company cars

Engine size	*Cost per mile*		
	Petrol	*Diesel*	*LPG*
from 1 December 2009			
1,400cc or less	**11p**	**11p**	**7p**
1,401–2,000cc	**14p**	**11p**	**8p**
Over 2,000cc	**20p**	**14p**	**12p**
from 1 July 2009			
1,400cc or less	10p	10p	7p
1,401–2,000cc	12p	10p	8p
Over 2,000cc	18p	13p	12p
from 1 January 2009			
1,400cc or less	10p	11p	7p
1,401–2,000cc	12p	11p	9p
Over 2,000cc	17p	14p	12p
from 1 July 2008			
1,400cc or less	12p	13p	7p
1,401–2,000cc	15p	13p	9p
Over 2,000cc	21p	17p	13p
from 1 January 2008			
1,400cc or less	11p	11p	7p
1,401–2,000cc	13p	11p	8p
Over 2,000cc	19p	14p	11p
1 August 2007–31 December 2007			
1,400cc or less	10p	10p	6p
1,401–2,000cc	13p	10p	8p
Over 2,000cc	18p	13p	10p
1 February 2007–31 July 2007			
1,400cc or less	9p	9p	6p
1,401–2,000cc	11p	9p	7p
Over 2,000cc	16p	12p	10p
1 July 2006–31 January 2007			
1,400cc or less	11p	10p	7p
1,401–2,000cc	13p	10p	8p
Over 2,000cc	18p	14p	11p
1 July 2005–30 June 2006			
1,400cc or less	10p	9p	7p
1,401–2,000cc	12p	9p	8p
Over 2,000cc	16p	13p	10p
6 April 2004 — 30 June 2005			
1,400cc or less	10p	9p	7p
1,401–2,000cc	12p	9p	8p
Over 2,000cc	14p	12p	10p

1 Advisory fuel rates can be used to negotiate dispensations for mileage payments from 28 January 2002 where:
(a) employers reimburse employees for business travel in their company cars; or
(b) employers require employees to repay the cost of fuel used for private travel.
(In the case of (b) the figures may be used for reimbursements of private travel from 6 April 2001.)

2 Payments at or below these rates are tax and NIC free. The table figures will be accepted for VAT purposes.

3 Other rates may be used if the employer can demonstrate that they are justified.

4 Rates are reviewed by HMRC every six months.

5 The 1 July 2008 rates can be used from 1 June 2008 if the employer wishes.

Authorised mileage rates

	Rate per business mile	
Cars	*First 10,000 miles*	*Over 10,000 miles*
2002–03 onwards[1]	**40p**	**25p**
Car passengers Allowance for each fellow passenger carried **2002–03 onwards**[1]		**5p**
Cycles and motorcycles **2002–03 onwards**[1]	Cycles **20p**	Motorcycles **24p**

1 Where the employer pays less than the authorised rate the employee can claim tax relief for the difference (ITEPA ss 229–232, 235, 236).

2 Up to 2001–02, simplified arrangements could be operated known as the Fixed Profit Car Scheme (FPCS) or the Car Allowances Enhanced Reporting Scheme (CAERS), under which an employee's taxable business mileage profit was determined by reference to the engine size and the excess of the mileage allowance paid over the authorised rates.

Charities

Gift Aid scheme

Under the Gift Aid scheme an individual donor can claim higher rate relief on the grossed up amount of a monetary donation against income tax and capital gains tax. The charity claims basic rate relief on the grossed up amount of the donation. Donors must make a declaration that they are UK taxpayers to allow the charity to reclaim the repayment. One declaration can cover a series of donations to the same charity and the declaration can be made by writing, by electronic means or orally. A declaration can be backdated for up to six years prior to the declaration for donations made after 5 April 2000. The basic rate tax deemed to have been deducted by the donor at source is clawed back if the donor's tax liability is insufficient to match it. Following the reduction of the basic rate to 20% for 2008–09 onwards, a transitional relief supplement of 2% of grossed up qualifying donations is payable to charities for 2008–09 to 2010–11.

Donors may elect in their self-assessment tax returns for donations made after 5 April 2003 to be treated as made in the preceding tax year for higher rate relief purposes. From April 2004, taxpayers can nominate a charity to receive all or part of any tax repayment due to them. The nomination is made on the taxpayer's self-assessment tax return for 2003–04 and later years, with an indication of whether Gift Aid should apply to the donation.

From 6 April 2002, the scheme is extended to gifts to Community Amateur Sports Clubs.

Relief for payments falling due after 5 April 2000 under charitable covenants is given under the Gift Aid scheme. (ITA 2007 ss 413–430)

Gifts in kind

Relief is available for gifts by companies to charities, community amateur sports clubs or educational establishments of goods produced or sold or of plant or machinery used for the purposes of the trade (TA 1988 ss 83A, 84; CAA 2001 s 63(2)–(4); ITTOIA 2005 ss 107–109; CTA 2009 ss 105–107; FA 2002 Sch 18 para 9(3)).

Gifts of land, shares and securities etc

Relief is available where a person disposes of listed shares and securities, unit trust units, AIM shares, etc or of freehold or leasehold interests in land to a charity by way of a gift or sale at an undervalue. The amount deductible from total income is the market value of the shares etc on the date of disposal plus incidental disposal costs less any consideration or value of benefits received by the donor or a connected person. This is in addition to any capital gains tax relief (ITA 2007, ss 431–446).

Payroll giving

Under the payroll giving scheme, employees authorise their employer to deduct charitable donations from their pay and receive tax relief on their donation at their top rate of tax. The government added a supplement to donations from 6 April 2000 to 5 April 2004. From 6 April 2004 to 31 December 2006, the first £10 donated by each employee every month will be matched for a period of six months. (FA 2000 s 38; FA 2003 s 148; ITEPA 2003 ss 713–715; SI 1986 No 2211.)

Inheritance tax relief see p 94. **Capital gains tax** see p 35.

Employment benefits

The following benefits on pp 74 to 77 cover some common benefits not detailed separately elsewhere. References to 'lower-paid' employees are to those whose annual remuneration plus benefits is less than £8,500.

Accommodation, supplies, etc used in employment duties

(ITEPA 2003 s 316)

The provision of accommodation, supplies or services used by employees in performance of employment duties is not taxable provided:

- (a) if the benefit is provided on premises occupied by the employer, any private use by the employee (or the employee's family or household) is not significant; or
- (b) in any other case, the sole purpose of providing the benefit is to enable the employee to perform those duties, any private use is not significant and the benefit is not an excluded benefit (eg the provision of a motor vehicle, boat or aircraft).

For leases of ten years or less entered into on or after 22 April 2009, a lease premium paid is to be treated as if it were rent and spread over the period of the lease accordingly. (FA 2009, s 71)

Assets given to employees

(ITEPA 2003 ss 203, 204)

If new, tax is chargeable on the cost to the employer (market value in the case of a 'lower-paid' employee). If used, tax is chargeable on the greater of:

- (a) market value at the time of transfer; and
- (b) where the asset is first applied for the provision of a benefit after 5.4.80 and a person has been chargeable to tax on its use, market value when first so applied less amounts charged to tax for use up to and including the year of transfer.

Buses to shops

(SI 2002/205)

The provision of buses for journeys of ten miles or less from the workplace to shops etc on a working day is not taxable.

Cheap loans

(ITEPA 2003 ss 174–190)

A taxable benefit arises on employer-related loans to directors or employees earning £8,500 or more a year, on the difference between the interest paid and interest payable at the 'official rate' below. There is no tax charge where:

- (a) all the employer-related loans (or all loans not qualifying for tax relief) do not exceed £5,000;
- (b) all the interest payable is or would be eligible for tax relief; and
- (c) the loans are ordinary commercial loans.

The 'official rate' is:

From 6 April 2010	*4.00%*
From 1 March 2009 to 5 April 2010	4.75%
From 6 April 2007 to 28 February 2009	6.25%
From 6 January 2002 to 5 April 2007	5.00%
From 6 March 1999 to 5 January 2002	6.25%

The average rate for the tax year is:

2009–10	*4.75%*
2008–09	6.10%
2007/08	6.25%
2002–2003 to 2006–07	5.00%
2001–2002	5.94%
1999–2000 to 2000–01	6.25%

From 2000–01 the official rate is set in advance for the whole of the following tax year, subject to review if the typical mortgage rates were to fall sharply during a tax year.

Christmas parties and annual functions

(ITEPA 2003 s 264; SI 2003/1361)

Not taxable if cost does not exceed £150 per head per tax year (£75 for 2002–03) and open to staff generally. Otherwise, fully taxable. Expenditure may be split between more than one function. (Not taxable on 'lower-paid' employees.)

Childcare provision

(ITEPA 2003 ss 318–318D; SI 2006/882)

From 2005–06, no liability arises:

(a) where the premises (which are not wholly or mainly used as a private dwelling) are made available by the employer or, where the scheme is provided under arrangements with other persons, by one or more of those persons; or

(b) where (a) does not apply, to the first £55 per week from 2006–07 or the first £50 per week for 2005–06 of registered or approved childcare.

Before 2005–06, broadly similar provisions to (*a*) applied.

Credit tokens

Where money goods or services are provided to employees through credit tokens, the cost to the employer, less any employee contribution, is taxable on the employee, except if they were used to buy certain non-taxable benefits.

Cyclists' breakfasts

Breakfast provided for employees arriving at the workplace by bicycle in recognition of having cycled to work is not taxable. No limit on number of such breakfasts per year.

Disabled employees

(ITEPA 2003 ss 246, 247; SI 2002/1596)

The provision of or payment for transport for disabled employees for ordinary commuting is tax free. From 9 July 2002, this also applies to the provision of equipment, services or facilities to disabled employees to help them carry out their duties of employment.

Emergency service vehicles

From 2004/05, there is no tax charge on any benefit arising from use of an emergency vehicle by an employee of an emergency service where private use is prohibited.

Employees' liability insurance

This is non-taxable.

Eye tests and corrective appliances

(ITEPA 2003 s 320A; FA 2006 s 62)

From 2006–07, no liability arises where the provision of tests or special corrective appliances are required under health and safety legislation and are available as required to employees generally.

Homeworkers

(ITEPA 2003 s 316A)

From 2003–04, employer contributions to additional household costs not taxable where employee works at home. Supporting evidence required if contributions exceed £3 per week (£156 per year). Before 6 April 2008 the limit was £2 per week (£104 per year).

Incidental overnight expenses

(ITEPA 2003 ss 99–108)

Not taxable where employee stays away from home on business and payment from employer does not exceed:

(a) £5 per night in the UK; or

(b) £10 per night overseas.

Living accommodation

A taxable benefit (the '*basic charge*') arises on the annual rental value (or actual rent if greater) less any sums made good by the employee. There is an *additional charge* (if the basic charge is not calculated on the full open market rental value) where the cost of accommodation (including costs of any capital improvements less amounts made good by the employee) exceeds £75,000. The additional charge is the excess cost over £75,000 multiplied by the official rate for cheap loans (see above) in force at the start of the tax year less any rent paid by the employee in excess of the basic charge.

The charges are apportioned in the case of multiple occupation or if the property is provided for only part of the year or part is used exclusively for business purposes.

Exemption: No taxable benefit arises where living accommodation is provided:

(a) for the proper performance of duties;

(b) by reason that it is customary to do so; or

(c) by reason of special threat to the employee's security.

The above exemptions apply to a full-time working director whose interest in the company does not exceed 5%, otherwise only exemption (c) applies to directors.

Living expenses

(ITEPA 2003 ss 313–315)

A taxable charge arises on the cost to the employer of the employee's living expenses. For the provision of assets such as furniture, see 'Use of employer's assets' on p 72.

Where the exemption for living accommodation above applies, the tax charge relating to living expenses (including the provision of furniture and items normal for domestic occupation) is restricted to 10% of the employee's net earnings from the related employment less any sums made good by the employee.

Expenditure on alteration and structural repairs which are normally the landlord's responsibility do not give rise to a taxable benefit.

Long service awards

(ITEPA 2003 s 323; SI 2003/1361)

Not taxable provided the employee has at least 20 years' service and cost to the employer does not exceed £50 (£20 where made before 13.6.03) for each year of service. No similar award may be made within ten years of such an award.

Meals

(ITEPA 2003 s 317)

Subsidised or free meals provided for staff generally at the workplace are not taxable.

Medical check-ups and insurance

(ITEPA 2003 s 325; HMRC Employment Income Manual EIM 21765)

2009–10 onwards: One screening and one check-up each year not taxable.

2007–08 and 2008–09: By concession, HMRC continued the previous concessionary practice not to collect tax and NICs which might arise from the previous regulations.

2006–07 and earlier years: Routine health checks and medical screenings for employee (or members of the family or household) are not taxable. Insurance premiums paid on behalf of employees (other than 'lower-paid' employees) are taxable unless for treatment outside the UK whilst the employee is performing duties abroad.

Personal expenses

(ITEPA 2003 ss 70–72, 336–340)

Unless covered by specific exemptions, payments to an employee by reason of his employment in respect of expenses or allowances are taxable. Deduction is allowed for expenses the employee is obliged to incur which are:

(a) qualifying travelling expenses (broadly those necessarily incurred other than for ordinary commuting or private travel); or

(b) other amounts incurred wholly, exclusively and necessarily in the performance of employment duties.

Relocation expenses

(ITEPA 2003 ss 271–289)

Qualifying removal expenses and benefits up to £8,000 per move in connection with job-related residential moves are not taxable. Included are expenses of disposal, acquisition, abortive acquisition, transport of belongings, travelling and subsistence, bridging loans and duplicate expenses (replacement domestic items).

Scholarships

An employee is taxable on the cost of any scholarship from a trust fund which does not satisfy a 25% distribution test or which is paid because of the employee's employment.

Third party gifts

(ITEPA 2003 ss 270, 324; SI 2003/1361)

Gifts during the tax year of goods and non-cash vouchers up to £250 (£150 for 2002–03) not taxable where provided by a party unconnected with the employer and not for services provided in connection with employment.

Use of employer's assets

(ITEPA 2003 ss 203–206, 242, 244, 320; FA 2005 s 17; FA 2006 ss 60, 61)

Tax is chargeable on the annual rental value of land and, for other assets, at 20% of the market value when they are first lent or the rental charge to the employer if higher. No taxable benefit arises on:

(a) the loan of a mobile phone for private use (from 6 April 2006 this is restricted to one mobile phone per employee and no longer extends to the employee's family or household but phones first loaned before 6 April 2006 are not affected by the change);

(b) the use of works buses (see p 69);

(c) bicycles and cycle safety equipment (see p 69);

(d) to 5 April 2006, the loan of computer equipment for private use, provided use is not restricted to directors or senior staff and value of benefit does not exceed £2,500 (computers made available for private use before 6 April 2006 are not affected by the change).

From 6 April 2005, no benefit arises on the subsequent purchase by an employee at market value of computer or cycling equipment previously on loan.

Vouchers

(ITEPA 2003 ss 73–89, 95, 96, 268–270, 362)

Vouchers are taxable as follows.

(a)	Cash vouchers	On amount for which voucher can be exchanged
(b)	Non-cash vouchers	On cost to employer less any contribution from employee (except where used to obtain certain non-taxable benefits)
(c)	Luncheon vouchers	On excess over 15p per working day
(d)	Transport vouchers	On cost to employer less any contribution from employee

Employment income

PAYE and national insurance thresholds

	2005–06	*2006–07*	*2007–08*	*2008–09*	*2009–10*	*2010–11*
	£	£	£	**£**	**£**	**£**
Weekly (NI only for 2009/10)	94	97	100	105	110	**110**
Weekly PAYE				116	125	**125**
Monthly (NI only for 2009/10)	408	420	435	453	476	**476**
Monthly PAYE				503	540	**540**

The 2008/09 PAYE figures apply from 7 September 2008.

PAYE settlement agreements

(ITEPA 2003, ss 61A-61J; FA 2007, s 25, Sch 3)

These are voluntary agreements between the employer and HMRC under which the employer agrees to meet the tax payable on certain expenses and benefits in kind that are given to his employees. Once an agreement has been signed for a tax year, there is no need to:

- enter the items covered on form P9D or P11D;
- operate PAYE on them, or
- calculate a liability for included items which are liable for Class 1 or Class1A NICs.

The employer pays Class 1B NICs on the items included in PAYE settlement agreements and on the total amount of tax payable. To be effective for a tax year, an agreement must be signed 6 July during the year and tax must be paid by 19 October following the end of the year. They are most suited for payments and benefits provided on an irregular basis, or where benefits are for a group of employees and apportionment is difficult.

Personal service companies

(ITEPA 2003, ss 48–61)

These provisions affect 2000/01 and subsequent years. They are commonly known under the name 'IR35' and apply where personal services are provided to a client through an intermediary – normally the worker's personal service company. The effect of the legislation is to treat the worker as an employee of the client for working out the 'deemed employment payment'. The computation involves taking into account all payments and benefits, including those paid direct to the worker for a tax year paid other than by the intermediary for his services. Certain, restricted, allowable expenses, are deducted from 'earnings'. Finally, any payments or benefits received by the worker from the intermediary are deducted. Tax (under PAYE) and NIC is calculated and the amounts due are payable by the worker and his company.

Managed service companies

(ITEPA 2003, ss 61A-61J; FA 2007, s 25, Sch 3)

Where an individual provides his services through a managed service company (as defined) all payments made to him by the company on or after 6 April 2007 are deemed to be employment income and PAYE and NIC have to be applied.

National minimum wage

(Hourly rate)

Age of worker	*Under 18**	*18–21***	*22 or more*
1.10.09–30.9.10	**£3.57**	**£4.83**	**£5.80**
1.10.08–30.9.09	£3.53	£4.77	£5.73
1.10.07–30.9.08	£3.40	£4.60	£5.52

Age of worker	Under 18*	18–21**	22 or more
1.10.06–30.9.07	£3.30	£4.45	£5.35
1.10.05–30.9.06	£3.00	£4.25	£5.05
1.10.04–30.9.05	£3.00	£4.10	£4.85

* Applies to all workers under 18 who are no longer of compulsory school age.
** Also applies to workers aged 22 or more, starting a new job with a new employer, doing accredited training.

Basis of assessment

(ITEPA 2003 ss 14–43)

	Services performed			
Persons domiciled in UK	*Wholly in UK*	*Partly in UK*	*Partly abroad*	*Wholly abroad*
Non-resident	All	That part	None	None
Resident but not ordinarily resident	All	That part	Remittances	Remittances
Resident and ordinarily resident	All	All*	All*	All*
Persons domiciled outside the UK				
UK employer	As for person domiciled in the UK			
Foreign employer				
Non-resident	All UK earnings			
Resident but not ordinarily resident	All UK earnings and remittances for duties performed outside UK			
Resident and ordinarily resident	Remittances for duties performed outside UK			

* Exemption for seafarers if at least half of qualifying period of over 364 days worked abroad (including 183 consecutive days) (FA 1998 s 63; ITEPA 2003 ss 378–385).

Termination payments

The following lump sum payments are exempt from tax:

(a) Payments in connection with the cessation of employment on the death, injury or disability of the employee.
(b) Payments under unapproved retirement benefits schemes where the employee has been taxed on the actual or notional contributions to provide the benefit.
(c) Payments under approved retirement benefits schemes which can properly be regarded as a benefit earned by past service.
(d) Certain payments of terminal grants to members of the armed forces.
(e) Certain benefits under superannuation schemes for civil servants in Commonwealth overseas territories.
(f) Payments in respect of foreign service where the period of foreign service comprises:
  (i) 75% of the whole period of service; or
  (ii) the whole of the last 10 years of service; or
  (iii) where the period of service exceeded 20 years, one-half of that period, including any 10 of the last 20 years.

  Otherwise, a proportion of the payment is exempt, as follows:

(g) The first £30,000 of genuine ex gratia payments (where there is no 'arrangement' by the employer to make the payment): (ITEPA 2003 ss 401–413).
(h) Statutory redundancy payments (included in computing £30,000 limit in (*g*) above).

Fixed rate expenses

For most classes of industry fixed rate allowances for the upkeep of tools and special clothing have been agreed between HMRC and the trade unions concerned. Alternatively, the individual employee may claim as a deduction his or her actual expenses (ITEPA 2003 s 367). (HMRC Employment Income Manual, EIM 32712.)

Industry	*Occupation*		*Deduction from 2004–05 to 2007–08*	*Deduction from 2008–09*
Agriculture	All workers[1]		70	100
Aluminium	(*a*)	Continual casting operators, process operators, de-dimplers, driers, drill punchers, dross unloaders, firemen[2], furnace operators and their helpers, leaders, mouldmen, pourers, remelt department labourers, roll flatteners	130	140
	(*b*)	Cable hands, case makers, labourers, mates, truck drivers and measurers, storekeepers	60	80
	(*c*)	Apprentices	45	60
	(*d*)	All other workers[1]	100	120
Banks and building societies	Uniformed doormen and messengers (£40 before 2004/05)		45	60
Brass and copper	Braziers, coppersmiths, finishers, fitters, moulders, turners and all other workers		100	120
Building	(*a*)	Joiners and carpenters	105	140
	(*b*)	Cement works, roofing felt and asphalt labourers	55	80
	(*c*)	Labourers and navvies (£40 before 2004/05)	45	60
	(*d*)	All other workers	85	120
Building materials	(*a*)	Stone masons	85	120
	(*b*)	Tilemakers and labourers (£40 before 2004/05)	45	60
	(*c*)	All other workers	55	80
Clothing	(*a*)	Lacemakers, hosiery bleachers, dyers, scourers and knitters, knitwear bleachers and dyers	45	60
	(*b*)	All other workers	45	60
Constructional engineering[3]	(*a*)	Blacksmiths and their strikers, burners, caulkers, chippers, drillers, erectors, fitters, holders up, markers off, platers, riggers, riveters, rivet heaters, scaffolders, sheeters, template workers, turners, welders	115	140
	(*b*)	Banksmen, labourers, shop-helpers, slewers, straighteners	60	80
	(*c*)	Apprentices and storekeepers	45	60
	(*d*)	All other workers	75	100
Electrical and electricity supply	(*a*)	Those workers incurring laundry costs only	45	60
	(*b*)	All other workers	90	120
Engineering (trades ancillary to)	(*a*)	Pattern makers	120	140
	(*b*)	Labourers, supervisory and unskilled workers	60	80
	(*c*)	Apprentices and storekeepers	45	60
	(*d*)	Motor mechanics in garage repair shops	100	120
	(*e*)	All other workers	100	120
Fire service	Uniformed firefighters and fire officers		60	80
Food	All workers		45	60
Forestry	All workers		70	100
Glass	All workers		60	80
Healthcare staff in the NHS, private hospitals and nursing homes	(*a*)	Ambulance staff on active service	110	140
	(*b*)	Nurses and midwives, chiropodists, dental nurses, occupational, speech and other therapists, phlebotomists and radiographers	70	100
	(*c*)	Plaster room orderlies, hospital porters, ward clerks, sterile supply workers, hospital domestics, hospital catering staff	60	100
	(*d*)	Laboratory staff, pharmacists, pharmacy assistants	45	60
	(*e*)	Uniformed ancillary staff: maintenance workers, grounds staff, drivers, parking attendants and security guards, receptionists and other uniformed staff	45	60
Heating	(*a*)	Pipe fitters and plumbers	100	120
	(*b*)	Coverers, laggers, domestic glaziers, heating engineers and their mates	90	120
	(*c*)	All gas workers, all other workers	70	100
Iron mining	(*a*)	Fillers, miners and underground workers	100	120
	(*b*)	All other workers	75	100

Industry	*Occupation*	*Deduction from 2004–05 to 2007–08*	*Deduction from 2008–09*
Iron and steel	(*a*) Day labourers, general labourers, stockmen, time keepers, warehouse staff and weighmen	60	80
	(*b*) Apprentices	45	60
	(*c*) All other workers	120	140
Leather	(*a*) Curriers (wet workers), fellmongering workers, tanning operatives (wet)	55	80
	(*b*) All other workers (£40 before 2004/05)	45	60
Particular engineering[4]	(*a*) Pattern makers	120	140
	(*b*) Chainmakers, cleaners, galvanisers, tinners and wire drawers in the wire drawing industry, tool-makers in the lock making industry	100	120
	(*c*) Apprentices and storekeepers	45	60
	(*d*) All other workers	60	80
Police force	Uniformed police officers (ranks up to and including Chief Inspector) (£110 for 2007–08 only)	55	140
Precious metals	All workers	70	100
Printing	(*a*) Letterpress section — electrical engineers (rotary presses), electrotypers, ink and roller makers, machine minders (rotary), maintenance engineers (rotary presses) and stereotypers	105	140
	(*b*) Bench hands (periodical and bookbinding section), compositors (letterpress section), readers (letterpress section), telecommunications and electronic section wire room operators, warehousemen (paper box making section)	45	60
	(*c*) All other workers	70	100
Prisons	Uniformed prison officers	55	80
Public service	(i) Dock and inland waterways		
	(*a*) Dockers, dredger drivers, hopper steerers	55	80
	(*b*) All other workers (£40 before 2004/05)	45	60
	(ii) Public transport		
	(*a*) Garage hands (including cleaners)	55	80
	(*b*) Conductors and drivers (£40 before 2004/05)	45	60
Quarrying	All workers	70	100
Railways	(See the appropriate category for craftsmen, eg engineers, vehicles etc.) All other workers	70	100
Seamen	Carpenters		
	(*a*) Passenger liners	165	165
	(*b*) Cargo vessels, tankers, coasters and ferries	130	140
Shipyards	(*a*) Blacksmiths and their strikers, boilermakers, burners, carpenters, caulkers, drillers, furnacemen (platers), holders up, fitters, platers, plumbers, riveters, sheet iron workers, shipwrights, tubers, welders	115	140
	(*b*) Labourers	60	80
	(*c*) Apprentices and storekeepers	45	60
	(*d*) All other workers	75	100
Textiles and textile printing	(*a*) Carders, carding engineers, overlookers and technicians in spinning mills	85	120
	(*b*) All other workers	60	80
Vehicles	(*a*) Builders, railway vehicle repairers, and railway wagon lifters	105	140
	(*b*) Railway vehicle painters and letterers, builders' and repairers' assistants	60	80
	(*c*) All other workers	45	60
Wood & furniture	(*a*) Carpenters, cabinet makers, joiners, wood carvers and woodcutting machinists	115	140
	(*b*) Artificial limb makers (other than in wood), organ builders and packing case makers	90	120
	(*c*) Coopers not providing own tools, labourers, polishers and upholsterers	45	60
	(*d*) All other workers	75	100

1 'All workers' and 'all other workers' refer only to manual workers who have to bear the cost of upkeep of tools and special clothing. They do not extend to other employees such as office staff.

2 'Firemen' means persons engaged to light and maintain furnaces.

3 'Constructional engineering' means engineering undertaken on a construction site, including buildings, shipyards, bridges, roads and other similar operations.

4 'Particular engineering' means engineering undertaken on a commercial basis in a factory or workshop for the purposes of producing components such as wire, springs, nails and locks.

Investment reliefs

Community investment tax credit

(ITA 2007 ss 333–382)

Investments made after 16 April 2002 by an individual or company in an accredited community development finance institution (CDFI) are eligible for tax relief up to 25%. The investment may be a loan or a subscription for shares or securities. Tax relief may be claimed for the tax year in which the investment is made and each of the four subsequent years. Relief for each year is the smaller of 5% of the invested amount, or the amount which reduces the investor's income tax liability for the year to nil.

Enterprise investment scheme

(ITA 2007 ss 156–257)

The EIS applies to investments in qualifying unquoted companies trading in the UK. Eligible shares must be held for at least three years from the issue date or commencement of trade if later (five years from the issue date for shares issued before 6 April 2000). The following reliefs apply subject to this and other conditions.

Relief on investment

Maximum investment:	From 2008–09	£500,000
	2006–07 to 2007–08	£400,000
	2004–05 to 2005–06	£200,000
	1998–99 to 2003–04	£150,000
Minimum investment:	From 1993–94	£500
Maximum carry-back to preceding year (up to 1/2 amount invested between 6 April and 5 October)	From 2006–07	£50,000
	1998–99 to 2005–06	£25,000
Rate of relief	From 1993–94	20%*

* Given as a deduction against income tax liability.

Other reliefs (TCGA 1992 ss 150A–150D, Schs 5B, 5BA)

(a) A gain on a disposal of shares on which EIS relief has been given and not withdrawn is exempt from capital gains tax.

(b) Deferral relief is available for gains on assets where the disposal proceeds are reinvested in eligible shares in a qualifying company one year before or three years after the disposal.

(c) A loss on a disposal of shares on which EIS relief has been given may be relieved against income tax or capital gains tax.

Venture capital trusts

(ITA 2007 ss 258–332)

An individual who subscribes for ordinary shares in a VCT obtains income tax reliefs at the rates in the table below subject to conditions. The shares must be held for at least five years (three years for shares issued before 6 April 2006 and five years for shares issued before 6 April 2000).

Relief on investment

Maximum annual investment:	From 2004–05	£200,000
	1995–96 to 2003–04	£100,000
Rate of relief:	From 2006–07	30%
	2004–05 to 2005–06	40%
	1995–96 to 2003–04	20%

Other reliefs

(a) Dividends on shares within investment limit exempt from income tax (unless the investor's main purpose is tax avoidance – from 9 March 1999).

(b) Capital gains reliefs (see p 35).

Urban Regeneration Companies

Relief is available from 1 April 2003 for expenditure incurred by businesses in making contributions to designated Urban Regeneration Companies (TA 1988 s 79B; FA 2003 s 180; ITTOIA 2005 ss 82, 86).

Individual savings accounts ('ISAs')

(TA 1988 s 333; ITTOIA 2005 ss 694–701; SI 1998/1870; SI 2001/908)

Savers can subscribe to an ISA up to the following limits per tax year.

Overall annual subscription limit	1999–2000 to 2007–08	£7,000	2008–09 to 2009–10*	£7,200	**2010–11**	**£10,200**
Cash limit	1999–2000 to 2007–08	£3,000	2008–09 to 2009–10*	£3,600	**2010–11**	**£5,100**
Life insurance limit	1999–2000 to 2004–05	£1,000	2008–09 to 2009–10*	N/A	**2010–11**	**N/A**

Before 2008–09 a limit of £4,000 (£3,000 before 2005–06) also applied to stocks and shares held in a mini-ISA. The subscription limit applies to each spouse or civil partner. Shares acquired under an approved share incentive plan, profit sharing scheme or SAYE option scheme may be transferred to a stocks and shares component of an ISA within 90 days without tax consequences. From 2008-09 PEPs are transferred into ISA accounts.

*For taxpayers aged 50 or over in 2009–10 the limits for 2010–11 apply for 2009–10 also, with effect from 6 October 2009.

Reliefs

(a) Investments under the scheme are free from income tax and capital gains tax.
(b) 10% tax credit paid until 5 April 2004 on dividends from UK equities.
(c) Withdrawals may be made at any time without loss of tax relief.

Personal equity plans ('PEPs')

(Subscriptions made **before 6 April 1999**: TA 1988 s 333; SI 1989/469; SI 1998/1869)

From 2008–09, all PEP accounts are transferred to ISA accounts.

Before 6 April 1999, subscriptions to PEPs could be made up to a maximum per year of £6,000 to a general plan and £3,000 to a single company plan. Dividend income is tax free and a 10% tax credit was payable until 5 April 2004 on dividends from UK equities. Interest on cash held is paid gross and is tax free if reinvested.

PEPs held at 5 April 1999 can continue to be held with the same tax advantages as an ISA (see above) and without affecting the amount that can be subscribed to an ISA.

National Savings Bank interest

The first £70 of any interest you receive from a National Savings Ordinary Account is tax free. It is not possible to open a new Ordinary Account after 28 January 2004.

Miscellaneous reliefs

Foster carers

(ITTOIA 2005 ss 803–828)

Generally, local authority payments to foster carers are not taxable to the extent they do no more than meet the actual costs of caring. In other cases, for 2003–04 onwards:

- where gross receipts do not exceed the 'individual limit', the carer is treated as having a nil profit and nil loss for the tax year concerned;
- where gross receipts exceed the 'individual limit', the carer can choose to either be taxed on the excess or compute profit or loss using the normal business rules.

The 'individual limit' is made up of a fixed amount of £10,000 per residence for a full tax year plus an amount per child for each week or part week that the individual provides foster care. The weekly amounts are £200 for a child under 11 years and £250 for a child of 11 or over.

Landlord's energy-saving allowance

(ITTOIA 2005 ss 312–314, SI 2007/831)

From 6 April 2004 to 5 April 2015 individual landlords who let residential property and pay income tax may claim a deduction from the property business profits for expenditure in the dwelling-houses let to install:

- loft insulation or cavity wall insulation; or
- (from 7 April 2005) solid wall insulation; or
- (from 6 April 2006) draught-proofing and insulation for hot water systems; or
- (from 6 April 2007) floor insulation.

Expenditure is restricted to £1,500 per building until 5 April 2007 and to £1,500 per dwelling-house from 6 April 2007.

The relief is extended to corporate landlords of residential property for expenditure on or after 8 July 2008.

Life assurance premium relief

(TA 1988 s 266, Sch 14 para 7)

Relief for premiums paid on qualifying life assurance policies for contracts made before 14 March 1984 is available by deduction of 12.5% from admissible premiums.

Maintenance payments

(ITTOIA 2005 ss 727, 729; ITA 2007 ss 453–456)

Where either party to the marriage was born before 6 April 1935 tax relief may be claimed by the payer in respect of the lower of:

- the amount of the payments in the year concerned and
- the minimum amount of the married couple's allowance for the year concerned (see p 66).

The relief is restricted to 10% of the relevant amount. The payment must be made to the divorced or separated spouse. It is made gross and is not taxable in the hands of the recipient.

Rent-a-room relief

(ITTOIA 2005 ss 784–802; F(No 2)A 1982 Sch 10)

Gross annual receipts from letting furnished accommodation in the only or main home are exempt from tax up to a maximum of £4,250 (provided no other taxable income is derived from a trade, letting or arrangement from which the rent-a-room receipts are derived).

If the gross receipts exceed £4,250, the taxpayer can pay tax on the net receipts after deduction of expenses. Alternatively, the taxpayer can elect to pay tax on the amount by which the gross receipts exceed £4,250, without relief for the actual expenses.

An individual's maximum is halved to £2,125 if during the 'relevant period' for the year (normally the tax year) some other person received income from letting accommodation in that property.

An election can be made to disapply the relief for a particular tax year (for example, if the individual would otherwise make an allowable loss).

Pension provision from 6 April 2006

(FA 2004 ss 149–284, Schs 28–36)

From 6 April 2006, a new pension scheme tax regime fully replaces pre-existing rules for occupational pension schemes, personal (and stakeholder) pension schemes and retirement annuity schemes.

Tax relief on contributions

Individual contributions: Contributions to registered schemes are not limited by reference to a fraction of earnings and there is no earnings cap. There is no provision for the carry-back or carry-forward of contributions to tax years other than the year of payment.

An individual may make unlimited contributions and tax relief is available on contributions up to the higher of:

- the full amount of relevant earnings; or
- £3,600 provided the scheme operates tax relief at source.

Employer contributions: Employer contributions to registered schemes are deductible for tax purposes, with statutory provision for spreading abnormally large contributions over a period of up to four years. The contributions are not treated as taxable income of the employee.

Special annual allowance charge: A special annual allowance charge applies for 2009–10 and 2010–11 for individuals with income of £130,000 or over. Tax relief above basic rate is recovered from pension savings above an individual's special annual allowance by the application of the special annual allowance charge. An individual's special annual allowance is the higher of their regular pension savings and £20,000 (or in certain circumstances, where contributions have been less regular than quarterly, £30,000).

Annual allowance

Each individual has an annual allowance as set out in the table below. If the annual increase in an individual's rights under all registered schemes exceeds the annual allowance, the excess is chargeable at 40%, the individual being liable for the tax.

Annual allowance	2006–07	2007–08	2008–09	2009–10	**2010–11**
	£215,000	£225,000	£235,000	£245,000	**£255,000**

Taxable benefits

'Tax-free' lump sum: The maximum 'tax-free' lump sum that can be paid to a member under a registered scheme is broadly the lower of:

- 25% of the value of the pension rights; and
- 25% of the member's lifetime allowance.

Lifetime allowance: Each individual has a lifetime allowance for contributions as set out in the table below. The excess over the lifetime allowance of the benefits crystallising (usually when a pension begins to be paid) is taxable at the following rates:

- 55% if taken as a lump sum;
- 25% in other cases.

Any tax due may be deducted from the individual's benefits.

Lifetime allowance	2006–07	2007–08	2008–09	2009–10	**2010–11**
	£1,500,000	£1,600,000	£1,650,000	£1,750,000	**£1,800,000**

Transitional. There are transitional provisions for the protection of lump sum and other pension rights accrued before 6 April 2006.

Age restrictions

Minimum pension age: The minimum pension age is 55 (50 before 6 April 2010). A pension cannot be paid before the minimum age except on grounds of ill health. Those with existing contractual rights to draw a pension earlier will have those rights protected and there is special protection for members of pre-6 April 2006 approved schemes with early retirement ages (see p 87). A reduced lifetime allowance will apply in the case of early retirement before minimum pension age except in the case of certain professions such as the police and the armed forces (to be prescribed by regulations).

Maximum benefit age: Benefits must be taken by the age of 75 at the latest. A member of a money purchase scheme may take a pension from the age of 75 by way of income withdrawal (known as an 'alternatively secured pension') instead of taking a scheme pension or purchasing a lifetime annuity. The maximum alternatively secured pension is 70% of a comparable annuity.

Personal pension schemes and retirement annuities

Provisions to 5 April 2006

1 July 1988 to 5 April 2006: Retirement annuity contracts were replaced by personal pension schemes, although retirement annuity premiums may continue to be paid, and tax relief obtained (TA 1988 ss 618–629). There are provisions for the carrying back (TA 1988 s 619) and the carrying forward (TA 1988 s 625) of relief, and these are not affected by FA 2000.

6 April 2001 to 5 April 2006: The personal pension scheme rules were adapted to accommodate the stakeholder pensions provisions (TA 1988 ss 630–655). From that date, personal pension and stakeholder pension contributions are subject to the same rules.

Tax relief on contributions

Retirement annuities: Premiums continue to be deducted from or set off against relevant earnings (TA 1988 s 619). The amount of relief available is based on a percentage of net relevant earnings (see maximum amount, below).

Personal pension schemes: Before 6 April 2001, premiums were deducted from or set off against relevant earnings (TA 1988 s 639, as enacted). The amount of relief available was based on a percentage of net relevant earnings (see maximum amount p 86).

Personal pension schemes/stakeholder pensions:

Contributions not exceeding the earnings threshold

(1) Contributions of up to £3,600 gross ('the earnings threshold') may be paid into a stakeholder pension by anyone who is not a member of an occupational pension scheme, regardless of the amount (if any) of their earnings (TA 1988 s 632A).

(2) An individual who is a member of an occupational pension scheme but who is not a controlling director and whose total annual remuneration is no more than £30,000 is allowed to pay into both an occupational scheme and a stakeholder pension and will receive tax relief on an annual contribution of up to £3,600 (gross) into the stakeholder pension (TA 1988 s 632B).

Contributions exceeding the earnings threshold

(1) Contributions in excess of the earnings threshold may be made. Tax relief is given on contributions up to a maximum based on a percentage of net relevant earnings (see maximum percentage below).

(2) For the purpose of supporting contributions in excess of the earnings threshold, a tax year for which evidence of relevant earnings can be provided may be nominated as the basis year and contributions based on the amount of those earnings may be paid in each of the next five years (TA 1988 s 646B). The provisions enable an individual to make pension contributions for up to five years after the relevant earnings ceased, by reference to the net relevant earnings of a basis year which may be any one of the six tax years preceding the first year for which there are no relevant earnings (TA 1988 s 646D).

Carry-back of relief

Carry-back of relief is provided for in TA 1988 s 641A. There is no carry forward of relief (FA 2000 Sch 13 para 19).

Basic and higher rate relief

From 6 April 2001, contributions are payable net of basic rate tax relief. Tax relief at the higher rate is given by extending the basic rate band by the amount of the contribution paid in the year of assessment (TA 1988 s 639).

From 2001–02, relief for contributions is given up to a maximum which is the greater of:

(a) the 'earnings threshold'; and

(b) the 'maximum percentage' of net relevant earnings for the year (TA 1988 s 640, as amended by FA 2000 Sch 13 para 16).

For the purposes of calculating the maximum percentage, net relevant earnings are subject to an earnings cap (TA 1988 s 640A).

Maximum amount

Personal pension schemes/ stakeholder pensions*(TA 1988 s 640)*	*Age in years at beginning of year of assessment*	*Maximum percentage*
	35 and below	17½
	36 to 45	20
	46 to 50	25
	51 to 55	30
	56 to 60	35
	61 or more	40
Earnings cap	£	
2005–06	105,600	
2004–05	102,000	
2003–04	99,000	
2002–03	97,200	
2001–02	95,400	
2000–01	91,800	
Retirement annuities (TA 1988 s 626)	*Age in years at beginning of year of assessment*	*Maximum percentage*
	50 and below	17½
	51 to 55	20
	56 to 60	22½
	61 or more	27½

Life insurance element (TA 1988 s 640(3), as amended)

The maximum amount of contributions in respect of life insurance on which tax relief can be given is limited to a percentage of net relevant earnings (retirement annuities; personal pension contracts taken out before 6 April 2001) or of total amount of relevant pension contributions (personal pensions/stakeholder pension contracts taken out after 5 April 2001).

	Maximum percentage of net relevant earnings
Retirement annuities (contracts for dependants or life insurance)	5%
Personal pension schemes (contract of life insurance made before 6 April 2001)	5%
	Maximum percentage of total relevant pension contributions
Personal pension schemes/stakeholder pensions	
Contract of life insurance made after 5 April 2001	10%

Approval of contracts – early retirement ages

Trades and professions for which an early retirement age was agreed by the Revenue under TA 1988 s 620(4)(*c*) for the purpose of the approval of retirement annuity contracts are set out below. Under the personal and stakeholder pensions legislation, individuals may not take benefits from their pension arrangements before the age of 50. The trades and professions listed below for which the Revenue has approved an earlier retirement age of 30, 35, 40 or 45 have been approved under TA 1988 s 634(3)(*b*) for the purposes of personal pension schemes and stakeholder pensions. (See p 84 for minimum age restrictions.)

Retirement age	*Profession or occupation*		
30	downhill skiers		
35	athletes badminton players boxers cyclists dancers footballers	ice hockey players models national hunt jockeys rugby league players rugby union players squash players	table tennis players tennis players (including real tennis players) wrestlers
40	cricketers divers (saturation, deep sea and free swimming)	golfers motorcycle riders (motorcross or road racing) motor racing drivers	speedway drivers trapeze artists WPBSA snooker players
45	flat racing jockeys	members of the reserve forces	
50	circus animal trainers croupiers interdealer brokers martial arts instructors moneybroker dealers	off-shore riggers (mechanical fitters, pipe fitters, riggers, platers, welders and roustabouts) Royal Navy reservists	rugby league referees territorial army members TV newsreaders
55	air pilots brass instrumentalists distant water trawlermen firemen (part-time) health visitors (female)	inshore fishermen midwives (female) moneybroker dealer managers and directors responsible for dealers nurses (female) physiotherapists (female)	psychiatrists (who are also maximum part-time specialists employed within the NHS solely in the treatment of the mentally disordered) singers

Share schemes

Share incentive plans ('SIPs')

(TCGA 1992 ss 236A, 238A, Schs 7C, 7D Pt 1; ITEPA 2003 ss 488–515, Sch 2; FA 2003 s 139, Sch 21)
Applications for approval of Share Incentive Plans could be made from 28 July 2000.

Free share plan

2000–01 onwards	*annual maximum*	£3,000

Partnership share plan

2000–01 to 2002–03	*monthly maximum*	£125 or 10% of monthly salary if lower
2003–04 onwards	*annual maximum*	£1,500 or 10% of annual salary if lower

Matching shares

2000–01 onwards	*Maximum number of shares given by employer to employee for each partnership share bought*	2

Shares are free of tax and NICs if held in the plan for five years. Dividends up to £1,500 per employee per tax year are tax free if reinvested in shares. Shares withdrawn from the plan at any time are exempt from capital gains tax and are treated as acquired by the employee at their market value at that time.

If shares are withdrawn within between three and five years (with exceptions such as on death, disability, normal retirement or redundancy), liability to income tax and NICs arises on the lower of their value on entering and on leaving the plan. If shares are withdrawn within three years (with similar exceptions), liability is on their value on leaving the plan.

Enterprise management incentives

(TCGA 1992 s 238A, Sch 7D Pt 4; ITEPA 2003 ss 527–541, Sch 5)

Certain independent trading companies with gross assets not exceeding £30 million may grant share options then worth up to £120,000 (£100,000 for options granted before 6 April 2008) to an eligible employee. The total value of shares in respect of which unexercised qualifying options exist must not exceed £3 million. An additional restriction, limiting the scheme to companies with fewer than 250 full-time equivalent employees, applies to options granted on or after 21 July 2008.

Where the conditions of the scheme are complied with:

(a) There is no charge to tax or NICs when the option is granted provided the option to acquire the shares is not at less than their market values at that date, and there is no charge on exercise providing the option is exercised within ten years.

(b) Capital gains tax will be payable when the shares are sold, but business assets taper relief (see p 33) will be available and starts from the date on which the options are granted.

Approved save as you earn (SAYE) share option schemes

(TCGA 1992 s 238A, Sch 7D Pt 2; ITEPA 2003 ss 516–520, Sch 3; FA 2003 s 139, Sch 21)

The scheme is linked to an approved savings scheme, on which bonuses are exempt from tax, to provide funds for the acquisition of shares when the option is exercised at the end of a three or five-year contract. A five-year contract may offer the option of repayment on the seventh anniversary.

Monthly contributions to SAYE scheme

Minimum	£5–£10[1]
Maximum	£250

[1] The company may choose a minimum savings contribution between £5 and £10.

See the Treasury website (www.hm-treasury.gov.uk) for the bonus rates.

Where the conditions of the scheme are complied with, no income tax charge arises on the employee in respect of:

(a) the grant of an option to acquire shares at a discount of up to 20% of the share price at time of the grant;

(b) the exercise of the option (options must not be exercised before the bonus date subject to cessation of employment due to injury, disability, redundancy, retirement or death); or

(c) any increase in the value of the shares.

Capital gains tax is chargeable on disposal of the shares: the CGT base cost is the consideration given by the employee for both the shares and the option.

Company share option plans ('CSOPs')

(TCGA 1992 s 238A, Sch 7D Pt 3; ITEPA 2003 ss 521–526, Sch 4; FA 2003 s 139, Sch 21)

Limit on value of shares under option held by employee at any one time

From 29 April 1996	£30,000

Scheme shares must be fully paid up, not redeemable and not subject to special restrictions. Only full-time directors or qualifying employees may participate in the scheme.

Where the conditions of the scheme are complied with, no tax charge arises on the employee in respect of:

(a) the grant of an option to acquire shares[1];
(b) the exercise of the option[2]; or
(c) any increase in the value of the shares.

Capital gains tax is chargeable on disposal of the shares: the CGT base cost is the consideration given by the employee for both the shares and the option.

1 At the time the option is granted the price at which shares can be acquired must not be less than the market value of shares of the same class at that time.

2 The option must be exercised between three and ten years after the grant (or may be exercised less than three years after the grant where the individual ceases to be an employee due to injury, disablement, redundancy or retirement). For options granted before 9 April 2003, the options must be exercised between three and ten years after the grant (without exception) and not less than three years after a previous exempt exercise of another option under the same or another approved company share option scheme.

Approved profit sharing schemes

(TA 1988 ss 186, 187, Schs 9, 10)

NOTE: The income tax relief in respect of awards of shares under approved profit sharing schemes was withdrawn for awards of shares made after 31 December 2002: FA 2000 s 49.

Annual limit on shares appropriated

From 1991–92	Greater of £3,000 or 10% of salary, up to £8,000

Schedule E charge on early disposal or receipt of capital from shares

Time of disposal or capital receipt	*Percentage charge*[1]
Before third anniversary of appropriation	100%[2]

1 Calculated on the appropriate percentage of the initial market value of the shares when appropriated (or the sales proceeds if less).

2 The charge is reduced to 50% where the employee reaches the retirement age specified in the scheme rules or leaves the employment due to injury, disability or redundancy before the shares are sold or capital is received.

Where the conditions of the scheme are satisfied, no tax charge arises on the employee in respect of:

(a) the value of the shares at the time of appropriation;
(b) any increase in the value of the shares; or
(c) any gain on the disposal of the shares (although capital gains tax is chargeable on any gain over the market value on appropriation).

Approved discretionary ('executive') share option schemes

Options held on 17 July 1995: (TA 1988 ss 185, 187, Sch 9)

Shares could be acquired at a discount of up to 15% of market value at the time of the grant where the employer also had an approved profit sharing scheme or an approved SAYE option scheme. No tax charge arose when the option was granted unless the price paid for the option plus the price at which the shares could be acquired was less than the market value of the shares, in which case, the discount was chargeable. In all other material respects, the rules are the same as for the CSOP schemes (see above).

The scheme was abolished for options granted after 16 July 1995.

Tax credits

From 6 April 2003, child tax credit and working tax credit replaced children's tax credit, working families' tax credit and disabled person's tax credit in addition to the child-related elements of certain social security benefits. Administered and paid by HMRC, they are non-taxable. Claims must be made after the commencement of the tax year and can be backdated for a maximum of three months. Claims must be renewed by 31 July.

Child tax credit and working tax credit

	2010–11 ***Annual amount***	*2009–10* *Annual amount*
Child tax credit	**£**	£
Family element[1]	**545**	545
Addition for child under age of one[1]	**545**	545
Child element (for each child or young person)	**2,300**	2,235
Addition for disabled child or young person	**2,715**	2,670
Enhancement for severe disabled child or young person	**1,095**	1,075
Working tax credit	**£**	£
Basic element	**1,920**	1,890
Lone parent and couple element	**1,890**	1,860
30-hour element	**790**	775
Disability element	**2,570**	2,530
Severe disability element	**1,095**	1,075
50+ element – 16–29 hours worked	**1,320**	1,300
50+ element – 30 or more hours worked[2]	**1,965**	1,935
Childcare element (up to 80% (70% for 2005/06) of eligible costs)	**Weekly**	Weekly
– maximum eligible cost for one child	**175**	175
– maximum eligible cost for two or more children	**300**	300

1 Where an individual qualifies for the 50+ (30+ hours) payment, they cannot also qualify for the 50+ (16–29 hours) payment.

2 Only one family element per family. Baby element payable in addition in the first year of the child's life.

Income thresholds and withdrawal rates	***2010–11***	***2009–10***
First income threshold for those entitled to CTC and WTC	**£6,420**	£6,420
First withdrawal rate	**39%**	39%
Second income threshold	**£50,000**	£50,000
Second withdrawal rate	**6.67%**	6.67%
First threshold for those entitled to CTC only	**£16,190**	£16,040
Income disregarded	**£25,000**	£25,000

Calculation of award. Tax credits are awarded on an annual basis. They are initially based on the income of the claimant or joint claimants for the preceding tax year and then adjusted based on actual income in the tax year in which the credit is claimed. Income broadly includes all taxable income excluding the first £300 of income from pensions, savings, property or foreign assets. If actual income is greater than the previous year's income by less than £25,000, the award is not adjusted. If actual income is less than the previous year's income or if it is greater than the previous year's income by £25,000 or more (£2,500 before April 2006), the award is adjusted to reflect actual income. Where circumstances change during a tax year and different rates apply, the award is recalculated on a proportional, daily basis. Such changes must be notified to HMRC within three months if tax credit entitlement will be reduced as a result. From April 2007, this time limit is reduced to one month.

Eligibility. CTC is payable to UK resident single parents and couples responsible for a child or young person. WTC is payable to UK residents who are at least 16 years old and who work (or in the case of a couple, one of whom works) at least 16 hours a week. Additionally, the claimant (or one of them if a couple) must either:

- be at least 25 years old and work at least 30 hours a week; or
- have a dependent child or children; or
- be over 50 and qualify for the 50+ element; or
- have a mental or physical disability which puts them at a disadvantage in getting a job and have previously been in receipt of some form of disability benefit.

Renewal claim. Claims for tax credit must be renewed by 31 July.

Inheritance tax

Rates of tax

From 15 March 1988 onwards

Cumulative gross transfer rate:	*Rate*
for gross transfers on death over the cumulative chargeable transfer limit	40%
for gross lifetime transfers over the cumulative chargeable transfer limit	20%
Grossing-up net transfer rate for each £1 over the chargeable transfer limit:	
for net transfers on death not bearing own tax	$^2/_3$
for net lifetime transfers	$^1/_4$

Cumulative chargeable transfer limits

Period	*Limit*	*Period*	*Limit*
	£		£
2010–11	**325,000**	1998–99	223,000
2009–10	325,000	1997–98	215,000
2008–09	312,000	1996–97	200,000
2007–08	300,000	1995–96	154,000
2006–07	285,000	10.3.92–5.4.95	150,000
2005–06	275,000	6.4.91–9.3.92	140,000
2004–05	263,000	1990–91	128,000
2003–04	255,000	1989–90	118,000
2002–03	250,000	15.3.88–5.4.89	110,000
2001–02	242,000	17.3.87–14.3.88	90,000
2000–01	234,000	18.3.86–16.3.87	71,000
1999–2000	231,000		

Capital transfer tax nil rate bands

Period	***Limit***	***Period***	***Limit***
	£		**£**
6.4.85–17.3.86	67,000	26.3.80–8.3.82	50,000
13.3.84–5.4.85	64,000	27.10.77–25.3.80	25,000
15.3.83–12.3.84	60,000	13.3.75–26.10.77	15,000
9.3.82–14.3.83	55,000		

Estate duty nil rate bands (England, Scotland and Wales)

Period	***Limit***	***Period***	***Limit***
	£		**£**
22.3.72–12.3.75	15,000	9.4.62–3.4.63	4,000
31.3.71–21.3.72	12,500	30.7.54–8.4.62	3,000
16.4.69–30.3.71	10,000	10.4.46–29.7.54	2,000
4.4.63–15.4.69	5,000	16.8.14–9.4.46	100

Any nil-rate band which is unused on a person's death can be transferred to their surviving spouse or civil partner for the purposes of the charge to tax on the death of the survivor on or after 9 October 2007.

Delivery of accounts: due dates

Type of transfer	*Due date*
Chargeable lifetime transfers	Later of: (*a*) 12 months after the end of the month in which the transfer took place; and (*b*) three months after the date on which the person delivering the account became liable
PETs which become chargeable	12 months after the end of the month in which the transferor died
Gifts with reservation chargeable on death	12 months after the end of the month in which the death occurred
Transfers on death	Later of: (*a*) 12 months after the end of the month in which the death occurred; and (*b*) three months after the date on which the personal representatives first act or the person liable first has reason to believe that he is liable to deliver an account
National heritage property	Six months after the end of the month in which the chargeable event occurred

Delivery of accounts: excepted transfers and estates

(SI 2002 No 1733; SI 2004 No 2543)

Date of transfer or death	*6 April 2000–5 April 2002*	*6 April 2002–5 April 2003*	*6 April 2003–31 Aug 2006*	*From 1 Sept 2006*
Excepted transfers:	*Value below*	*Value below*	*Value below*	*Value below*
Total chargeable transfers since 6 April	£10,000	£10,000	£10,000	£10,000
Total chargeable transfers during last ten years	£40,000	£40,000	£40,000	£40,000
Excepted estates:				
Total gross value	£210,000[1].	£220,000[1]	£240,000[1] (see (*a*) below)	(see (*a*) below)
Total gross value of property outside UK	£50,000	£75,000	£75,000	£100,000
Aggregate value of 'specified transfers'[2]	£75,000	£100,000	£100,000	£150,000
Settled property passing on death	–	£100,000	£100,000	£150,000

For chargeable transfers after 5 April 2007, no account need be delivered where:

(a) the transfer is of cash or quoted shares or securities and the value of the transfer and other chargeable transfers made in the preceding seven years does not exceed the IHT threshold; or

(b) the value of the transfer and other chargeable transfers made in the preceding seven years does not exceed 80% of the IHT threshold and the value of the transfer does not exceed the net amount of the threshold available to the transferor at the time of the transfer.

Excepted estates

For deaths occurring after 5 April 2004, no account need be delivered where the deceased died domiciled in the UK provided either conditions (*a*) or (*b*) below are met, and both conditions (*c*) and (*d*) below are met.

(a) the aggregate of the gross value of the estate, and of any 'specified transfers' or 'specified exempt transfers'[3] does not exceed the appropriate IHT threshold;

(b) the aggregate of the gross value of the estate, and of any 'specified transfers' or 'specified exempt transfers'[3] does not exceed £1,000,000; and after deducting from that aggregate figure any exempt spouse and charity transfers and total estate liabilities, it does not exceed the appropriate IHT threshold;

(c) the gross value of settled property or foreign assets do not exceed the above limits; and

(d) there were no chargeable lifetime transfers in the seven years before death other than specified transfers not exceeding the above limits.

For deaths occurring after 31 August 2006, an estate will not be an excepted estate if the provisions for alternatively secured pension funds in IHTA 1984 ss 151A–151C apply by reason of the individual's death.

For deaths after 5 April 2002 and before 6 April 2004, no account need be delivered where the deceased died domiciled in the UK provided that:

(i) the aggregate of the gross value of the estate, and of any 'specified transfers' does not exceed the above limits; and

(ii) the gross value of settled property or foreign assets do not exceed the above limits; and

(iii) there were no chargeable lifetime transfers in the seven years before death other than specified transfers not exceeding the above limits.

Where the deceased was never domiciled in the UK, no account need be delivered for deaths after 5 April 2002 provided that:

- the value of the estate in the UK is wholly attributable to cash and quoted shares and securities not exceeding £150,000 (£100,000 before 1 September 2006); and
- for deaths occurring after 31 August 2006, the provisions for alternatively secured pension funds in IHTA 1984 ss 151A–151C do not apply by reason of the individual's death.

1 This limit applies to the aggregate gross value of the estate and of 'specified transfers'[3].

2 'Specified transfers' are transfers of cash, quoted shares and securities and, after 6 April 2002, interests in or over land and, after 5 April 2004, personal chattels or corporeal moveable property.

3 'Specified exempt transfers' are transfers in the seven years before death between spouses, gifts to charity, political parties or housing associations, transfers to maintenance funds for historical buildings, etc or to employee trusts.

Excepted settlements

No account need be delivered of property comprised in an excepted settlement (i.e. one with no qualifying interest in possession) where a chargeable event occurs after 5 April 2007 and cash not exceeding £1,000 is the only property comprised in the settlement. Other conditions to be fulfilled are that, the settlor has not provided further property, the trustees are UK resident throughout the settlement's existence and there are no related settlements.

Reliefs

The following is a summary of the main reliefs and exemptions under the Inheritance Tax Act 1984. The legislation should be referred to for conditions and exceptions.

Agricultural property

Transfer with vacant possession (or right to obtain it within 12 months); transfer on or after 1 September 1995, of land let (or treated as let) on or after that date	100% of agricultural value
Any other case	50% of agricultural value

Note: The 100% relief is extended in limited circumstances by Concession F17

Annual gifts £3,000

Business property

Unincorporated business.	100%		
Unquoted shares (including shares in AIM or USM companies) (held for 2 years or more).[1]	100%	Controlling holding in fully quoted companies.	50%
Unquoted securities which alone, or together with other such securities and unquoted shares, give the transferor control of the company (held for 2 years or more).[1]	100%	Land, buildings, machinery or plant used in business of company or partnership.	50%
Settled property used in life tenant's business.	100%		

1 Tax charges arising and transfers occurring after 5 April 1996. 10 March 1992–5 April 1996 minority holding of shares or securities of up to 25% in unquoted or USM company qualified for 50% relief; larger holdings qualified for 100% relief.

Charities, gifts to		Exempt
From 1 April 2002, Community Amateur Sports Clubs are treated as charities.		
Marriage gifts		
Made by:	parent	£5,000
	remoter ancestor	£2,500
	party to marriage	£2,500
	other person	£1,000
National purposes		
Property given or bequeathed to bodies listed in IHTA 1984 Sch 3.		Exempt
Political parties, gifts to		Exempt

Potentially exempt transfers

Exempt if made 7 or more years before the date of death. Except for gifts with reservation etc, they include:

(a) transfers by individuals to other individuals or certain trusts for the disabled;
(b) transfers after 21 March 2006 by individuals to a bereaved minor's trust on the coming to an end of an immediate post-death interest;
(c) transfers before 22 March 2006 by individuals to accumulation and maintenance trusts;
(d) transfers by individuals into interest in possession trusts in which, for transfers after 21 March 2006, the beneficiary has a disabled person's interest; and
(e) certain transfers on the termination or disposal of an individual's beneficial interest in possession in settled property (in restricted circumstances following FA 2006).

Quick succession relief

Estate increased by chargeable transfer followed by death within 5 years.	
Death within 1st year.	100%
Each additional year: decreased by	20%
Small gifts to same person	£250
Spouses/civil partners with separate domicile (one not being in the UK)	
Total exemption	£55,000

Tapering relief

The value of the estate on death is taxed as the top slice of cumulative transfers in the 7 years before death. Transfers on or within 7 years of death are taxed on their value at the date of the gift on the death rate scale, but using the scale in force at the date of death, subject to the following taper:

Years between gift and death	*Percentage of full charge at death rates*
0–3	100
3–4	80
4–5	60
5–6	40
6–7	20

Penalties see p 14.

National insurance contributions

From 6 April 2010

Class 1 contributions[1]				
Earnings limits and threshold		Weekly £	Monthly £	Yearly £
Lower earnings limit		97	421	5,044
Earnings threshold		110	476	5,715
Upper earnings limit		844	3,656	43,875
Upper accruals point		770	3,337	40,040
Not contracted out		**Employees' contributions**		**Employers' contributions**
Weekly earnings:	£110.01–£844	11%		12.8%
	Over £844	1%		12.8%
Contracted out			*Salary-related schemes*	*Money purchase schemes*
Weekly earnings:	£110.01–£770	9.4%	9.1%	11.4%
	£770–£844	11%	12.8%	12.8%
	Over £844	1%	12.8%	12.8%
	– rebate £97–£110	1.6%[2]	3.7%	1.4%
Women at reduced rate				
Weekly earnings:	£110.01–£844	4.85%	*as above*	
	Over £844	1%	*as above*	
Class 1A and Class 1B contributions				12.8%

1 Employees' rates are nil for children under 16 and those over state pensionable age but employers' contributions are still payable. NICs are not payable on earnings up to the earnings threshold.

2 The rebate is given on earnings between the lower earnings limit and the earnings threshold. The rebate for employees is given to employers to the extent that insufficient contributions have been paid by the employee for offset.

6 April 2009–5 April 2010

Class 1 contributions[1]				
Earnings limits and threshold		Weekly £	Monthly £	Yearly £
Lower earnings limit		95	412	4,940
Earnings threshold		110	476	5,715
Upper earnings limit		844	3,656	43,875
Upper accruals point		770	3,337	40,040
Not contracted out		**Employees' contributions**		**Employers' contributions**
Weekly earnings:	£110.01–£844	11%		12.8%
	Over £844	1%		12.8%
Contracted out			*Salary-related schemes*	*Money purchase schemes*
Weekly earnings:	£110.01–£770	9.4%	9.1%	11.4%
	£770–£844	11%	12.8%	12.8%
	Over £844	1%	12.8%	12.8%
	– rebate £95–£110	1.6%[2]	3.7%	1.4%
Women at reduced rate				
Weekly earnings:	£110.01–£844	4.85%	*as above*	
	Over £844	1%	*as above*	
Class 1A and Class 1B contributions				12.8%

1 Employees' rates are nil for children under 16, men over 65 and women over 60 but employers' contributions are still payable. NICs are not payable on earnings up to the earnings threshold.

2 The rebate is given on earnings between the lower earnings limit and the earnings threshold. The rebate for employees is given to employers to the extent that insufficient contributions have been paid by the employee for offset.

6 April 2008–5 April 2009

Class 1 contributions[1]				
Earnings limits and threshold		Weekly £	Monthly £	Yearly £
Lower earnings limit		90	390	4,680
Earnings threshold		105	453	5,435
Upper earnings limit		770	3,337	40,040
Not contracted out		**Employees' contributions**		**Employers' contributions**
Weekly earnings:	£105.01–£770	11%		12.8%
	Over £770	1%		12.8%
Contracted out			*Salary-related schemes*	*Money purchase schemes*
Weekly earnings:	£105.01–£770	9.4%	9.1%	11.4%
	Over £770	1%	12.8%	12.8%
	– rebate £90–£105	1.6%[2]	3.7%	1.4%
Women at reduced rate				
Weekly earnings:	£105.01–£770	4.85%	*as above*	
	Over £770	1%	*as above*	
Class 1A and Class 1B contributions				12.8%

1 Employees' rates are nil for children under 16, men over 65 and women over 60 but employers' contributions are still payable. NICs are not payable on earnings up to the earnings threshold.

2 The rebate is given on earnings between the lower earnings limit and the earnings threshold. The rebate for employees is given to employers to the extent that insufficient contributions have been paid by the employee for offset.

6 April 2007–5 April 2008

Class 1 contributions[1]				
Earnings limits and threshold		Weekly £	Monthly £	Yearly £
Lower earnings limit		87	377	4,524
Earnings threshold		100	435	5,225
Upper earnings limit		670	2,904	34,840
Not contracted out		**Employees' contributions**		**Employers' contributions**
Weekly earnings:	£100.01–£670	11%		12.8%
	Over £670	1%		12.8%
Contracted out			*Salary-related schemes*	*Money purchase schemes*
Weekly earnings:	£100.01–£670	9.4%	9.1%	11.4%
	Over £670	1%	12.8%	12.8%
	– rebate £87–£100	1.6%[2]	3.7%	1.4%
Women at reduced rate				
Weekly earnings:	£100.01–£670	4.85%	*as above*	
	Over £670	1%	*as above*	
Class 1A and Class 1B contributions				12.8%

1 Employees' rates are nil for children under 16, men over 65 and women over 60 but employers' contributions are still payable. NICs are not payable on earnings up to the earnings threshold.

2 The rebate is given on earnings between the lower earnings limit and the earnings threshold. The rebate for employees is given to employers to the extent that insufficient contributions have been paid by the employee for offset.

6 April 2006–5 April 2007

Class 1 contributions[1]				
Earnings limits and threshold		Weekly	Monthly	Yearly
		£	£	£
Lower earnings limit		84	364	4,368
Earnings threshold		97	420	5,035
Upper earnings limit		645	2,795	33,540
Not contracted out		**Employees' contributions**		**Employers' contributions**
Weekly earnings:	£97.01–£645	11%		12.8%
	Over £645	1%		12.8%
Contracted out			*Salary-related schemes*	*Money purchase schemes*
Weekly earnings:	£97.01–£645	9.4%	9.3%	11.4%
	Over £645	1%	12.8%	12.8%
	– rebate £84–£97	1.6%[2]	3.5%	1%
Women at reduced rate				
Weekly earnings:	£97.01–£645	4.85%		*as above*
	Over £645	1%		*as above*
Class 1A and Class 1B contributions				12.8%

1 Employees' rates are nil for children under 16, men over 65 and women over 60 but employers' contributions are still payable. NICs are not payable on earnings up to the earnings threshold.

2 The rebate is given on earnings between the lower earnings limit and the earnings threshold. The rebate for employees is given to employers to the extent that insufficient contributions have been paid by the employee for offset.

6 April 2005–5 April 2006

Class 1 contributions[1]				
Earnings limits and threshold		Weekly	Monthly	Yearly
		£	£	£
Lower earnings limit		82	356	4,264
Earnings threshold		94	408	4,895
Upper earnings limit		630	2,730	32,760
Not contracted out		**Employees' contributions**		**Employers' contributions**
Weekly earnings:	£94.01–£630	11%		12.8%
	Over £630	1%		12.8%
Contracted out			*Salary-related schemes*	*Money purchase schemes*
Weekly earnings:	£94.01–£630	9.4%	9.3%	11.8%
	Over £630	1%	12.8%	12.8%
	– rebate £82–£94	1.6%[2]	3.5%	1%
Women at reduced rate				
Weekly earnings:	£94.01–£630	4.85%		*as above*
	Over £630	1%		*as above*
Class 1A and Class 1B contributions				12.8%

1 Employees' rates are nil for children under 16, men over 65 and women over 60 but employers' contributions are still payable. NICs are not payable on earnings up to the earnings threshold.

2 The rebate is given on earnings between the lower earnings limit and the earnings threshold. The rebate for employees is given to employers to the extent that insufficient contributions have been paid by the employee for offset.

Class 2, 3 and 4 contributions

	2010–11	*2009–10*	*2008–09*
Class 2 (self-employed)			
Flat rate—per week	**£2.40**	£2.40	2.30
Share fishermen—per week	**£3.05**	£3.05	2.95
Volunteer development workers—per week	**£4.85**	£4.75	4.50
Small earning exception—per year	**£5,075**	£5,075	4,825
Class 3 (voluntary contributions)			
Flat rate—per week	**£12.05**	£12.05	8.10
Class 4 (self-employed)[1]			
Lower annual profits limit	**£5,715**	£5,715	£5,435
Upper annual profits limit	**£43,875**	£43,875	£40,040
Rate between lower and upper limits	**8%**	8%	8%
Rate on profits above upper limit	**1%**	1%	1%
Maximum contributions			
Class 1 or Class 1/Class 2[2]	**4,279.22**	4,279.22	3,876.95
– plus rate on earnings above upper limit	**1%**	1%	1%
Class 4 limiting amount[3]	**3,180.00**	3,180.00	2,890.30
– plus rate on profits above upper limit	**1%**	1%	1%

1 Not payable if pensionable age is reached by the beginning of the tax year.

2 Where an earner has more than one employment (including self-employment), liability for Class 1 or Class 1 and Class 2 contributions cannot exceed a maximum amount equal to 53 employees' Class 1 contributions at the maximum standard rate, plus, from 2003–04 onwards, 1% on earnings over the individual's upper earnings limit (which varies depending on individual circumstances).

3 Where Class 4 contributions are payable in addition to Class 1 and/or Class 2 contributions, liability for Class 4 contributions cannot exceed such an amount as, when added to the Class 1/Class 2 contributions payable (after applying the maximum if appropriate), equals the limiting amount. The limiting amount is the maximum Class 4 contributions payable (including, from 2003–04 onwards, 1% on earnings over the upper profit limit) plus 53 Class 2 contributions.

	2007–08	*2006–07*	*2005–06*
Class 2 (self-employed)			
Flat rate—per week	£2.20	£2.10	£2.10
Share fishermen—per week	£2.85	£2.75	£2.75
Volunteer development workers—per week	£4.35	£4.20	£4.10
Small earning exception—per year	£4,635	£4,465	£4,345
Class 3 (voluntary contributions)			
Flat rate—per week	£7.80	£7.55	£7.35
Class 4 (self-employed) [1]			
Lower annual profits limit	£5,225	£5,035	£4,895
Upper annual profits limit	£34,840	£33,540	£32,760
Rate between lower and upper limits	8%	8%	8%
Rate on profits above upper limit	1%	1%	1%
Maximum contributions			
Class 1 or Class 1/Class 2 [2]	£3,323.10	£3,194.84	£3,124.88
– plus rate on earnings above upper limit	1%	1%	1%
Class 4 limiting amount [3]	£2,485.80	£2,391.70	£2,340.50
– plus rate on profits above upper limit	1%	1%	1%

1 Not payable if pensionable age is reached by the beginning of the tax year.

2 Where an earner has more than one employment (including self-employment), liability for Class 1 or Class 1 and Class 2 contributions cannot exceed a maximum amount equal to 53 employees' Class 1 contributions at the maximum standard rate, plus, from 2003–04 onwards, 1% on earnings over the individual's upper earnings limit (which varies depending on individual circumstances).

3 Where Class 4 contributions are payable in addition to Class 1 and/or Class 2 contributions, liability for Class 4 contributions cannot exceed such an amount as, when added to the Class 1/Class 2 contributions payable (after applying the maximum if appropriate), equals the limiting amount. The limiting amount is the maximum Class 4 contributions payable (including, from 2003–04 onwards, 1% on earnings over the upper profit limit) plus 53 Class 2 contributions.

Employers' contributions: benefits in kind

Class 1A national insurance contributions are payable by employers on most taxable benefits in kind, excluding benefits:

(1) which are covered by a dispensation;
(2) included in a PAYE settlement agreement;
(3) provided to employees not earning more than £8,500 pa (including benefits in kind and expenses payments);
(4) otherwise not required to be included on a P11D;
(5) on which Class 1 national insurance contributions were due.

Class 1B contributions are payable by employers by reference to the value of any items included in a PAYE settlement agreement (PSA) which would otherwise be earnings for Class 1 or Class 1A, including the amount of tax paid. Income tax and Class 1B contributions on a PSA are payable by 19 October after the end of the tax year to which the PSA relates.

Common benefits subject to Class 1 and Class 1A NICs (CWG5 2006)

Benefit	*NICs Class*	*PAYE or P11D*
Assets/gifts given to employees*	1A	P11D
Assets loaned to employees	1A	P11D
Car or van fuel supplied for private motoring	1A	P11D
Cars or vans available for private use	1A	P11D
Car parking other than at or near place of work or as part of business travel*	1A	P11D
Christmas gifts – cash	1	PAYE
– benefits	1A	P11D
Clothing and uniforms		
– cash payment for clothing that can be worn at any time	1	PAYE
– cash payment for clothing that can only be worn at work or non-durable items such as tights or stockings	–	PAYE
– clothing provided by employer that can be worn at any time	1A	P11D
Computers provided for private use where value exceeds £2,500 (all computers provided for private use after 5.4.06)	1A	P11D
Credit cards and tokens – personal expenses not reimbursed	1	P11D
Entertaining – non-business staff expenses/allowances*	1A	P11D
Holidays provided*	1A	P11D
Living accommodation (beneficial)	1A	P11D
Loans – at low interest or interest-free	1A	P11D
– written off	1	P11D
Meals provided other than at canteen or at business premises open to all staff on a reasonable scale	1A	P11D
Medical insurance or treatment provided in the UK by employer	1A	P11D
Notional payments	1	PAYE
Payments in kind convertible to cash	1	PAYE
Payments of employees' personal liabilities	1	PAYE
Prize money	1	PAYE
Relocation payments – qualifying over £8,000	1A	P11D
– non-qualifying benefits	1A	P11D
– non-qualifying expenses	1	P11D
Round sum allowances (not identified as business expense)	1	PAYE
Scholarships awarded to students because of parent's employment or payment of school fees*	1A	P11D
Services supplied	1A	P11D
Tax paid for and not reimbursed by employee	1	P11D
Telephone rental and private calls – employer subscribes*	1A	P11D
Vouchers (other than exceptions for childcare, meals, etc)	1	P11D

* Reimbursement of or payment for goods or services for personal use by employee or payment of personal expenses or allowances where the employee contracts with the supplier is subject to Class 1 NICs and is reportable on form P11D.

Overseas

Average rates of exchange

Average for year ending	***31.03.07***	***31.12.07***	***31.03.08***	***31.12.08***	***31.03.09***
Algeria (Dinar)	136.9221	139.34	137.08	119.634	112.768
Argentina (Peso)	5.8223	6.2363	6.283	5.8413	5.559
Australia ($A)	2.4739	2.3907	2.3153	2.1869	2.1814
Bahrain (Dinar)	0.7141	0.754	0.7562	0.6979	0.6472
Bangladesh (Taka)	131.2303	138.02	138.23	126.837	117.481
Barbados (BD$)	3.7884	4.0023	4.0151	3.7036	3.4337
Bolivia (Boliviano)	15.1462	15.7073	15.5431	13.4418	12.2272
Botswana (Pula)	11.4887	12.2795	12.4328	12.5687	12.2141
Brazil (Real)	4.0789	3.8951	3.7214	3.3579	3.3307
Brunei ($)	2.9649	3.0127	2.9581	2.6016	2.4531
Bulgaria (Lev)		2.8506	2.7593	2.4496	2.3525
Burundi (Franc)	1,932.3958	2,180.06	2,246.85	2,196.36	2,060.04
Canada (Can$)	2.1567	2.1484	2.0725	1.9615	1.9112
Cayman Islands (CI$)	1.6242	1.7029	1.6912	1.5166	1.4031
Chile (Peso)	1,010.6452	1,043.21	1,007.89	956.952	946.012
China (Renminbi Yuan)	14.9935	15.2109	14.944	12.8301	11.7475
Colombia (Peso)	4,441.0926	4,150.21	4,009.40	3,608.31	3,535.02
Congo Dem Rep (Zaire) (Congolese Franc)	935.6975	1,111.48	1,116.84	1,032.28	1,023.63
Costa Rica (Colon)	981.3863	1,033.37	1,025.41	973.351	928.677
Cuba (Peso)	1.901	1.9787	1.9719	1.826	1.7008
Cyprus (£)	0.8508	0.8494	0.84398		
1.4.07 to 21.12.07			0.84398		
Euro from 1.1.08					
Czech Republic (Koruna)	41.5989	40.4435	38.2403	31.2163	30.6209
Denmark (Krone)	11.0014	10.8900	10.5702	9.3823	8.971
Egypt (£)	10.8563	11.2921	11.226	10.0716	9.3599
El Salvador (Colon)	16.6369	17.5503	17.6071	16.1864	14.9744
Ethiopia (Birr)	16.7003	18.0963	18.4057	17.8542	17.1711
European Union (Euro)	1.475	1.4604	1.4178	1.2586	1.2042
Fiji Islands (F$)	3.2532	3.2178	3.1500	2.9203	2.8305
French Cty/Africa (CFA franc)	967.3428	956.12	925.47	821.42	788.89
French Pacific Is (CFP franc)	175.8587	173.82	168.25	149.33	143.417
Gambia (Dalasi)	53.0478	49.573	46.5553	40.9522	39.7935
Ghana (Cedi)	17,447.0667	16,916.4967	17,447.0667	1.9891	1.9975
1.1.07 to 30.6.07		18,264.02			
1.7.07 to 31.12.07		1.927			
1.4.07 to 30.6.07			18,434.15		
1.7.07 to 31.3.08			1.9257		
Grenada/Wind. Isles (EC$)	5.1144	5.4032	5.4204	4.9999	4.6356
Guyana (G$)	365.1609	406.10	409.02	377.743	349.056
Honduras (Lempira)	35.9179	37.8929	38.016	34.9474	32.3282
Hong Kong (HK$)	14.724	15.6114	15.659	14.4291	13.354
Hungary (Forint)	388.1129	366.12	356.86	312.999	311.844
Iceland (Krona)	133.7177	127.99	128.36	159.163	167.632
India (Rupee)	85.6028	82.6063	80.7528	79.9647	78.1871
Indonesia (Rupiah)	17,253.2658	18,294.55	18,425.14	17,758.16	17,352.65
Iran (Rial)	17,424.415	18,566.81	18,630.05	17,472.49	16,415.66
Iraq (Dinar)	2,685.7928	2,510.79	2,479.81	2,209.16	2,024.15
Israel (Shekel)	8.2179	8.2105	7.9471	6.6178	6.2823
Jamaica (J$)	125.8431	138.11	140.35	134.301	130.009

Average for year ending	***31.03.07***	***31.12.07***	***31.03.08***	***31.12.08***	***31.03.09***
Japan (Yen)	221.4527	235.6273	229.3116	192.26	173.793
Jordan (Dinar)	1,3422	1.4178	1.4222	1.3114	1.2159.
Kenya (Shilling)	135.298	134.68	134.00	126.93	122.243
Korea South (Won)	1,794.2808	1,861.77	1,877.73	2,016.25	2,052.65
Kuwait (Dinar)	0.5483	0.5687	0.5618	0.4978	0.468
Laos (New Kip)	18,804.8133	19,225.02	18,955.83	16,140.15	14,709.12
Latvia (lats)		1.0206	0.9855	0.8802	0.848
Lebanon (£)	2,859.8993	3,026.21	3,035.80	2,792.83	2,584.94
Libya (Dinar)	2.4467	2.519	2.4937	2.2503	2.1135
Lithuania (Litas)		5.0329	4.8715	4.3238	4.1526
Malawi (Kwacha)	262.3102	280.16	281.54	260.21	241.322
Malaysia (Ringgit)	6.832	6.8706	6.7553	6.1456	5.858
Malta (Lira)	0.6338				
Up to 31.12.07		0.6271			
1.4.07 to 31.12.07			0.62236		
Euro from 1.1.08					
Mauritius (Rupee)	60.4041	62.0963	59.8987	52.2565	50.51
Mexico (Peso)	20.8418	21.8598	21.8287	20.4908	20.3173
Morocco (Dirham)	16.3655	16.3605	15.9354	14.2196	13.5629
Myanmar (Burma) (Kyat)	12.1615	12.8474	12.8986	11.9263	11.0485
Nepal (Rupee)	137.3187	132.02	129.13	128.535	125.743
N'nd Antilles (Guilder)	3.4027	3.5895	3.6011	3.3106	3.0628
New Zealand(NZ$)	2.8853	2.7195	2.6436	2.6107	2.657
Nicaragua (Gold Cordoba)	33.5507	37.0597	37.6291	35.8091	33.5155
Nigeria (Naira)	242.9804	251.46	246.92	219.909	214.921
Norway (Krone)	11.9303	11.7296	11.3122	10.3359	10.1688
Oman (Rial Omani)	0.7293	0.7702	0.7726	0.7129	0.661
Pakistan (Rupee)	114.5979	121.51	122.81	129.686	127.419
Papua New Guinea (Kina)	5.6454	5.8123	5.7172	4.8787	4.5214
Paraguay (Guarani)	10,251.0069	10,055.95	9,823.32	8,020.51	7,557.59
Peru (New Sol)	6.1252	6.2554	6.1231	5.3906	5.1117
Philippines (Peso)	95.5121	92.1586	88.695	81.9749	78.9259
Poland (Zloty)	5.7668	5.4989	5.2082	4.3869	4.5008
Qatar (Riyal)	6.8958	7.2833	7.3053	6.7405	6.2508
Romania (Leu)	5.1239	4.8646	4.8313	4.6269	4.5851
Russia (Rouble-Market)	50.6508	51.1028	50.1627	45.8837	46.5529
Rwanda (R Franc)	1,042.4532	1,096.84	1,098.52	1,011.52	944.62
Saudi Arabia (Riyal)	7.1037	7.4983	7.5217	6.9462	6.4408
Seychelles (Rupee)	10.8403	13.6354	14.6353	17.1243	19.1079
Sierra Leone (Leone)	5,631.4166	5,972.91	5,987.38	5,518.12	5,152.67
Singapore (S$)	2.966	3.0131	2.9616	2.613	2.4609
Slovakia (Koruna) to 31.12.08		49.234	47.1771	39.0363	37.7155
Euro from 1.1.09					(1.4.08 to 31.12.08)
Solomon Islands (SI$)	13.9149	14.509	14.6865	14.1409	13.2045
Somali Republic (Shilling)	2,599.6275	2,745.39	2,270.69	2,594.15	2,388.10
South Africa (Rand)	13.341	14.1085	14.3067	15.1357	14.8671
Sri Lanka (Rupee)	200.1501	221.39	221.61	200.476	188.497
Sudan (Dinar to 30.6.07, £ thereafter)	397.5664		397.5664		
1.1.07 to 30.6.07		397.24			
1.7.07 to 31.12.07		4.1168			
1.4.07 to 30.6.07			400.6417		
1.7.07 to 31.3.08			4.0913		
1.1.08 to 31.12.08				3.8614	
1.4.08 to 31.3.09					3.6671
Surinam (Dollar)	5.218	5.5045	5.5224	5.0768	4.6968

Average for year ending	31.03.07	31.12.07	31.03.08	31.12.08	31.03.09
Swaziland (Lilangeli)	13.4435	14.0461	14.3204	15.1142	14.863
Sweden (Krona)	13.593	13.5236	13.1967	12.0887	12.0213
Switzerland (Franc)	2.3425	2.4010	2.3261	1.9979	1.8833
Syria (Pound)	99.2471	103.71	103.50	92.5003	83.5987
Taiwan (New T$)	61.8966	65.7326	65.258	58.2406	54.854
Tanzania (Shilling)	2,411.6028	2,481.21	2,437.04	2,213.92	2,111.78
Thailand (Baht)	69.3549	68.5207	67.7565	61.599	58.3223
Tonga Islands (Pa'Anga)	3.8224	3.908	3.8389	3.521	3.3988
Trinidad and Tobago (TT$)	11.9098	12.6152	12.6561	11.5893	10.7217
Tunisia (Dinar)	2.4998	2.5590	2.5108	2.2674	2.1824
Turkey (Lira)	2.7546	2.6067	2.5166	2.3965	2.3961
Uganda (New Shilling)	3,440.7299	3,451.92	3,429.98	3,164.28	3,045.77
United Arab Emirates (Dirham)	6.9571	7.3481	7.3712	6.8011	6.3059
Uruguay (Peso Uruguayo)	45.5669	46.9076	45.3662	38.4107	36.5457
USA (US$)	1.8932	2.0020	2.0080	1.8511	1.7138
Venezuela (Bolivar to 31.12.07, Bolivar Fuerte thereafter)	5,747.9573	5,357.25		3.9764	3.6867
1.4.07 to 31.12.07			4,665.73		
1.1.08 to 31.3.08			4.2501		
Vietnam (Dong)	30,455.15	32,241.04	32,340.43	30,510.83	28,859.78
Yemen (Rial)	376.1672	398.84	400.27	368.639	341.543
Zambia (Kwacha)	7,244.9871	7,984.03	7,769.02	6,878.11	6,952.69
Zimbabwe (Dollar)					
1.4.06 to 3.8.06	185,137.83				
4.8.06 to 31.3.07	481.06				
1.1.07 to 5.9.07		496.04			
6.9.07 to 31.12.07		61,053.83			
1.4.07 to 5.9.07			500.60		
6.9.07 to 31.3.08			60,335.72		

Rates of exchange on year-end dates

	30.03.07	31.12.07	31.03.08	31.12.08	31.03.09
Australia ($A)	2.4279	2.2671	2.1773	2.0622	2.0630
Canada (Can$)	2.2627	1.9646	2.0393	1.7749	1.8034
Denmark (Krone)	10.9789	10.1522	9.3536	7.6987	8.0409
European Union (Euro)	1.4735	1.3615	1.2543	1.0344	1.0796
Hong Kong (HK$)	15.3265	15.5215	15.4685	11.1429	11.1085
Japan (Yen)	231.586	222.380	197.826	130.332	141.572
Norway (Krone)	11.9723	10.8087	10.1000	10.0673	9.6781
South Africa (Rand)	14.2247	13.6045	16.1515	13.2920	13.6312
Sweden (Krona)	13.7611	12.8656	11.7858	11.3697	11.8499
Switzerland (Franc)	2.3945	2.2536	1.9658	1.5303	1.6298
USA (US$)	1.9614	1.9906	1.9875	1.4378	1.4334

Note: The material on p 103–105 is reproduced from information provided by HMRC and is Crown copyright.

Double taxation agreements (including protocols and regulations)

Agreements in force covering taxes on income and capital gains

Country	*SI/SR & O*
Antigua & Barbuda	**1947/2865**
	1968/1096
Argentina	**1997/1777**
Armenia[1]	
Australia	**2003/3199**
Austria	**1970/1947**
	1979/117
	1994/768
Azerbaijan	**1995/762**
Bangladesh	**1980/708**
Barbados	**1970/952**
	1973/2096
Belarus[1]	**1986/224**
Belgium	**1987/2053**
Belize	**1947/2866**
	1968/573
	1973/2097
Bolivia	**1995/2707**
Bosnia Herzegovina[2]	**1981/1815**
Botswana	**2006/1925**
Brunei	**1950/1977**
	1968/306
	1973/2098
Bulgaria	**1987/2054**
Canada	**1980/709**
	1980/1528
	1980/1996
	1985/1996
	2003/2619
Chile	**2003/3200**
China[4]	**1984/1826**
	1996/3164
Croatia[2]	**1981/1815**
Cyprus	**1975/425**
	1980/1529
Czech Republic[3]	**1991/2876**
Denmark	**1980/1960**
	1991/2877
	1996/3165
Egypt	**1980/1091**
Estonia	**1994/3207**
Falkland Islands	**1997/2985**
Faroes	**2007/3469**
Fiji	**1976/1342**
Finland	**1970/153**
	1973/1327
	1980/710
	1985/1997
	1991/2878
	1996/3166
France	**2009/226**
Georgia[1]	**2004/3325**
Germany	**1967/25**
	1971/874
Ghana	**1993/1800**
Greece	**1954/142**
Grenada	**1949/361**
	1967/1490
	1968/1867
Guernsey	**1952/1215**
	1994/3209
Guyana	**1992/3207**
Hungary	**1978/1056**
Iceland	**1991/2879**
India	**1993/1801**
Indonesia	**1994/769**
Irish Republic	**1976/2151**
	1976/2152
	1995/764
	1998/3151
Isle of Man	**2009/228**
Israel	**1963/616**
	1971/391
Italy	**1990/2590**
Ivory Coast	**1987/169**
Jamaica	**1973/1329**
Japan	**2006/1924**
Jersey	**1952/1216**
	1994/3210
Jordan	**2001/3924**
Kazakhstan	**1994/3211**
	1998/2567
Kenya	**1977/1299**
Kiribati (and Tuvalu)	**1950/750**
	1968/309
	1974/1271
Korea (South)	**1996/3168**
Kuwait	**1999/2036**
Kyrgyzstan[1]	
Latvia	**1996/3167**
Lesotho	**1997/2986**
Lithuania[1]	**2001/3925**
	2002/2847
Luxembourg	**1968/1100**
	1980/567
	1984/364
Macedonia[2]	**2007/2127**
Malawi	**1956/619**
	1964/1401
	1968/1101

Country	*SI/SR & O*
Gambia	**1980/1963**
Malta	**1995/763**
Mauritius	**1981/1121**
	1987/467
	2003/2620
Mexico	**1994/3212**
Moldova[1]	**2008/1795**
Mongolia	**1996/2598**
Montenegro[2]	**1981/1815**
Montserrat	**1947/2869**
	1968/576
Morocco	**1991/2881**
Myanmar (Burma)	**1952/751**
Namibia	**1962/2352**
Netherlands	**2009/227**
New Zealand	**2008/1793**
Nigeria	**1987/2057**
Norway	**2000/3247**
Oman	**1998/2568**
Pakistan	**1987/2058**
Papua New Guinea	**1991/2882**
Philippines	**1978/184**
Poland	**2006/3323**
Portugal	**1969/599**
Romania	**1977/57**
Russian Federation	**1994/3213**
St Kitts and Nevis	**1947/2872**
Saudi Arabia	**2008/1770**
Serbia[2]	**1981/1815**
Sierra Leone	**1947/2873**
	1968/1104
Singapore	**1997/2988**
Slovak Republic[3]	**1991/2876**
Slovenia[2]	**2008/1796**

Country	*SI/SR & O*
	1979/302
Malaysia	**1997/2987**
Solomon Islands	**1950/748**
	1968/574
	1974/1270
South Africa	**2002/3138**
Spain	1976/1919
	1995/765
Sri Lanka	**1980/713**
Sudan	**1977/1719**
Swaziland	**1969/380**
Sweden	**1984/366**
Switzerland	**2007/3465**
Taiwan	**2002/3137**
Tajikistan[1]	**1986/224**
Thailand	**1981/1546**
Trinidad and Tobago	**1983/1903**
Tunisia	**1984/133**
Turkey	**1988/932**
Turkmenistan[1]	**1986/224**
Tuvalu (and Kiribati)	**1950/750**
	1968/309
	1974/1271
Uganda	**1993/1802**
Ukraine	**1993/1803**
USA	**2002/2848**
Uzbekistan	**1994/770**
Venezuela	**1996/2599**
Vietnam	**1994/3216**
Zambia	**1972/1721**
	1981/1816
Zimbabwe	**1982/1842**

1 Following the dissolution of the USSR, new agreements have come into force with Azerbaijan, Estonia, Kazakhstan, Latvia, Lithuania, Moldova the Russian Federation, Ukraine and Uzbekistan. *SI 1986 No 224* (the former USSR agreement) is treated as continuing to apply to Belarus, Tajikistan and Turkmenistan (in the case of Belarus until the coming into force of *SI 1995 No 2706*). It was similarly so treated by the UK until 31 March 2002 in the case of Armenia, Georgia, Kyrgyzstan and Lithuania (none of which considered itself bound by that convention) but as ceasing so to apply after that date (although new treaties are in force with Lithuania and Georgia). (SP 4/01.)

2 *SI 1981 No 1815* (the former Yugoslavia agreement) is treated as remaining in force between the UK and, respectively, Bosnia-Herzegovina, Croatia and Serbia and Montenegro. (SP 3/2004.) Negotiations for a new double taxation convention are taking place with Croatia, Serbia and Montenegro and Slovenia (Revenue Press Release, 29 September 2004).

3 *SI 1991 No 2876* (the former Czechoslovakia agreement) is treated as remaining in force between the UK and, respectively, the Czech Republic and the Slovak Republic. (SP 5/93.)

4 *SI 1984 No 1826* does not apply to the Hong Kong Special Administrative Region.

Agreements in force covering shipping and air transport profits

Country	*SI/SR & O*	*Country*	*SI/SR & O*
Algeria (air)	**1984/362**	Iran (air)	**1960/2419**
Armenia (USSR air)*	**1974/1269**	Kyrgyzstan (USSR air)*	**1974/1269**
Belarus (USSR air)*	**1974/1269**	Lebanon	**1964/278**
Brazil	**1968/572**	Moldova (USSR air)*	**1974/1269**
Cameroon (air)	**1982/1841**	Saudi Arabia (air)	**1994/767**
China (air)	**1981/1119**	Tajikistan (USSR air)*	**1974/1269**
Congo Democratic Republic	**1977/1298**	Turkmenistan (USSR air)*	**1974/1269**
Ethiopia (air)	**1977/1297**		
Georgia (USSR air)*	**1974/1269**		
Hong Kong (air)	**1998/2566**		
(shipping)	**2000/3248**		

* HMRC have confirmed that this Arrangement will be treated in the same way as the Convention covering income and capital gains (SI 1986/224). See note 1 above.

Agreements in force covering estates, inheritances and gifts

France*	**1963/1319**	Pakistan*	**1957/1522**
India*	**1956/998**	South Africa	**1979/576**
Ireland	**1978/1107**	Sweden	**1981/840**
Italy*	**1968/304**		1989/986
Netherlands	**1980/706**	Switzerland	**1994/3214**
	1996/730	USA	**1979/1454**

* Agreements pre-date UK inheritance tax/capital transfer tax.

Overseas income – basis of assessment

	Professions, trades, etc	Pensions	Other income
Non-residents	Exempt	Exempt	Exempt
Residents			
(1) **Foreign domicile**	Remittance	Remittance	Remittance
(2) **UK domicile**			
(*a*) Non Commonwealth citizen[1]	Arising	90%[3] arising	Arising
(*b*) Commonwealth citizen[2]			
(i) ordinarily resident	Arising	90%[4] arising	Arising
(ii) not ordinarily resident	Remittance	Remittance	Remittance

1 But not citizen of the Republic of Ireland.
2 Or citizen of the Republic of Ireland.
3 Pensions paid by the governments of the Federal Republic of Germany or of Austria to victims of Nazi persecution are exempt.
4 Where from 6 April 2008, an individual with a domicile outside the UK who has overseas income or gains in excess of £2,000 claims the remittance basis, he will not qualify for personal allowances or the capital gains tax annual exemption. The claim for remittance basis must be made annually. If the individual is not UK domiciled or ordinarily resident in a year and has been resident in the UK for seven out of the last nine years and has overseas income or gains in excess of £2,000, there is an additional charge of £30,000.

Employment income liability of non-resident employees see p 78.

Tax-free (FOTRA) securities

Interest on all government stock is exempt from tax where the beneficial owner is not ordinarily resident in the UK (FA 1996 s 154; FA 1998 s 161; ITTOIA 2005 ss 713, 714). Except in the case of 3½% War Loan 1952 or after, the exemption does not apply where the securities are held for the purposes of a trade or business carried on in the UK.

Social security benefits

Taxable state benefits

	Weekly 12.4.10	Total 2010–11 (52 weeks)	Weekly 6.4.09	Total 2009–10 (52 weeks)
	£	£	£	£
Bereavement benefits[1]				
Standard rate (widow's pension)	**97.65**	**5,077**	95.25	4,953
Widowed parent's allowance	**97.65**	**5,077**	95.25	4,953
Carer's allowance	**53.90**	**2,802**	53.10	2,761
– Adult dependency increase	**31.70**	**1,648**	31.70	1,648
Employment and support allowance[6]				
–under 25	**51.85**	**–**	50.95	–
–25 or over	**65.45**	**–**	64.30	–
Incapacity benefit[6]				
Long-term (after 52 weeks)	**91.40**	**4,752**	89.80	4,669
– Adult dependency increase	**53.10**	**2,761**	53.10	2,761
– Age increase: higher rate	**15.00**	**780**	15.65	814
lower rate	**5.80**	**301**	6.55	340
Short term				
– Under pension age: higher rate	**81.60**	**–**	80.15	–
– Adult dependency increase	**41.35**	**–**	41.35	–
– Over pension age: higher rate	**91.40**	**–**	89.80	–
– Adult dependency increase	**51.10**	**–**	51.10	–
Industrial death benefit[2]				
Widow's pension: higher rate	**97.65**	**5,077**	95.25	4,953
lower rate	**29.30**	**1,523**	28.58	1,486
Widower's pension	**97.65**	**5,077**	95.25	4,953
Invalidity allowance[3]				
Higher rate	**15.00**	**780**	15.65	814
Middle rate	**8.40**	**436**	9.10	473
Lower rate	**5.45**	**283**	5.35	278
Jobseeker's allowance[4]				
Single: under 25	**51.85**	**–**	50.95	–
25 or over	**65.45**	**–**	64.30	–
State pension				
Single person (Category A or B)	**97.65**	**5,077**	95.25	4,953
Adult dependency increase	**57.05**	**2,966**	57.05	2,966
Non-contributory pension				
– single (Category C or D)	**58.50**	**3,042**	57.05	2,966
Age addition (over 80) (each)	**0.25**	**13**	0.25	13
Statutory adoption pay				
Rate[5]	**124.88**	**–**	123.06	–
Earnings threshold	**97.00**	**–**	95.00	–
Statutory maternity pay				
Rate[5]	**124.88**	**–**	123.06	–
Earnings threshold	**97.00**	**–**	95.00	–
Statutory paternity pay				
Rate[5]	**124.88**	**–**	123.06	–
Earnings threshold	**97.00**	**–**	95.00	–
Statutory sick pay				
Rate	**79.15**	**–**	79.15	–
Earnings threshold	**97.00**	**–**	95.00	–

1 Paid to widows and widowers for up to 52 weeks.
2 For deaths before 11 April 1988 only.
3 When paid with retirement pensions. See note below on non-taxable benefits on p 111.
4 Where the allowance exceeds the amount shown above, the excess is not taxable.
5 The allowance is 90% of average weekly earnings if less than the above amount. In the first six weeks the rate of SMP is 90% of average weekly earnings even if higher than the standard rate.
6 Employment and support allowance replaces incapacity benefits for new claimants on or after 27 October 2008. Only contributory employment and support allowance is taxable. Income related allowance is not taxable.

Non-taxable state benefits

Weekly rates from			*12.4.10*	*6.4.09*
			£	**£**
Attendance allowance				
Higher rate (day and night)			**71.40**	70.35
Lower rate (day or night)			**47.80**	47.10
Child benefit				
Eldest child			**20.30**	20.00
Each subsequent child			**13.40**	13.20
Child dependency addition				
Paid with retirement pension, bereavement benefit, carer's allowance, incapacity benefit, higher rate industrial death benefit			**11.35**	11.35
Disability living allowance				
Care component	higher rate		**71.40**	70.35
	middle rate		**47.80**	47.10
	lower rate		**18.95**	18.65
Mobility component	higher rate		**49.85**	49.10
	lower rate		**18.95**	18.65
Guardian's allowance			**14.30**	14.10
Incapacity benefit (short-term)*				
Under pension age – lower rate (first 28 weeks)			**68.95**	67.75
– Adult dependency increase			**41.35**	41.35
Over pension age – lower rate (first 28 weeks)			**87.75**	86.20
– Adult dependency increase			**51.10**	51.10
Maternity allowance (where SMP not available)				
Standard rate			**124.88**	123.06
MA threshold			**30.00**	30.00
– Adult dependency increase			**41.35**	41.35
Severe disablement allowance				
Basic rate			**59.45**	57.45
Age-related addition		higher rate	**15.00**	15.65
		middle rate	**8.40**	9.10
		lower rate	**5.45**	5.35
– Adult dependency increase			**31.90**	31.90

* Incapacity benefit replaced invalidity allowance from April 1995. The benefits are taxable except those paid in the first 28 weeks of incapacity and those paid to persons already receiving invalidity benefit on 13 April 1995 so long as they remain incapable of work.

Other non-taxable benefits include:

- Bereavement payment (lump sum £2,000)
- Child tax credit (see Tax Credits, p 90)
- Christmas bonus (with retirement pension)
- Cold weather payments
- Council tax benefit (income related)
- Earnings top-up
- Housing benefit (income related)
- Income support (income related)
- Industrial death benefit
- Industrial injuries disablement pension
- Jobfinder's grant
- Pension credit
- Pneumoconiosis, byssinosis and miscellaneous disease benefits
- Redundancy payment
- Social fund payments
- Television licence payment
- Vaccine damage (lump sum)
- War pensions
- Winter fuel payment (£200 plus £100 for those aged over 80)
- Working tax credit (see Tax Credits, p 90)

Stamp taxes

Stamp duty land tax

Stamp duty land tax applies to contracts entered into (or varied) after 10.7.03 and completed after 30.11.03 and to leases granted after that date. With effect from 22.7.04, it also applies to the transfer of an interest in land into, or out of, a partnership and to the acquisition of an interest in a partnership where the partnership property includes an interest in land. With effect from 19.7.06, it applies to transfers of partnership interests only where the sole or main activity of the partnership is investing or dealing in interests in land.

Land transactions	*Consideration*[1]		
Effective date	*Residential property*	*Non-residential or mixed property*	*Rate*
From 1.1.10	**Up to £125,000**	**Up to £150,000**	**Nil**
	£125,001–£250,000[2]	**£150,001–£250,000**	**1%**
	£250,001–£500,000	**£150,001–£250,000**	**3%**
	£500,001 or more[3]	**£500,001 or more**	**4%**
3.9.08–31.12.09	Up to £175,000	Up to £150,000	Nil
	£175,001–£250,000	£150,001–£250,000	1%
	£250,001–£500,000	£150,001–£250,000	3%
	£500,001 or more	£500,001 or more	4%
23.3.06–2.9.08	Up to £125,000	Up to £150,000	Nil
	£125,001–£250,000	£150,001–£250,000	1%
	£250,001–£500,000	£250,001–£500,000	3%
	£500,001 or more	£500,001 or more	4%
17.3.05–22.3.06	Up to £120,000	Up to £150,000	Nil
	£120,001–£250,000	£150,001–£250,000	1%
	£250,001–£500,000	£250,001–£500,000	3%
	£500,001 or more	£500,001 or more	4%
1.12.03–16.3.05	Up to £60,000	Up to £150,000	Nil
	£60,001–£250,000	£150,001–£250,000	1%
	£250,001–£500,000	£250,001–£500,000	3%
	£500,001 or more	£500,001 or more	4%
Lease rentals	*On net present value of rent over term of lease (applying a discount rate of 3.5%)*[4]		
Effective date	*Residential property*	*Non-residential or mixed property*	*Rate*
1.1.10	Up to £125,000	Up to £150,000	**Nil**
	£125,001 or more	£150,001 or more	**1%**
3.9.08–31.12.09	Up to £175,000	Up to £150,000	Nil
	£175,001 or more	£150,001 or more	1%
23.3.06–2.9.08	Up to £125,000	Up to £150,000	Nil
	£125,001 or more	£150,001 or more	1%
17.3.05–22.3.06	Up to £120,000	Up to £150,000	Nil
	£120,001 or more	£150,001 or more	1%
1.12.03–16.3.05	Up to £60,000	Up to £150,000	Nil
	£60,001 or more	£150,001 or more	1%

Premiums
The same tax is payable for a premium granted as for a land transaction. Special rules apply to a premium in respect of non-residential property where the rent exceeds £1,000 a year. For transactions before 12 March 2008, the rules applied to all property where the rent exceeded £600 a year.

1 Rates apply to the full consideration, not only to that in excess of the previous band.
2 For residential property, purchases by first-time buyers between 25 March 2010 and 24 March 2012 inclusive attract a nil rate of SDLT for purchase consideration up to £250,000.
3 A new 5% band for residential property only is to be introduced for purchases after 5 April 2011 where the purchase consideration exceeds £1 million.
4 Rates apply to the amount of npv in the slice, not the whole value.

Exemptions and reliefs

No SDLT (or stamp duty) is chargeable on:

(1) transfers to charities for use for charitable purposes.
(2) transfers to bodies established for national purposes.
(3) gifts inter vivos.
(4) land transfers within groups of companies.
(5) land transferred in exchange for shares on company reconstruction and acquisitions.
(6) transfers of intellectual property.
(7) certain transfers to registered social landlords (registered providers of social housing from Royal Assent to Finance Bill 2009).
(8) certain leases granted by registered social landlords.
(9) transfers of goodwill (after 21.4.02).
(10) sale and leaseback arrangements involving commercial property (after 30.11.03) (extended with effect from 22.7.04 to residential property and lease and leaseback transactions).
(11) certain acquisitions of residential property by house building companies or property traders when people move into a new dwelling or a chain of transactions break down, or by employers involving employee relocations (after 31.11.03) (extended with effect from 22.7.04 for people buying a new home and unable to move into it immediately).
(12) (after 30.11.03 and before 22.3.06) initial acquisition of assets by trustees of a unit trust scheme.
(13) transfers of property to beneficiaries under a will or an intestacy (after 30.11.03).
(14) certain transfers on divorce.
(15) transfers on sale of residential property for a consideration of up to £150,000 in disadvantaged parts of the UK. This also applies to leases broadly, where the relevant rental value does not exceed £150,000 and to premiums unless the annual rent exceeds £600.
(16) from 1.10.06 until 30.9.12 for new zero carbon homes and from 1.10.07 for new zero carbon flats with a purchase price of up to £500,000, there is no SDLT charged. Where the purchase price is in excess of £500,000, the SDLT liability on the purchase price will be reduced by £15,000.

Stamp duty

For contracts entered into (or varied) after 10 July 2003 and completed after 30 November 2003 and for leases granted after that date, stamp duty is abolished for all transfers other than stocks and marketable securities, and interests in partnerships. From 22 July 2004 stamp duty is also abolished for certain partnership transactions involving an interest in land. From those dates, transfers of land are subject to stamp duty land tax (see p 113).

Transfers of stock and marketable securities		***0.5%***
For instruments executed on or after 12 March 2008, stamp duty is not chargeable where the amount or value of the consideration is less than £1,000.		
Other transfers *(including land transactions before the introduction of SDLT)*		
	16.3.99–27.3.00	28.3.00–30.11.03
On transfer made pursuant to contract after	9.3.99	21.3.00
Conveyance or transfer on sale with certificate of value[1]		
Not exceeding £60,000	Nil	Nil
£60,001–£250,000	1.0%	1%
£250,001–£500,000	2.5%	3%
£500,001 or more	3.5%	4%
Conveyance or transfer on sale without certificate of value	3·5%	4%
Lease premiums The same duty is payable for a premium granted as for a conveyance or transfer on sale (except that special rules apply to a premium where the rent exceeds £600 a year). For instruments executed on or after 12 March 2008, stamp duty is not chargeable where the amount or value of the consideration is less than £1,000.		
Lease rentals (before the introduction of SDLT)		
Furnished residential accommodation for definite term of less than one year at rent in excess of £5,000	£5	
Leases not exceeding seven years, or for an indefinite term:		
– Up to £5,000 (£500 before 28.3.00) pa	Nil	
– Over £5,000 (£500 before 28.3.00) pa	1%	
Leases over seven years and up to 35 years	2%	
Leases over 35 years and up to 100 years	12%	
Leases over 100 years	24%	

[1] These rates apply to the full consideration, not only to that in excess of the previous band.

Rounding

Stamp duty is rounded up to the next multiple of £5 in all cases other than for SDRT.

Fixed duties (before the introduction of SDLT)

Leases other than above	£5
Declaration of trust; duplicate or counterpart; exchange or partition; release or renunciation; surrender	£5

Stamp Duty Reserve Tax (SDRT)

Agreements to transfer chargeable securities for money or money's worth (eg renounceable letters of allotment)[1]	0.5%
Chargeable securities put into a clearance service[2] or converted into depositary receipts	1.5%
Dealings of units in unit trusts and shares in open-ended investment companies[3]	0.5%
Transfers of foreign currency bearer shares and agreements to transfer sterling or foreign currency convertible or equity-related loan stock issued by UK companies	0.5%

1 If the transaction is completed by a duly stamped instrument within six years from the date on which the charge is imposed, the SDRT will be cancelled or repaid.

2 Where the operator of a clearance service elects to collect and account for SDRT on the normal rate of 0.5% on dealing within the system the higher SDRT charge of 1.5% does not apply.

3 From 6 April 2001 transfers of units in a unit trust and surrenders of shares in open-ended investment trusts are exempt when held within individual pension accounts.

Interest on unpaid tax

Stamp duty land tax. *From 26 September 2005*: Interest runs from the end of 30 days after the effective date of transaction (normally completion), or the date of a disqualifying event, until the tax is paid. In the case of a deferred payment, interest runs from the date the payment is due until the tax is paid. A penalty carries interest from the date determined until the date of payment.

Stamp duty. *For instruments executed from 1 October 1999*: Interest runs from the end of 30 days after the date the instrument is executed until the tax is paid. Amounts less than £25 are not charged.

Stamp duty reserve tax. Interest is charged from 14 days after the transaction date for exchange transactions and otherwise from seven days after the end of the month of the transaction. Amounts less than £25 are not charged.

Rates: see p 5.

Repayment supplement

Stamp duty land tax. *From 26 September 2005*: Interest is added to repayments of overpaid stamp duty land tax and runs from the date tax was paid or an amount was lodged with HMRC, or the date a penalty was made, to the date the order for repayment is issued.

Stamp duty. *For instruments executed from 1 October 1999*: Interest is added to repayments of overpaid stamp duty and runs from 30 days after the date the instrument is executed or the date of payment if later. Amounts less than £25 are not paid.

Stamp duty reserve tax. Interest is paid from 14 days after the transaction date for exchange transactions and otherwise from seven days after the end of the month of the transaction.

Rates: see p 8.

Penalties

Offence	*Penalty*
For liabilities to stamp duty land tax arising after 31 March 2010, returns or information provided by the taxpayer or a third party and containing a careless or deliberate inaccuracy, (FA 2007, Sch 24).	An amount arrived at by applying a percentage to the potential lost revenue — up to 30% for a careless error, up to 70% for a deliberate but unconcealed error and up to 100% for a deliberate and concealed error
Stamp duty – for instruments executed from 1 October 1999	
Failure to present instrument for stamping within 30 days after execution (or the day in which it is first received in the UK if executed outside the UK) (Stamp Act 1891 s 15B; SI 1999/2537). (Extended to instruments executed from 24 July 2002 for transfers of UK land and buildings, wherever executed (FA 2002 s 114).)	If presented within one year after the end of the 30-day period: the lower of £300 or the amount of the unpaid duty. If presented more than one year after the end of the 30-day period: the greater of £300 or the amount of unpaid duty.
Stamp duty land tax – contracts completed after 30 November 2003	
Failure to deliver a land transaction return by the filing date (FA 2003 Sch 10 paras 3, 4).	£100 if return delivered within three months of filing date, otherwise £200. If not delivered within 12 months, penalty up to amount of tax chargeable.
Failure to comply with notice to deliver return within specified period (FA 2003 Sch 10 para 5).	Up to £60 for each day on which the failure continues after notification.
Fraudulently or negligently delivering an incorrect return or failing to remedy an error without unreasonable delay (FA 2003 Sch 10 para 8).	Up to the difference between the amount payable and the amount that would have been chargeable on the basis of the return delivered. Repealed and replaced by penalty under FA 2007, Sch 24 above after 31 March 2010.
Fraudulently or negligently giving a self-certificate for a chargeable transaction or failing to remedy an error in respect of such certificate without unreasonable delay (FA 2003 Sch 11 para 3).	Up to the amount of tax chargeable.
Failure to keep and preserve records under FA 2003 Sch 10 para 9 or Sch 11 para 4 (FA 2003 Sch 10 para 11, Sch 11 para 6).	Up to £3,000 unless the information is provided by other documentary evidence.
Failure to comply with notice to produce documents etc under FA 2003 Sch 10 para 14 or Sch 11 para 9 (FA 2003 Sch 10 para 16, Sch 11 para 11).	(*a*) Initial penalty of £50; (*b*) further penalty for each day the failure continues up to £30 if penalty determined by HMRC, or £150 if determined by the court.
Failure (From 1 August 2005) to disclose certain SDLT proposals or arrangements (SI 2008/1868; SI 2008/1869).	(*a*) Initial penalty up to £5,000; (*b*) further penalty up to £600 per day while failure continues.

Value added tax

Rates

	From 1.1.10		1.12.2008– 31.12.09		Pre 1.12.08	
	Rate	VAT Fraction	Rate	VAT Fraction	Rate	VAT fraction
Standard rate	17.5%	7/47	15.0%	3/23	17.5%	7/47
Reduced rate (see p 118)	5.0%	1/21	5.0%	1/21	5.0%	1/21
Flat-rate scheme for farmers	4.0%*		4.0%*		4.0%*	

* Flat rate addition to sale price

Registration limits

UK taxable supplies

A person who makes taxable supplies is liable to be registered:
(a) at the end of any month, or
(b) at any time, if:

	(a) turnover in the past year[1] *(b) turnover in the next 30 days*[2] *exceeds:*	*Unless, in the case of (a), turnover for next year not expected to exceed:*
1.4.10 onwards	**£70,000**	**£68,000**
1.5.09–31.3.10	£68,000	£66,000
1.4.08–30.4.09	£67,000	£65,000
1.4.07–31.3.08	£64,000	£62,000
1.4.06–31.3.07	£61,000	£59,000
1.4.05–31.3.06	£60,000	£58,000
1.4.04–31.3.05	£58,000	£56,000

1 The value of taxable supplies in the year then ending.
2 If there are reasonable grounds for believing the value of taxable supplies will exceed limit.

Supplies from other EC countries ('distance selling')

A business person in another EC country not registered or liable to be registered in the UK is liable to be registered on any day if, in the period beginning with 1 January in that year, the value of supplies by that person to non-taxable persons in the UK exceeds:

1.1.93 onwards	**£70,000**

Acquisitions from other EC countries

A person not registered or liable to be registered under the above rules is liable to be registered:

(a) at the end of any month if, in the period beginning with 1 January in that year, the value of taxable goods acquired by that person for business purposes (or for non-business purposes if a public body, charity, club, etc) from suppliers in other EC countries exceeds the following limits; or

(b) at any time, if there are reasonable grounds for believing the value of such acquisitions in the next 30 days will exceed the following limits:

1.4.10 onwards	**£70,000**
1.5.09–31.3.10	£68,000
1.4.08–30.4.09	£67,000
1.4.07–31.3.08	£64,000
1.4.06–31.3.07	£61,000
1.4.05–31.3.06	£60,000
1.4.04–31.3.05	£58,000
10.4.03–31.3.04	£56,000

Deregistration limits

UK taxable supplies

A registered taxable person ceases to be liable to be registered if, at any time, HMRC are satisfied that the value of taxable supplies in the year then beginning will not exceed:

1.4.10 onwards	**£68,000**
1.5.09–31.3.10	£66,000
1.4.08–30.4.09	£65,000
1.4.07–31.3.08	£62,000
1.4.06–31.3.07	£59,000
1.4.05–31.3.06	£58,000
1.4.04–31.3.05	£56,000
10.4.03–31.3.04	£54,000
25.4.02–9.4.03	£53,000
Unless the reason for not exceeding the limit during that year is that the person will cease making taxable supplies or suspend making taxable supplies for 30 days or more.	

Supplies from other EC countries ('distance selling')

A person registered under these provisions ceases to be liable to be registered if, at any time:

(a) relevant supplies in year ended 31 December last before that time did not exceed following limit; and

(b) HMRC are satisfied that value of relevant supplies in year immediately following that year will not exceed following limit:

1.1.93 onwards	**£70,000**

Acquisitions from other EC countries

A person registered under these provisions ceases to be liable to be registered if, at any time:

(a) relevant acquisitions in year ended 31 December last before that time did not exceed following limits; and

(b) HMRC are satisfied that value of relevant acquisitions in year immediately following that year will not exceed following limits:

1.4.10 onwards	**£70,000**
1.5.09–31.3.10	£68,000
1.4.08–30.4.08	£67,000
1.4.07–31.3.08	£64,000
1.4.06–31.3.07	£61,000
1.4.05–31.3.06	£60,000
1.4.04–31.3.05	£58,000
10.4.03–31.3.04	£56,000
25.4.02–9.4.03	£55,000
1.4.01–24.4.02	£54,000

Annual accounting scheme

A business may, subject to conditions, complete one VAT return a year. Before 1 April 2006, only businesses with taxable turnover up to £150,000 could join the scheme immediately; other businesses had to have been registered for 12 months.

	Can join if taxable supplies in next year not expected to exceed:	*Must leave at end of accounting year if taxable supplies exceeded:*
1.4.06 onwards	**£1,350,000**	**£1,600,000**
1.4.04–31.3.06	£660,000	£825,000
1.4.01–31.3.04	£600,000	£750,000

Cash accounting scheme

A business may, subject to conditions, account for and pay VAT on the basis of cash paid and received. It can join the scheme at any time as follows.

	Can join if taxable supplies in next year not expected to exceed:	*Must leave at end of accounting year if taxable supplies exceed:*	*Unless turnover for next year not expected to exceed:*
1.4.07 onwards	**£1,350,000**	**£1,600,000**	**£1,350,000**
1.4.04–31.3.07	£660,000	£825,000	£660,000
1.4.01–31.3.04	£600,000	£750,000	£600,000

Flat-rate scheme for small businesses

A business which expects its taxable supplies in the next year to be no more than £150,000 and (before 1 April 2009) its total business income to be no more than £187,500 (including VAT) can opt to join a flat-rate scheme. The appropriate percentage below is applied to total turnover generated, including exempt income, to calculate net VAT due.

Category of business	*Appropriate %*		
	after 31.12.09	***1.12.08–31.12.09***	***before 1.12.08***
Accountancy or book-keeping	13	11.5	13
Advertising	10	8.5	9.5
Agricultural services	10	7	7.5
Any other activity not listed elsewhere	10.5	9	10
Architect	13	11	12.5
Boarding or care of animals	10.5	9.5	10.5
Business services that are not listed elsewhere	10.5	9.5	11
Catering services, including restaurants and takeaways	11	10.5	12
Civil and structural engineer or surveyor	13	11	12.5
Computer and IT consultancy or data processing	13	11.5	13
Computer repair services	9.5	10	11
Dealing in waste or scrap	9.5	8.5	9.5
Entertainment or journalism	11	9.5	11
Estate agency and property management services	10.5	9.5	11
Farming or agriculture that is not listed elsewhere	6	5.5	6
Film, radio, television or video production	11.5	9.5	10.5
Financial services	12	10.5	11.5
Forestry or fishing	9.5	8	9
General building or construction services	8.5	7.5	8.5
Hairdressing or other beauty treatment services	11.5	10.5	12
Hiring or renting goods	8.5	7.5	8.5
Hotel or accommodation	9.5	8.5	9.5
Investigation or security	10.5	9	N/A
Labour-only building or construction services[1]	13	11.5	13.5
Laundry or dry-cleaning services	10.5	9.5	11
Lawyer or legal services	13	12	13
Library, archive, museum or other cultural activity	8.5	7.5	7.5
Management consultancy	12.5	11	12.5
Manufacturing fabricated metal products	9.5	8.5	10
Manufacturing food	8	7	7.5
Manufacturing that is not listed elsewhere	8.5	7.5	8.5
Manufacturing yarn, textiles or clothing	8	7.5	8.5
Membership organisation	7	5.5	5.5
Mining or quarrying	9	8	9
Packaging	8	7.5	8.5
Photography	10	8.5	9.5
Post Offices	4.5	2	2
Postal and courier services		N/A	5.5
Printing	7.5	6.5	7.5
Publishing	10	8.5	9.5
Pubs	6	5.5	5.5

Category of business	*Appropriate %*		
	after 31.12.09	***1.12.08–31.12.09***	***before 1.12.08***
Real estate activity not listed elsewhere	12.5	11	12
Repairing personal or household goods	9	7.5	8.5
Repairing vehicles	7.5	6.5	7.5
Retailing food, confectionery, tobacco, newspapers or children's clothing	3.5	2	2
Retailing pharmaceuticals, medical goods, cosmetics or toiletries	7	6	7
Retailing that is not listed elsewhere	6.5	5.5	6
Retailing vehicles or fuel	6	5.5	7
Secretarial services	11.5	9.5	11
Social work	10	8	8.5
Sport or recreation	7.5	6	7
Transport or storage, couriers, freight, removals and taxis	9	8	9
Travel agency	9.5	8	9
Veterinary medicine	10	8	9.5
Wholesaling agricultural products	7	5.5	6
Wholesaling food	6.5	5	5.5
Wholesaling that is not listed elsewhere	7.5	6	7

1 That is, services where value of materials supplied is less than 10% of turnover of such services; any other services are 'general building or construction services'.

Partial exemption

A registered person who makes taxable and exempt supplies is partly exempt and may not be able to deduct (or reclaim) all his input tax. Where, however, input tax attributable to exempt supplies in a prescribed accounting period or tax year is within the de minimis limits below, all such input tax is attributable to taxable supplies and recoverable (subject to the normal rules).

De minimis limits	£625 per month on average and 50% of all input tax for the period concerned

Capital goods scheme

Input tax adjustment following change in taxable use of capital goods

Item	*Value*	*Adjustment period*
Computer equipment	£50,000 or more	Five years
Land and buildings	£250,000 or more	Ten years (five years where interest had less than ten years to run on acquisition)

Adjustment formula

The adjustment percentage is the percentage change in the extent to which the item is used (or treated as used) in making taxable supplies between the first interval in the adjustment period and a subsequent interval. (The first interval generally ends on the last day of the tax year in which the input tax was incurred.)

Zero-rated supplies

A zero-rated supply is a taxable supply, but the rate of tax is nil (VATA 1994 Sch 8).

Group 1 – Food
Group 2 – Sewerage services and water
Group 3 – Books etc
Group 4 – Talking books for the blind and handicapped and wireless sets for the blind
Group 5 – Construction of buildings etc
Group 6 – Protected buildings
Group 7 – International services
Group 8 – Transport
Group 9 – Caravans and houseboats
Group 10 – Gold
Group 11 – Bank notes
Group 12 – Drugs, medicines, aids for the handicapped etc
Group 13 – Imports, exports etc
Group 15 – Charities etc
Group 16 – Clothing and footwear

Reduced rate supplies

(VATA 1994 Sch 7A, SI 2007 No 1601)

Group 1 – Domestic fuel and power
Group 2 – Installation of energy-saving materials
Group 3 – Grant-funded installation of heating equipment or security goods or connection of a gas supply
Group 4 – Women's sanitary products
Group 5 – Children's car seats and bases
Group 6 – Residential conversions
Group 7 – Residential renovations and alterations
Group 8 – Contraceptive products (from 1 July 2006)
Group 9 – Welfare advice or information (from 1 July 2006)
Group 10 – Installation of mobility aids for the elderly (from 1 July 2007)
Group 11 – Smoking cessation products (from 1 July 2007)

Exempt supplies

(VATA 1994 Sch 9)

Group 1 – Land
Group 2 – Insurance
Group 3 – Postal services
Group 4 – Betting, gaming and lotteries
Group 5 – Finance
Group 6 – Education
Group 7 – Health and welfare
Group 8 – Burial and cremation
Group 9 – Subscriptions to trade unions, professional and other public interest bodies
Group 10 – Sport, sports competitions and physical education
Group 11 – Works of art etc
Group 12 – Fund-raising events by charities and other qualifying bodies
Group 13 – Cultural services etc
Group 14 – Supplies of goods where input tax cannot be recovered
Group 15 – Investment gold

Car fuel

VAT-inclusive scale figures are used to assess VAT due on petrol provided at below cost price for private journeys by registered traders or their employees, where the petrol has been provided from business resources. The figures represent the tax-inclusive value of the fuel supplied to each individual and relate to return periods beginning on the dates shown.

	12 months £	*3 months* £	*1 month* £
From 1 May 2010: CO_2 band			
120 or below	570	141	47
125	850	212	70
130	850	212	70
135	910	227	75
140	965	241	80
145	1,020	255	85
150	1,080	269	89
155	1,135	283	94
160	1,190	297	99
165	1,250	312	104
170	1,305	326	108
175	1,360	340	113
180	1,420	354	118
185	1,475	368	122
190	1,530	383	127
195	1,590	397	132
200	1,645	411	137
205	1,705	425	141
210	1,760	439	146
215	1,815	454	151
220	1,875	468	156
225	1,930	482	160
230 or above	1,985	496	165

	12 months £	3 months £	1 month £
1 May 2009 to 30 April 2010: CO_2 band			
120 or below	505	126	42
125	755	189	63
130	755	189	63
135	755	189	63
140	805	201	67
145	855	214	71
150	905	226	75
155	960	239	79
160	1,010	251	83
165	1,060	264	88
170	1,110	276	92
175	1,160	289	96
180	1,210	302	100
185	1,260	314	104
190	1,310	327	109
195	1,360	339	113
200	1,410	352	117
205	1,465	365	121
210	1,515	378	126
215	1,565	390	130
220	1,615	403	134
225	1,665	416	138
230	1,715	428	142
235 or above	1,765	441	147

	12 months £	3 months £	1 month £
1 May 2008–30 April 2009: CO_2 band			
120 or below	555	138	46
125	830	207	69
130	830	207	69
135	830	207	69
140	885	221	73
145	940	234	78
150	995	248	82
155	1,050	262	87
160	1,105	276	92
165	1,160	290	96
170	1,215	303	101
175	1,270	317	105
180	1,325	331	110
185	1,380	345	115
190	1,435	359	119
195	1,490	373	124
200	1,545	386	128
205	1,605	400	133
210	1,660	414	138
215	1,715	428	142
220	1,770	442	147
225	1,825	455	151
230	1,880	469	156
235 or above	1,935	483	161

	12 months £	3 months £	1 month £
1 May 2007–30 April 2008: CO_2 band			
140 or below	730	182	60
145	780	195	65
150	830	207	69
155	880	219	73
160	925	231	77
165	975	243	81
170	1,025	256	85
175	1,075	268	89
180	1,120	280	93
185	1,170	292	97
190	1,220	304	101
195	1,270	317	105
200	1,315	329	109
205	1,365	341	113
210	1,415	353	117
215	1,465	365	121
220	1,510	378	126
225	1,560	390	130
230	1,610	402	134
235	1,660	414	138
240 or above	1,705	426	142

	12 months £	VAT due per car £	3 months £	VAT due per car £	1 month £	VAT due per car £
1 May 2006–30 April 2007						
Diesel engine						
2,000cc or less	1,040	154.89	260	38.72	86	12.81
Over 2,000cc	1,325	197.34	331	49.30	110	16.38
Any other type of engine						
1,400cc or less	1,095	163.09	273	40.66	91	13.55
Over 1,400cc up to 2,000cc	1,385	206.28	346	51.53	115	17.13
Over 2,000cc	2,035	303.09	508	75.66	169	25.17
1 May 2005–30 April 2006						
Diesel engine						
2,000cc or less	945	140.74	236	35.15	78	11.62
Over 2,000cc	1,200	178.72	300	44.68	100	14.89
Any other type of engine						
1,400cc or less	985	146.70	246	36.64	82	12.21
Over 1,400cc up to 2,000cc	1,245	185.43	311	46.32	103	15.34
Over 2,000cc	1,830	272.55	457	68.06	152	22.64
1 May 2004–30 April 2005						
Diesel engine						
2,000cc or less	865	128.82	216	32.17	72	10.72
Over 2,000cc	1,095	163.08	273	40.65	91	13.55
Any other type of engine						
1,400cc or less	930	138.51	232	34.55	77	11.46
Over 1,400cc up to 2,000cc	1,175	175.00	293	43.63	97	14.44
Over 2,000cc	1,730	257.65	432	64.34	144	21.44

Interest and penalties

Default interest

(VATA 1994 s 74)

Interest runs on the amount of any VAT assessed (or paid late by voluntary disclosure):

- from the reckonable date (normally the latest date on which a return is required for the period in question);
- until the date of payment (although in practice it runs to the date shown on the notice of assessment or notice of voluntary disclosure if paid within 30 days of that date).

The period of interest cannot commence more than three years before the date of assessment or payment.

The rates of interest are as follows:

Period	*Rate*
From 29 September 2009	**3%**
24 March 2009–28 September 2009	2.5%
27 January 2009–23 March 2009	3.5%
6 January 2008–26 January 2009	4.5%
6 December 2008–5 January 2009	5.5%
6 November 2008–5 December 2008	6.5%
6 January 2008–5 November 2008	7.5%
6 August 2007–5 January 2008	8.5%
6 September 2006–5 August 2007	7.5%
6 September 2005–5 September 2006	6.5%
6 September 2004–5 September 2005	7.5%
6 December 2003–5 September 2004	6.5%
6 August 2003–5 December 2003	5.5%

Interest on VAT overpaid in cases of official error

(VATA 1994 s 78)

Where VAT has been overpaid or underclaimed due to an error by HMRC, then on a claim HMRC must pay interest:

- from the date they receive payment (or authorise a repayment) for the return period in question;
- until the date on which they authorise payment of the amount on which interest is due.

This provision does not require HMRC to pay interest on an amount on which repayment supplement is due.

The rates of interest are as follows:

Period	*Rate*
from 29 September 2009	**0.5%**
27 January 2009–28 September 2009	0%
6 January 2009–26 January 2009	1%
6 December 2008–5 January 2009	2%
6 November 2008–5 December 2008	3%
6 January 2008–5 November 2008	4%
6 August 2007–5 January 2008	5%
6 September 2006–5 August 2007	4%
6 September 2005–5 September 2006	3%
6 September 2004–5 September 2005	4%
6 December 2003–5 September 2004	3%
6 August 2003–5 December 2003	2%*
6 November 2001–5 August 2003	3%

* Due to an administrative error the rate of default and statutory interest was too high by one percentage point between 6 August 2003 and 5 September 2003. HMRC will not seek to recover amounts overpaid by HMRC and will seek to identify businesses overcharged (see Business Brief 17/05 as of 9 September 2005).

Repayment supplement – VAT

(VATA 1994 s 79)

Where a person is entitled to a repayment the payment due is increased by a supplement of the greater of:

(i) 5% of that amount; or

(ii) £50.

The supplement will only be paid if:

(a) the return or claim is received by HMRC not later than the last day on which it is required to be made;

(b) HMRC do not issue a written instruction making the refund within the relevant period; and

(c) the amount shown on the return or claim does not exceed the amount due by more than 5% of that amount or £250, whichever is the greater.

The 'relevant period' is 30 days beginning with the receipt of the return or claim or, if later, the day after the last day of the VAT period to which the return or claim relates.

Penalties and surcharges

Offence	*Penalty*
Delivery of return containing a careless or deliberate error (FA 2007, s 97, Sch 24) for period beginning on or after 1 April 2008 and ending on or after 1 April 2009.	An amount arrived at by applying a percentage to the potential lost revenue — 30% for a careless error, 70% for a deliberate but unconcealed error and 100% for a deliberate and concealed error. Reductions may be made for unprompted disclosure, down to nil, 20% and 30% respectively and for unprompted disclosure down to and 15%, 35% and 50% for a prompted disclosure.
Failure to notify obligation to register for VAT or change in supplies made by person exempted from registration (FA 2008, s 123, Sch 41) on or after 1 April 2010.	An amount arrived at by applying a percentage to the potential lost revenue — 30% for a careless error, 70% for a deliberate but unconcealed error and 100% for a deliberate and concealed error. Reductions may be made for unprompted disclosure, down to nil, 20% and 30% respectively and for unprompted disclosure down to and 15%, 35% and 50% for a prompted disclosure.

Offence	*Penalty*
Delivery by a taxpayer of a document containing a relevant inaccuracy due to information supplied by a third party. where the VAT period begins on or after 1 April 2009 and the filing date is on or after 1 April 2010 (FA 2007, Sch 24).	An amount arrived at by applying a percentage to the potential lost revenue — 30% for a careless error, 70% for a deliberate but unconcealed error and 100% for a deliberate and concealed error. Reductions may be made for unprompted disclosure, down to nil, 20% and 30% respectively and for unprompted disclosure down to and 15%, 35% and 50% for a prompted disclosure.
Failure to submit return or pay VAT due within time limit (where a return is late but the VAT is paid on time or no VAT is due, a default is recorded but no surcharge arises) (VATA 1994 s 59). Failure to pay tax due under the payment on account scheme on time (VATA 1994 s 59A).	The greater of £30 and a specified percentage of outstanding VAT for period, depending on number of defaults in surcharge period: first default in period 2%, second default 5%, third default 10%, fourth and further defaults 15%. (Surcharge assessments are not issued for sums of less than £200 unless the rate of the surcharge is 10% or more.)
Evasion of VAT: conduct involving dishonesty (VATA 1994 s 60).	Amount of tax evaded or sought to be evaded (subject to mitigation). Repealed and replaced for periods beginning on or after 1 April 2008 and ending on or after 1 April 2009.
Issuing incorrect certificate stating that certain supplies fall to be zero-rated or taxed at the reduced rate (VATA 1994 s 62).	Difference between tax actually charged and tax which should have been charged. Repealed and replaced for periods beginning on or after 1 April 2008 and ending on or after 1 April 2009.
Misdeclaration or neglect (VATA 1994 s 63).	15% of VAT which would have been lost if inaccuracy had not been discovered. Repealed and replaced for periods beginning on or after 1 April 2008 and ending on or after 1 April 2009.
Repeated misdeclarations (VATA 1994 s 64).	15% of VAT which would have been lost if second and subsequent inaccuracies within penalty period had not been discovered. Repealed and replaced for periods ending on or after 1 April 2008 and ending on or after 1 April 2009.
Material inaccuracy in EC sales statement (VATA 1994 s 65).	£100 for each material inaccuracy in two-year penalty period (which commences following notice of second material inaccuracy).
Failure to submit an EC sales statement (VATA 1994 s 66).	Greater of £50 or a daily penalty (maximum 100 days) £5 for the first, £10 for the second, £15 for the third or subsequent failure in the default period.
Failure to notify liability for registration or a change in nature of supplies by person exempted from registration (VATA 1994 s 67).	Greater of £50 and a specified percentage of the tax for which the person would have been liable, depending on the period of failure: nine months or less 5%; over nine and up to 18 months 10%; over 18 months 15%. Repealed after 31 March 2010.
Failure to notify acquisition of excise duty goods or new means of transport (VATA 1994 s 67).	Greater of £50 and: 5% of the tax for which the person would have been liable if period of failure is three months or less, 10% if over three and up to six months and 15% if over six months.
Unauthorised issue of invoices (VATA 1994 s 67).	Greater of £50 and 15% of amount shown as or representing VAT.
Breach of walking possession agreement (VATA 1994 s 68).	50% of VAT due or amount recoverable.
Failure to preserve records for prescribed period.	£500.
Failure to preserve records specified in HMRC direction (VATA 1994 ss 69, 69B).	£200 for each day of failure (maximum 30 days).
Breaches of regulatory provisions, including failure to notify cessation of liability or entitlement to be registered, failure to keep records and non-compliance with any regulations made under VATA 1994 (VATA 1994 s 69).	Greater of £50 and a daily penalty (maximum 100 days) of a specified amount depending on number of failures in preceding two years: £5* per day if no previous failures; £10* per day if one previous failure; £15* per day if two or more previous failures.
Where failure consists of not paying VAT or not making a return in the required time.	*$^1/_6$, $^1/_3$ and $^1/_2$ of 1% of the VAT due respectively, if greater.

Offence	*Penalty*
Breaches of regulatory provisions involving failure to pay VAT or submit return by due date (VATA 1994 s 69).	Greater of £50 and a daily penalty (for no more than 100 days) of a specified amount depending on number of failures in preceding two years: greater of £5 and $^1/_6$% of VAT due if no previous failures; greater of £10 and $^1/_3$% of VAT due if one previous failure; greater of £15 and $^1/_2$% of VAT due if two or more previous failures.
Failure to comply with the requirements of the investment gold scheme (FA 2000 s 137).	17.5% of the value of transactions concerned.
Import VAT (FA 2003 ss 24–41):	From 27 November 2003:
– failures relating to non-compliance	maximum penalty of £2,500
– evasion.	maximum penalty equal to VAT sought to be evaded.
Failure to notify the use of a designated avoidance scheme (VATA 1994 Sch 11A paras 10, 11).	15% of the tax avoided (applies to businesses with supplies of £600,000 or more from 1 August 2004).
Failure to disclose certain schemes within 30 days of the due date or the first return affected (VATA 1994 Sch 11A paras 10, 11).	£5,000 (applies to businesses with supplies exceeding £10 million from 1 August 2004).

*Penalties under VATA 1994 s 60 will continue to be charged for acts or omissions not relating to an inaccuracy in a document or failure to notify HMRC of an under-assessment.

Index

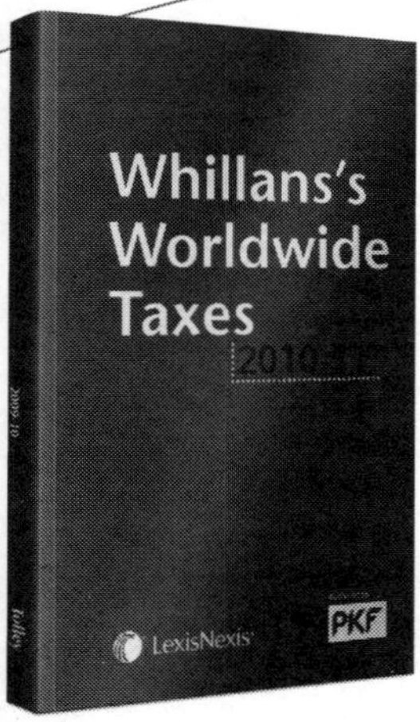

Seeking information on taxes payable, company tax or interest deductions in different countries?

Whillans's Worldwide Taxes 2010-11

This essential guide forms the first point of reference for tax managers seeking information on tax positions, rates, and processes in 95 of the world's key trading nations and tax havens. With 6-10 pages of coverage on the key corporate and personal taxes in each country, you will immediately understand the practical issues and pitfalls for your clients. **Whillans's Worldwide Taxes** is an essential purchase for any adviser who needs to understand the tax implications of their clients' overseas activities. Categories covered for each country include taxes payable, company tax, interest deductions and much more.

"...a great source of reference and is a must for any practitioner who has clients with international interests... With so much useful material all in one place; this should dramatically reduce the time spent researching."

Simon Gray, Partner, Henton & Co

Purchase this title today!

Quote AD11196 when you visit www.lexisnexis.org.uk/taxannuals, email orders@lexisnexis.co.uk or call +44 (0)845 370 1234

SOLUTIONS FOR KNOWLEDGE-DRIVEN PROFESSIONALS

Client Development | Research & Knowledge Solutions | Practice & Productivity Management | Risk & Compliance

LexisNexis